AQA GCSE SPANISH

Higher

John Halksworth
Viv Halksworth
José Antonio García Sánchez
Tony Weston

OXFORD
UNIVERSITY PRESS

OXFORD
UNIVERSITY PRESS

Great Clarendon Street, Oxford, OX2 6DP, United Kingdom

Oxford University Press is a department of the University of Oxford. It furthers the University's objective of excellence in research, scholarship, and education by publishing worldwide. Oxford is a registered trade mark of Oxford University Press in the UK and in certain other countries.

First published in 2024

British Library Cataloguing in Publication Data
Data available

978-1-38-204600-8

978-1-38-204601-5 (ebook)

10 9 8 7 6 5 4 3 2

The manufacturing process conforms to the environmental regulations of the country of origin.

Printed in Great Britain by Bell and Bain Ltd., Glasgow

Acknowledgements

The publisher and authors would like to thank the following for permission to use photographs and other copyright material:

Cover artwork by Sua Balac.

Artwork by Javier Joaquin, Martyn Cain, Andrew Painter, Daniel Klein, Mauro Marchesi and Sua Balac

Photos: Beatriz Gascon J; **p14(a):** Jacob Lund/Shutterstock; **p14(b):** AJR_photo / Shutterstock; **p14(c):** Krakenimages.com / Shutterstock; **p14(d):** ViDI Studio/ Shutterstock; **p17(a):** BAZA Production/Shutterstock; **p17(b):** Christian Bertrand/ Shutterstock; **p17(c):** M_Agency/Shutterstock; **p17(d):** Alexey Bakharev/ Shutterstock; **p17(e):** Fractal Pictures/Shutterstock; **p17(f):** Drazen Zigic/ Shutterstock; **p17(g):** Drazen Zigic/Shutterstock; **p18:** otnaydur / Shutterstock; **p19(tl):** RossHelen / Shutterstock; **p19(tr):** fizkes / Shutterstock; **p19(bl):** Dejan Dundjerski / Shutterstock; **p19(br):** Ahturner / Shutterstock; **p22:** MIKHAIL GRACHIKOV/Shutterstock; **p26(l):** Studio Romantic / Shutterstock; **p26(m):** Andrey Yurlov / Shutterstock; **p26(r):** dotshock / Shutterstock; **p28(t):** AJR_photo / Shutterstock; **p28(m):** Krakenimages.com / Shutterstock; **p28(b):** Cast Of Thousands / Shutterstock; **p30(t):** Asier Romero / Shutterstock; **p30(m):** Krakenimages.com / Shutterstock; **p30(b):** Prostock-studio / Shutterstock; **p30(inset):** Irina Strelnikova/Shutterstock; **p32(t):** Studioshots / Alamy Stock Photo; **p32(m):** Studioimagen73/Shutterstock; **p32(b):** Lecker Studio/Shutterstock; **p34(l):** LightField Studios / Shutterstock; **p34(m):** Monkey Business Images / Shutterstock; **p34(r):** dotshock / Shutterstock; **p36:** Monkey Business Images / Shutterstock; **p38:** eamesBot / Shutterstock; **p39:** Drazen Zigic / Shutterstock; **p40**: fizkes / Shutterstock; **p41:** Odua Images/Shutterstock; **p42(t):** Sandra Polo / Shutterstock; **p42(a):** Victor Velter / Shutterstock; **p42(b):** Bettmann / Contributor / Getty Images; **p42(c):** Aflo Co. Ltd. / Alamy Stock Photo; **p42(d):** D. Clarke Evans / Contributor / Getty Images; **p42-43(bkg):** carlos castilla / Shutterstock; **p43(m):** Anastasiya Alexeeva / Shutterstock; **p43(b):** mimohe/Shutterstock; **p55(t):** Hero Images Inc. / Alamy Stock Photo; **p55(b):** Gorodenkoff / Shutterstock; **p60:** Tint Media/Shutterstock; **p61:** DFree / Shutterstock; **p61(bkg):** Lamax / Shutterstock; **p62:** Monkey Business Images / Shutterstock; **p64(a):** Zoonar GmbH / Alamy Stock Photo; **p64(b):** Tetra Images, LLC / Alamy Stock Photo; **p64(c):** Helmut Corneli / Alamy Stock Photo; **p64(d):** Batareykin / Alamy Stock Photo; **p65:** Jag_cz/Shutterstock; **p67:** Tomas Loutocky/Shutterstock; **p69:** geostanegeo / Shutterstock; **p70(t):** BrAt82 / Shutterstock; **p70(ml):** New Africa / Shutterstock; **p70(mr):** Krakenimages.com / Shutterstock; **p70(b):** Rosa Irene Betancourt / Alamy Stock Photo; **p71:** Europa Press News / Contributor / Getty Images; **p72(l):** Yuganov Konstantin / Shutterstock; **p72(ml):** Roman / Alamy Stock Photo; **p72(mr):** NurPhoto SRL / Alamy Stock Photo; **p72(r):** Anna Kraynova / Alamy Stock Photo; **p73(t):** Luis Pizarro Ruiz / Shutterstock; **p73(bl):** fernandocomet / Shutterstock; **p73(br):** Pixel-Shot / Shutterstock; **p74(tl):** Cookie Studio / Shutterstock; **p74**(tr): Prostock-studio / Shutterstock; **p74(bl):** Ground Picture / Shutterstock; **p74(br):** Wavebreak Media / Shutterstock; **p75:** ezellhphotography / Shutterstock; **p76(t):** Eve Orea / Shutterstock; **p76(b):** Orchid photho / Shutterstock; **p77:** Roberto Epifanio / Shutterstock; **p78(t):** Pavel L Photo and Video / Shutterstock; **p78(b):** VDV / Shutterstock; **p79:** Sonya illustration/Shutterstock; **p80(t):** Christian Bertrand / Alamy Stock Photo; **p80(b):** Album / Alamy Stock Photo; **p82:** Sipa US / Alamy Stock Photo; **p83(l):** Christian Bertrand / Shutterstock; **p83(m):** Sipa US / Alamy Stock Photo; **p83(r):** DFree / Shutterstock; **p84(t):** Kathy Hutchins / Shutterstock; **p84(b):** AB Images / Shutterstock; **p85:** Saolab Press / Shutterstock; **p86:** Associated Press / Alamy Stock Photo; **p87(t):** Tim Martotrana/ Alamy; **p87(b):** astonphoto / Shutterstock; **p88(t):** Something Special / Shutterstock ;**p88**(b): Festival de Viña del Mar; **p88(bkg):** dwphotos / Shutterstock ; **p89(t):** Jose Luis Stephens/Shutterstock; **p89(a):** Lev Dolgachov / Alamy Stock Photo ; **p89(b):** Hugo Brizard - YouGoPhoto / Shutterstock; **p89(c):** abogdanska / Shutterstock; **p89(bkg):** dwphotos / Shutterstock ; **p101(t):** kelseyannvere/ Pixabay; **p101(b):** Nuva Frames / Shutterstock; **p106:** PeopleImages.com - Yuri A/ Shutterstock; **p108(t):** klyaksun/Shutterstock; **p108(b):** trabantos / Shutterstock; **p109:** Jesus Noguera photography / Shutterstock; **p110(tl):** carballo / Shutterstock; **p110(tr):** Paul Hakimata Photography / Shutterstock; **p110(m):** Tutatamafilm / Shutterstock; **p110(bl):** fizkes / Shutterstock; **p110(br):** logoboom / Shutterstock; **p112(a):** Karrrtinki / Shutterstock; **p112(b):** M Dorta / Shutterstock; **p112(c):** eddie-hernandez.com / Shutterstock; **p112(d):** NavinTar / Shutterstock; **p112(e):** RealPeopleStudio / Shutterstock; **p114(tl):** Emanuele Capoferri / Alamy Stock Photo; **p114(tr):** Oleg Medvedytskov / Shutterstock; **p114(bl):** Darren Baker / Shutterstock; **p114(br):** Pavel L Photo and Video/Shutterstock; **p116(t):** Alex Cimbal / Shutterstock; **p116(b):** marketa1982 / Shutterstock; **p118:** POM POM / Shutterstock; **p119:** Nikodash/Shutterstock; **p120:** DavideAngelini / Shutterstock; **p124:** Alex_Traksel / Shutterstock; **p125:** Dmytro Zinkevych / Shutterstock; **p128:** GranTotufo / Shutterstock; **p130:** Viktoriia Hnatiuk / Shutterstock; **p132:** Man As Thep / Shutterstock; **p133:** lala firdaa /Shutterstock; ; **p134-135(bkg):** underworld / Shutterstock; **p134(t):** Peter Hermes Furian / Shutterstock; **p134(b):** underworld / Shutterstock; **p135(t):** SL-Photography/Shutterstock; **p135(a):** Tommaso Boddi / Stringer / Shutterstock; **p135(b):** fckncg / Shutterstock; **p135(c):** Gorodenkoff / Shutterstock; **p147(t):** Dogora Sun / Shutterstock; **p147(b):** lhorintson / Shutterstock; **p155(t):** 4 PM production / Shutterstock; **p155(b):** Unai Huizi Photography / Shutterstock

Every effort has been made to contact copyright holders of material reproduced in this book. Any omissions will be rectified in subsequent printings if notice is given to the publisher.

This textbook has been approved by AQA for use with our qualification. This means that we have checked that it broadly covers the specification and we are satisfied with the overall quality. Full details of our approval process can be found on our website.

We approve textbooks because we know how important it is for teachers and students to have the right resources to support their teaching and learning. However, the publisher is ultimately responsible for the editorial control and quality of this book.

Please note that when teaching the AQA GCSE Spanish course, you must refer to AQA's specification as your definitive source of information. While this book has been written to match the specification, it cannot provide complete coverage of every aspect of the course.

A wide range of other useful resources can be found on the relevant subject pages of our website: aqa.org.uk

Contents

Contents

Introducing AQA GCSE Spanish

Learning vocabulary	Sound–spelling links	Translation skills	Writing	Reading & reading aloud
Dictation	Speaking	Culture	Grammar knowledge	Listening

Understanding how the specification works

The AQA GCSE Spanish specification is divided into three main subject areas, called Themes. This book is divided up in the same way, with colour-coding to help you know where you are.

Theme 1	Theme 2	Theme 3
People and lifestyle	Popular culture	Communication and the world around us

Each Theme is divided into three Topics, making a total of nine Topics to study during the course. The exam is divided up according to the four Language Skills: Listening, Speaking, Reading and Writing. Each one of these has its own separate exam, in the form of an end-of-course paper.

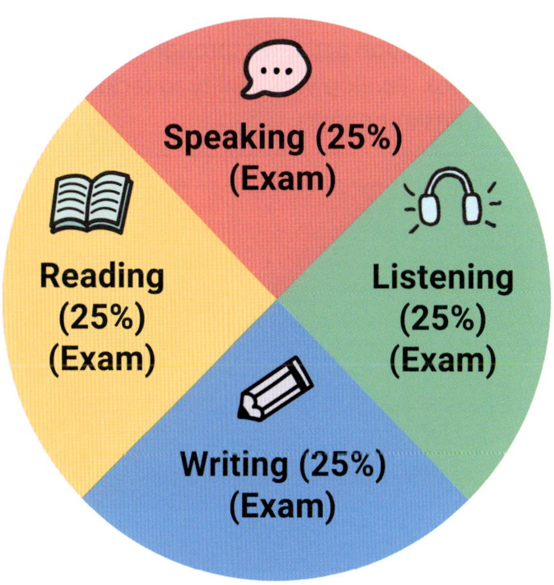

Useful language

The section on pages 10–11 provides useful key vocabulary and phrases which are commonly used in real-life, everyday situations.

Phonics and sound–spelling links

- The section on pages 12–13 groups together all the sounds included in the *Fonética* boxes and provides tips on how to pronounce widely used words and phrases to speak Spanish confidently and clearly. Your knowledge of how spelling represents sounds will be tested through dictation and a read-aloud task in the exam.
- The *Fonética* boxes cover all the common sounds in the Spanish language and the sound–spelling links included in the specification, and include pronunciation tips.

Pronunciación

gue, gui

When the letter *g* is followed by *ue* or *ui*, the *g* is hard, like the 'g' in 'garden'. The *u* is not pronounced, just like the 'u' in the English word 'guess' is not pronounced.

Themes and topics

Each Theme is divided into three Topics. Each Theme starts with two introductory double-page spreads introducing key themes, core vocabulary and structures that you may have covered at Key Stage 3. These pages provide an opportunity to recap and practise important language and/or lay the foundations for further learning.

The three Topics are then each covered over four double-page spreads, two at Foundation level and two at Higher level. Each spread introduces specification vocabulary and features a verb focus and a grammar focus. All the key skills required in the specification are also covered, including phonics and cultural knowledge.

Learning vocabulary

Vocabulary support is provided in various ways throughout the book and on Kerboodle:

- Vocabulary lists – the introductory double-page spreads at the start of each Theme include lists of key words and phrases practised in the texts and on the page. Vocabulary from each of the core spreads and the culture pages is listed in the vocabulary pages at the end of each Theme. Items highlighted in grey are words that are useful but do not appear in the specification. It is important that you learn the specification vocabulary.
- Vocabulary tasks – these help to build the vocabulary required in each topic of the specification.
- Interactive activities – the vocabulary builders on Kerboodle provide activities with instant feedback.*
- Glossary – the glossary at the back of the book combines the vocabulary from the Themes' vocabulary pages.

Features

Reading

The Student Book contains plenty of Spanish reading material on the Themes and Topics included within the specification. The activities that follow the reading passages help develop your comprehension skills so that you can access unfamiliar texts in the future.

Listening

Activities with a listening icon next to them help you to improve listening comprehension skills. The audio can be accessed through Kerboodle.

Speaking

The speaking activities are designed to build your confidence in speaking Spanish and to practise using the vocabulary you've learnt in the unit or Theme. There are also practice role plays and photo card activities throughout the book.

Writing

The writing icon indicates an activity that will help you to use the language you've learnt to build sentences and paragraphs of written Spanish.

Translation

Translation activities throughout the book develop your ability to tackle translation tasks.

Language support in speaking and writing

Examples of language to be used or language structure boxes are provided for some speaking and writing tasks. These can be used as models to build your own sentences.

Para estar en forma,	*tienes que*	*cuidar …*
		hacer …
Para llevar una vida sana,	*es importante*	*beber …*
		comer …

6 Look back at the vocabulary on these two pages and work with a partner to give health advice.

This grid will give you some ideas for starting

Building grammar knowledge

- Understanding grammar is key to understanding Spanish and building your own phrases. *AQA GCSE Spanish* helps you to consolidate and deepen your grammar knowledge in a logical way with no assumption of prior learning.
- Grammar boxes outline key grammar points, with accompanying activities on the same page to put theory into practice.

Gramática

Subject pronouns

Spanish verbs don't usually need the subject pronoun (I, you, he, we, they, etc). This is because all

- Additional grammar practice is also provided in two double-page spreads at the end of each Theme.
- Interactive activities on Kerboodle provide further consolidation with instant feedback.*
- There is a grammar section at the back of the Student Book to refer to whenever you need to.

Verbs

Specific emphasis is given to the formation of verbs and tenses, and how they are used.

Los verbos

The immediate future

To talk about what is **going to** happen, use the verb *ir* (to go), add *a* and then the infinitive of the verb:

Culture

- Culture boxes throughout the book highlight aspects of Hispanic culture relevant to each topic.

Cultura

The Mediterranean diet has come about because of the foods that are plentiful in southern Europe.

- There is a *Culture* double-page spread at the end of each Theme showcasing aspects of Francophone history, literature and contemporary culture.

Language tips

These boxes give extra support and information about what to look out for or how to do a particular activity.

Consejo

On occasions, there may be more than one way of translating a word. For example, if you don't know

Test and revise

There are regular revision and practice opportunities throughout the book in the four test and revise sections (one test per Theme and a cross-Theme test at the end of the book). Each test offers exam-style activities in the four skill areas.

Kerboodle

Kerboodle for *AQA GCSE Spanish* provides resources focused on developing key grammar, vocabulary, phonics and all the language-learning and exam skills required at GCSE. This includes auto-marked interactive activities and tests, worksheets, listening activities with downloadable transcripts, practice questions and assessments, and comprehensive teacher support.

Interactive activities can be completed on tablets or mobile devices.

Kerboodle Books

Kerboodle Books are digital versions of the Student Books, which can be accessed on a range of devices and tablets.

Activities and audio can be launched directly from the page and individual users have their own digital notebook for use within their Kerboodle Book, in which they can use various tools and annotate pages to create their own personalised copy.

*These resources are not part of the AQA approval process.

Useful language

Numbers

0 *cero*	**15** *quince*	**30** *treinta*
1 *uno*	**16** *dieciséis*	**40** *cuarenta*
2 *dos*	**17** *diecisiete*	**41** *cuarenta y uno*
3 *tres*	**18** *dieciocho*	**50** *cincuenta*
4 *cuatro*	**19** *diecinueve*	**52** *cincuenta y dos*
5 *cinco*	**20** *veinte*	**60** *sesenta*
6 *seis*	**21** *veintiuno*	**63** *sesenta y tres*
7 *siete*	**22** *veintidós*	**70** *setenta*
8 *ocho*	**23** *veintitrés*	**75** *setenta y cinco*
9 *nueve*	**24** *veinticuatro*	**80** *ochenta*
10 *diez*	**25** *veinticinco*	**86** *ochenta y seis*
11 *once*	**26** *veintiseis*	**90** *noventa*
12 *doce*	**27** *veintisiete*	**97** *noventa y siete*
13 *trece*	**28** *veintiocho*	
14 *catorce*	**29** *veintinueve*	

Large Numbers

100 *cien*	**600** *seiscientos*
200 *doscientos*	**700** *setecientos*
300 *trescientos*	**800** *ochocientos*
400 *cuatrocientos*	**900** *novecientos*
500 *quinientos*	

1,000	*mil*
1,000,000	*un millón*
1,000,000,000	*mil millones*

Days and dates

- Remember that the days of the week are written with small letters in Spanish.

  lunes, martes, miércoles, jueves, viernes, sábado, domingo

- The same is true of the months.

  enero, febrero, marzo, abril, mayo, junio, julio, agosto, septiembre, octubre, noviembre, diciembre

- To say the date, simply use *el* + number + *de* + month.

  el cuatro de septiembre, el veintidós de mayo

Greetings and ages

¡Hola!	Hello!
¡Buenos días!	Hello / Good morning!
¡Buenas tardes!	Good afternoon!
¡Buenas noches!	Good evening / night!
¡Adiós!	Goodbye!
¡Hasta luego!	See you later!
¡Buenas noches!	Good night!
¿Qué tal?	How are you?
Bien, gracias.	Fine, thanks.
¿Cuántos años tienes?	How old are you?
Tengo dieciséis años.	I'm sixteen.
¿Y tú?	And you?

Time

There aretwo ways of telling the time in Spanish: the traditional 12-hour clock method and the 24-hour clock method, which is often used in Spanish, particularly to discuss travel times.

- To say what time it is using the traditional 12-hour clock, start with *Son las…*

- As in English, when using the 24-hour clock, use numbers such as *trece, dieciocho, etc.:*

a las veinte diez	at 20.10
A mediodía.	At midday.
A medianoche.	At midnight.
Es la una.	It's one o'clock.

- To ask the time:
  ¿Qué hora es? What time is it? / What's the time?

Interrogatives

¿Quién?	Who?
¿Cuándo?	When?
¿Cómo?	How? / What … like?
¿Por qué?	Why?
¿Cuánto?	How much?
¿Cuántos …? ¿Cuántas …?	How many?
¿Qué?	What?
¿Cuáles …?	Which …?

Conjunctions

y	and
pero	but
o	or
porque	because
donde	where
cuando	when

Intensifiers

bastante	quite
más	more
muy	very
menos	less
demasiado	too

Adverbs of frequency

nunca	never
raramente	rarely
de vez en cuando	from time to time
normalmente	normally
a veces	sometimes
frecuentemente	often
siempre	always

Sound-spelling links

The new GCSE Exams involve a reading-aloud task and a dictation task to test your knowledge and understanding of sound-symbol correspondences. Learning how spelling represents sounds and using clear pronunciation when speaking Spanish will be a key part of your success at GCSE. It is important that you are confident with pronunciation and know how to pronounce words correctly to speak Spanish confidently.

Sound	Example	Page
ce	***ce**ntro, do**ce***	19
ci	*fá**ci**l, difí**ci**l*	19
ñ	*Espa**ñ**a, se**ñ**or, a**ñ**o*	21
z	***za**pato, **zo**na, a**zu**l, actri**z***	22
ll	*po**ll**o, me **ll**amo*	27
gue	*hambur**gue**sa*	30
gui	*se**gui**r, **gui**tarra, al**gui**en*	30
que	***que**, **que**rer, par**que***	34
qui	***qui**en, e**qui**po, **qui**nce*	34
cu + vowel	***cua**ndo, **cua**tro, cin**cue**nta, **cue**rpo, es**cue**la*	39
ga	*ju**ga**ndo*	65
go	***go**bierno*	65
gu	***gu**star*	65
ca	***ca**da*	69
co	***co**ncurso*	69
cu	***cu**ltural*	69
-r-, -r	*favo**r**ito, du**r**ante, t**r**aer*	72
ch	*Que**ch**ua, **Ch**ile, co**ch**e*	77
a	***a**ño*	81
e	***e**s*	81
i	*n**i**ño*	81
o	*s**olo***	84
u	***U**r**u**g**u**ay*	84
j	***j**ugar, naran**j**a, **j**amón, me**j**or, hi**j**o*	111
ge	***ge**nial, co**ge**r, **ge**nte, **ge**neral*	114
gi	***gi**mnasio, cole**gi**o, re**gi**ón*	114
rr, r-, -r-*	*El pe**rr**o de San **R**oque no tiene **r**abo porque **R**amón **R**odríguez se lo ha **r**obado.*	119
silent h	***h**orario, **h**otel, **h**ijos, **h**ablar* *a**h**ora, pro**h**ibir, a**h**orrar, en**h**orabuena*	123
tu	*insti**tu**to, si**tu**ación, cul**tu**ra, ac**tu**al, tempera**tu**ra*	126
v	***v**erano, **v**oy, **v**amos, **v**iernes, **v**iaje, **v**ender, **v**ale, **v**isitar*	130

Fonética

a, e ,i

Spanish vowels are shorter in duration than their English equivalents. The vowels 'a', 'e' and 'i' sound a bit like those taught to young children as part of the English phonetic alphabet ('a' as in 'apple', 'e' as in 'net' and 'i' as in 'meet'.

Examples: año, es, niño, América,

Fonética

o,u

The Spanish vowel sound 'o' is much shorter and less pronounced that the distinct English 'o'. The 'u' is similar to the 'oo' in the English word 'moon', with the lips rounded, almost closed.

Saying the 'o' and the 'u' correctly is essential for a good Spanish accent.

Examples: solo, Uruguay, mucho

Fonética

g + vowel sounds

g

When it comes directly before the vowels 'a', 'o' and 'u', the 'g' makes a hard sound, just as itdoes in English.

Examples: jugando, gobierno, gustar

ge / gi

The letter 'g' when followed by 'e' or 'i' sounds like the 'ch' in the Scottish word 'loch'.

Examples: gimnasio, colegio, región, coger, gente, general

gue, gui

When the letter *g* is followed by *ue* or *ui*, the *g* is hard, like the 'g' in 'garden'. The *u* is not pronounced, just like the 'u' in the English word 'guess' is not pronounced.

Examples: *hambur**gue**sa, se**gui**r, **gui**tarra, al**gui**en*

Tip box

To sound as fluent as possible in Spanish, it is important to think not just about what you say, but also how you say it. You also need to think about 'stress' (where the emphasis is placed within words); 'rhythm' (the beat and flow of the language in sentences) and 'pitch' (varying the tone of your language). Listen to as much authentic Spanish as possible and imitate as best as you can!

Tip box

Reading aloud in Spanish poses challenges when you come across new words, or sometimes words just come out wrong when you read them off the page!

- Try to read and understand the sentence before you start.
- Work with a partner and seek their advice once you have finished.
- Practise reading aloud regularly.
- Record yourself and listen to it with a critical ear!

Tip box

The rules of stress and accents

- Words that end in a vowel (a, e, i, o, u), an 'n' or an 's' are stressed on the last but one syllable.

  Examples: trabajo ⟶ tra-ba-jo, practican ⟶ prac-ti-can, amigos ⟶ a-mi-gos
- Words that end in any other consonant are stressed on the last syllable.

  Examples: compartir ⟶ com-par-tir, principal ⟶ prin-ci-pal, dificultad ⟶ di-fi-cul-tad

If a word has an accent on, it means that it does not follow the rule above and that you should stress it on the accented vowel. Examples: sábado, jóvenes, matemáticas.

Question words have accents (¿dónde?, ¿cómo?) and some words have accents to differentiate them from otherwise identical words: te (you), té (tea).

Theme 1
People and lifestyle

Identity and relationships with others

el pelo	hair	*corto/a*	short
las gafas	glasses	*negro/a*	black
largo/a	long	*rojo/a*	red

1 **Read the email from Graciela and match each name in bold to the correct person in the photo.**

¡Hola!

Esta es una foto de mi familia. Yo soy **Graciela** y vivo con todos ellos en Oaxaca. Tengo el pelo largo y negro. Tengo un hermano pequeño, **Lucas**, que solo tiene cuatro años. Mi madre se llama **Teresa** y también tiene el pelo largo y negro. Mi padre, **Juan**, tiene el pelo corto y es una persona alegre. Vivimos con mis abuelos. Mi abuela **María** tiene el pelo rojo. Mi abuelo **José** tiene gafas.

Un besito

Graciela

2 **Graciela sends a text with a photo. Read the message and answer the questions.**

a Who is the woman in the photo?

b What is the woman's relationship to the man in the photo?

c How old is the baby?

Mi prima Lorena y su marido tienen un bebé. Se llama Miguel y tiene cuatro meses.

3 **Graciela sends another text with a photo. Read the message and answer the questions.**

a Who is Sandra?

b How is Ana related to Sandra?

c Where do they live?

Esta es mi tía Sandra con su pareja Ana. Viven en un piso cerca de mi casa.

la familia	family
la madre	mother
la madrastra	stepmother
el padre	father
el padrastro	stepfather
el hermano	brother
el hermanastro	stepbrother
la hermana	sister
la hermanastra	stepsister
el abuelo	grandfather
la abuela	grandmother
los abuelos	grandparents
el primo	cousin (male)
la prima	cousin (female)
el marido	husband
la mujer	woman, wife
el bebé	baby
el tío	uncle
la tía	aunt
el/la pareja	partner

4 Listen to these people talking about members of their family. Choose the correct adjective from the table to describe each family member.

A	boring
B	fun
C	good
D	happy
E	interesting

F	lively
G	nice
H	popular
I	silly
J	sporty

1 aunt, uncle
2 grandfather, grandmother
3 brother, stepsister
4 boy cousin, girl cousin
5 mother, stepfather

bueno/a	good
deportivo/a	sporty
interesante	interesting
popular	popular
simpático/a	nice, friendly
feliz	happy
aburrido/a	boring
tonto/a	silly
animado/a	lively
divertido/a	fun

Healthy living and lifestyle

5 Read what each person says about their lifestyle. Choose the correct number for the food / drink that each one mentions and the correct letter for the exercise.

a **Andrés**
Juego al baloncesto todos los sábados. Mi problema es que como demasiados caramelos.

b **Daniela**
Yo como cinco porciones de fruta y verduras cada día, pero no hago mucho ejercicio.

c **Rodrigo**
No me puedo resistir a las hamburguesas con patatas fritas. Doy un paseo todos los días.

d **Laura**
Tomo el café con mucho azúcar. Soy miembro de un equipo de fútbol.

1	burger and fries
2	fruit and veg
3	too many sweets
4	sugary coffee

A	plays basketball
B	doesn't do much exercise
C	goes for walks
D	member of football team

jugar	to play
el baloncesto	basketball
hacer	to do, make
el ejercicio	exercise
dar un paseo	to go for a walk
el miembro	member
el equipo	team
el fútbol	football
ir	to go
la bicicleta	bicycle
la comida	food
la bebida	drink
el caramelo	sweet
la fruta	fruit
las verduras	vegetables
la sal	salt
el café	coffee
el azúcar	sugar
la hamburguesa	burger
las patatas fritas	chips, fries
demasiado(s)	too much, too many

6 Listen to five people talking about what they eat or drink and what they don't like. Copy and complete the table with the correct letters for each speaker (1–5).

	Eats / drinks	Does not eat / drink
1		

Education

7 Pablo is describing a typical Monday for him, but his sentences are out of order. Put them in the correct order (1–12).

A	A las tres, como con mi familia.
B	Después de la tercera clase, hay un recreo.
C	Después del inglés tenemos religión.
D	Durante el recreo como un bocadillo.
E	La segunda clase es inglés.
F	Las clases terminan a las dos y media.
G	Me lavo y me visto.
H	Me levanto a las siete.
I	Mi primera clase empieza a las ocho.
J	Tenemos tres clases más, después del descanso.
K	Desayuno antes de ir al colegio.
L	Vuelvo a casa.

comer	to eat	*vestirse*	to get dressed
la comida	food, meal	*levantarse*	to get up
después de	after	*empezar*	to start, begin
la clase	class	*tener*	to have
el recreo	break, break time	*más*	more
el bocadillo	sandwich	*el descanso*	rest, break
primero	first	*el desayuno*	breakfast
segundo	second	*el colegio*	school
terminar	to finish, to end	*volver*	to return, go back
lavarse	to have a wash	*la casa*	house, home

8 🎧 **Listen to five people (1–5) describing what they do in different subjects at school. Which subject is each one describing? Write the correct letter from the table.**

A	biología	E	geografía
B	dibujo	F	historia
C	educación física	G	informática
D	francés	H	matemáticas

el inglés	English
la religión	Religious Education (R.E.)
la biología	Biology
la educación física	P.E.
el francés	French
la geografía	Geography
la historia	History
la informática	ICT
las matemáticas	Maths
las ciencias	Science

Work

9 📖 **Match these descriptions to the correct pictures.**

1 Trabajo en una empresa grande. Uso el ordenador mucho, contesto el teléfono y organizo el horario de mi jefe.

2 Escribo artículos para revistas y periódicos; también entrevisto a personas importantes. El trabajo es muy interesante.

3 Yo ayudo a las personas que están enfermas o que han tenido un accidente. Organizo sus medicinas y les doy consejos sobre su salud.

4 Cuando la gente viene a cenar, los llevo a la mesa, les sirvo la comida y las bebidas y les doy la cuenta.

5 Trabajo en un colegio y enseño matemáticas a los alumnos. Preparo las clases y corrijo los deberes.

6 Puedes verme andando por las calles de la ciudad, normalmente con otro colega. Somos responsables de evitar la violencia y los robos, y de proteger a la gente.

7 Toco la guitarra y soy miembro de un grupo. Hacemos conciertos en muchos sitios, a veces también en estadios.

a

b

c

d

e

f

g
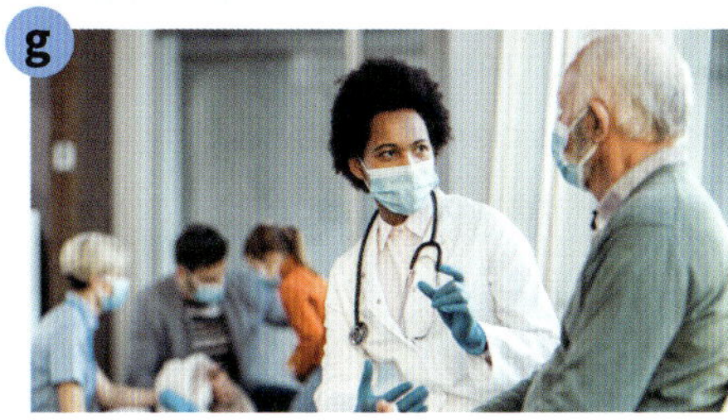

10 📖 **Now choose the correct word in Spanish for each picture.**

1 el / la médico / a
2 el / la profesor / a
3 el / la empleado / a de oficina
4 el / la camarero / a
5 el / la policía
6 el / la músico
7 el / la periodista

1.1F ¿Qué tipo de persona eres?

OBJECTIVES
- Talking about personality
- Adjective agreement
- *ser* and *estar*
- Pronunciation *ce, ci*

1 **A new TV series set in a high school is starting in Argentina. Read the descriptions of the main characters and answer the questions.**

Estos cinco estudiantes son buenos amigos. Graciela es una chica feliz, pero un poco nerviosa – especialmente con los animales. En el instituto, es perezosa. Óscar es muy listo y responsable; es muy trabajador y piensa que las ciencias son fáciles. Silvia es fuerte e independiente. Le gusta mucho el baloncesto y es miembro de un club deportivo. Raúl es muy divertido y gracioso; tiene una personalidad alegre y simpática. Miguel es más práctico que los otros y es muy artístico. Es un chico tranquilo.

Which character would say each of the following?

a I want to do it on my own.
b My favourite subjects are Physics and Chemistry.
c I really enjoy drawing.
d I don't really feel like doing my homework.
e Let's go and cheer up our friend who is upset.
f Don't worry, I know how to solve this difficulty.
g Shall we have a game of basketball?
h I've just heard a really good joke!
i I can't walk past that house where there is a big dog.
j Hey, I got 100% in the Physics exam!

2 **Complete the sentences with the correct form of the adjectives in brackets and then translate the sentences into English.**

a Los perros están muy ___ (*tranquilo*) hoy.
b Mis hijas son muy ___ (*listo*) y ___ (*serio*).
c Creo que las ciencias son muy ___ (*difícil*).
d Los estudiantes nunca son ___ (*perezoso*).
e Mi hermana es ___ (*responsable*) y ___ (*trabajador*).
f Mis amigos son ___ (*alegre*) y ___ (*simpático*).
g Antonio es un chico bastante ___ (*independiente*).
h Mi madre es ___ (*artístico*) y ___ (*simpático*).
i Los estudiantes de esta clase son ___ (*trabajador*) y ___ (*feliz*).
j María es una persona ___ (*fuerte*) y ___ (*práctico*).

Gramática

Adjective agreement

As well as adjectives ending in *-o*, there are other types, too. This is how they all agree:

masc. sing.	fem. sing.
*-o (list**o**)*	*-a (list**a**)*
*-e (responsabl**e**)*	*-e (responsabl**e**)*
*-l (fáci**l**)*	*-l (fáci**l**)*
*-r (trabajado**r**)*	*-ra (trabajado**ra**)*
*-z (feli**z**)*	*-z (feli**z**)*

masc. pl.	fem. pl.
*-os (list**os**)*	*-as (list**as**)*
*-es (responsabl**es**)*	*-es (responsabl**es**)*
*-les (fáci**les**)*	*-les (fáci**les**)*
*-res (trabajado**res**)*	*-ras (trabajado**ras**)*
*-ces (feli**ces**)*	*-ces (feli**ces**)*

3 Listen to four people describing themselves. Which three adjectives do each of them use? Write the correct letters from the table.

1 Paula
2 Luis
3 Sofía
4 Jorge

A	active	**E**	fun	**I**	independent	**M**	practical
B	artistic	**F**	funny	**J**	lazy	**N**	responsible
C	calm	**G**	happy	**K**	nervous	**O**	serious
D	difficult	**H**	hard-working	**L**	nice	**P**	sporty

4 Listen to this short description and write it down in Spanish. You will hear it three times: once in full, then in sections and finally in full one more time.

5 Choose the correct form of *ser* or *estar* to complete the sentences.

a Mis hermanos **sois / son / estamos** prácticos.
b Muy bien, Carlos; ¡**es / estáis / eres** muy listo!
c Los perros **son / estamos / están** en el jardín.
d Tengo un examen hoy y **soy / estoy / eres** muy nervioso.
e Normalmente Ana **eres / es / están** muy alegre, pero hoy **está / es / soy** un poco seria.
f En general yo **soy / es / estoy** muy activa, pero esta mañana **soy / estoy / está** cansada.
g Mis amigos y yo **están / somos / estamos** en mi dormitorio, jugando a videojuegos.

6 Work with a partner and use your imagination to describe the personalities of these young people.

7 Choose three people that you know, either friends or family. Write two sentences about each one to describe their personality.

Pronunciación

ce, ci

In Spanish pronunciation, when *c* is followed by *e* or *i*, it is pronounced like 'th' in the English word 'thin'.
Examples: *fá**ci**l, difí**ci**l, **ce**ntro, do**ce***

In Central and South America, *c* followed by *e* or *i* is pronounced just like 's'.

Los verbos

ser* and *estar

The two verbs 'to be' in Spanish are *ser* and *estar*. When they are followed by an adjective, *ser* is used if the adjective describes a permanent characteristic (like 'clever' or 'artistic'). *Estar* is used if the adjective is a temporary state (like 'nervous' because you have a test, or 'serious' because you are concentrating on something).

When you are saying where someone or something is, always use *estar*.

Estoy en casa. I am at home.
El libro está en la mesa. The book is on the table.

This is the present tense of *ser* and *estar*:

ser	***estar***	
soy	*estoy*	I am
eres	*estás*	you (sing.) are
es	*está*	he/she/it
somos	*estamos*	we are
sois	*estáis*	you (pl.) are
son	*están*	they are

1.1H Personalidad y aspecto físico

OBJECTIVES
- Describing people
- The definite article
- Present tense of *tener*
- Pronunciation *ñ*

1 **Carlos is writing an email about his new friends at university. Which two adjectives match each person?**

a Hugo
b Rafael
c Bruno
d Álex

A	ambitious	**F**	lively
B	angry	**G**	practical
C	boring	**H**	proud
D	capable	**I**	serious
E	different	**J**	timid

carlos@claromail.es

Hay un chico que se llama Hugo. Tiene el pelo largo y moreno y los ojos verdes. Hasta ahora, parece un poco orgulloso y serio; tiene una cara triste y no es popular entre los otros. Hay un chico muy alto, Rafael, con el pelo negro y ojos grises. Parece muy capaz y práctico, y tiene una actitud positiva y optimista. Bruno es una persona interesante con sus tatuajes y su pelo azul. Parece muy animado y los otros piensan que es muy ambicioso. Álex es distinto de los otros; no le gusta hablar con gente desconocida porque no tiene mucha confianza. Con su pelo corto y rubio y sus ojos marrones, tiene un aspecto muy agradable.

2 **Complete the sentences with the correct form of the definite article.**

a Mi madre tiene ___ pelo largo.
b Soy rubia y tengo ___ ojos morenos.
c Jordi tiene ___ gafas azules.
d Después de estar al sol, Laura tiene ___ piel muy roja.
e En la foto, Emma tiene ___ camiseta blanca.
f Para ir a la fiesta, Álex lleva ___ pantalón gris.
g Nuestro gato tiene ___ pelo negro y blanco.
h ¿Qué pasa con Rodrigo? Tiene ___ cara muy seria.

Gramática

The definite article

When referring to your own or someone else's body parts or items of clothing, you need to insert the definite article (*el*, *la*, *los*, *las*) before the noun. For example, if a person has blue eyes, the definite article needs to be added before 'eyes': *tiene* ***los*** *ojos azules*.

3 **A casting director is looking for people to star in a new film. She describes the appearance of the actors she needs and the personality of the character each one will play. Complete the table.**

	Character name	Physical characteristics (x2)		Aspects of personality (x2)	
a	Mauricio				
b	Josefina				
c	Eduardo				
d	Esther				
e	Mariana				

4 **Translate these sentences into Spanish.**

a You (sing.) have a very positive attitude.
b My parents have very different personalities.
c I have brown eyes and black hair.
d Ricardo has a very interesting tattoo.
e Do you (pl.) have a small grey dog?
f My sisters and I have blue eyes and blond hair.
g Tomás is a very tall man and he has a pleasant face.
h You (masc. sing.) are very capable and hard-working, and you have confidence.
i She is not a calm person; she has a nervous personality.

¡Atención!

When translating 'very positive attitude, 'positive' is the adjective so it will go after the noun 'attitude'. 'Very' goes with 'positive'. The word order will be 'attitude very positive'. Bear this in mind for the other sentences, too.

Pronunciación

ñ

The *ñ* sound in *pequeño* is pronounced like the 'ni' in 'onion'.

Examples: *España, señor, año*

Los verbos

Present tense of *tener*

This is the present tense of the irregular verb *tener*.

tengo	I have
tienes	you (sing.) have
tiene	he/she/it has
tenemos	we have
tenéis	you (pl.) have
tienen	they have

This is a very important verb used to express ownership. It implies that someone 'owns' or 'possesses' something, such as 'I have brown eyes' or 'We have a small dog'. It is also used to express age: *Tengo dieciséis años* – I am sixteen (literally 'I have sixteen years'). It is not used to create tenses like 'I have seen the film'. The verb *haber* is used for this purpose, and you will learn about it later on in the course.

5 **In pairs, take turns to describe someone you know. You can use this grid for ideas.**

Mi	*amigo/a* *padre/madre* *hermano/a* *abuelo/a* *padrastro/madrastra* *hermanastro/a*	*es*	*alto/a* *bajo/a* *pequeño/a* *moreno/a* *delgado/a*	*y* *con*	*moreno/a.* *rubio/a.* *el pelo marrón/moreno/ negro/rubio.*
Tiene los ojos	*azules* *grises* *verdes* *marrones*	*y es*	*alegre* *feliz* *serio/a* *trabajador/a* *práctico/a* *capaz* *fuerte* *animado/a* *gracioso/a* *divertido/a* *positivo/a* *optimista*	*y*	*alegre.* *feliz.* *serio/a.* *trabajador/a.* *práctico/a.* *capaz.* *fuerte.* *animado/a.* *gracioso/a.* *divertido/a.* *positivo/a.* *optimista.*

1.2F Los amigos

OBJECTIVES
- Relationships with friends
- Possessive adjectives
- Reflexive verbs
- Pronunciation *z*

1 Julia has done a magazine quiz. Read the answers that she has ticked and answer the questions.

¿Eres un buen amigo?

¿Cómo te llevas con tus amigos?
- Nuestras relaciones son bastantes buenas.
- Me llevo muy, muy bien con mis amigos. ✓
- A veces discutimos.

¿Escuchas a tus amigos?
- Escucho a mis amigos cuando tienen problemas. ✓
- Sí, pero hablan demasiado.
- Claro, y ellos me escuchan a mí también.

¿Te pones en contacto con ellos con frecuencia?
- Sí, hablo con mis amigos todos los días. ✓
- Cuando me acuerdo.
- Solo en el instituto.

¿Hay algo en tus relaciones con tus amigos que te preocupa?
- Me preocupo si mis amigos no contestan mis mensajes de texto. ✓
- Sí, cuando mis amigos salen sin mí.
- No, no hay ningún problema.

¿Guardas secretos?
- No, en eso soy fatal.
- Normalmente, pero no siempre.
- Siempre guardo los secretos de mis amigos. ✓

¿Te peleas con tus amigos?
- Al menos una vez a la semana.
- Con algunos, sí, porque me molestan.
- Raramente me peleo con mis amigos. ✓

¿Cuál es la definición de 'buen amigo'?
- Siempre está ahí para sus amigos. ✓
- Te ayuda si tienes un problema.
- Tenéis mucho en común.

How do you know that Julia...?

a is a good listener
b is not argumentative
c has a good relationship with friends
d can be trusted not to gossip about her friends
e keeps in touch with her friends
f sometimes gets anxious about her friendships
g would be a good friend to have, according to her definition

2 A boy is telling his father about two friends, Mateo and Pablo. What does he mention about each one? Write down the correct letters for each friend. You will not need all the options.

A	can't be trusted	F	fighting
B	gets on very well	G	very different
C	has a lot in common	H	a good listener
D	is good fun	I	patient
E	quite sporty	J	lazy

Pronunciación

z

In Spanish pronunciation, the letter *z* is always pronounced like 'th' in 'thin' (just like the *c* in *ci* and *ce*.) The sound *z* is used instead of *c* when the following vowels are *a*, *o* or *u*; also, when the 'th' sound comes at the end of the word.

Examples: ***z**apato, **z**ona, a**z**ul, actri**z***

In Central and South America (and some parts of southern Spain), the letter *z* is pronounced just like 's'.

3 Listen to a short description and write it down in Spanish. You will hear it three times: once in full, then in sections and finally in full one more time.

4 Choose the correct possessive adjective to complete the sentences.

a Creo que **nuestro** / **nuestros** / **nuestras** padres son muy pacientes.
b A veces me peleo con **mi** / **mis** / **sus** amiga.
c ¿Te llevas bien con **tu** / **tus** / **mi** amigos?
d Los niños se preocupan por **vuestros** / **mis** / **su** perro.
e Carlos, te pareces mucho a **sus** / **vuestra** / **tu** hermano.
f Mi hija se lleva bien con **su** / **sus** / **mi** amigas.
g Voy al estadio con **mi** / **vuestro** / **mis** amigos.
h Hijos, ¿por qué os peleáis con **vuestro** / **vuestros** / **vuestras** primos?
i Mi hermano y yo vamos al fútbol con **nuestro** / **su** / **nuestros** padrastro.
j El profesor siempre escucha **nuestro** / **nuestros** / **nuestras** ideas.

5 Complete the sentences with the correct pronoun (***me***, ***te***, ***se***, ***nos***, ***os***).

a Mi hermano ___ parece mucho a nuestro padre.
b Tú ___ levantas muy temprano.
c Yo ___ preocupo por mi amiga.
d El actor ___ divorcia de su mujer.
e ¿Cómo ___ llamas?
f Yo ___ peleo con mis compañeros todo el rato.
g Laura ___ casa con Martina el sábado.
h Mis padres ___ preocupan mucho por mi hermano.
i Los domingos ___ levantáis tarde.
j Daniel y yo ___ casamos el año próximo.

6 Work with a partner. Look back at the vocabulary in the quiz in activity 1. Take turns to tell your partner what a marvellous friend you are!

7 Write six sentences beginning with the phrase ***El amigo ideal…*** or ***La amiga ideal….***

pelearse	to fight
preocuparse por	to worry about
casarse con	to get married to
levantarse	to get up
divorciarse	to get divorced
parecerse a	to look like
llevarse bien / mal con	to get on well / badly with

Gramática

Possessive adjectives

These adjectives agree with the **following** word.

	masc. sing.	fem. sing.
my	*mi*	
your (sing.)	*tu*	
his/her/its	*su*	
our	*nuestro*	*nuestra*
your (pl.)	*vuestro*	*vuestra*
their	*su*	

	masc. pl.	fem. pl.
my	*mis*	
your (sing.)	*tus*	
his/her/its	*sus*	
our	*nuestros*	*nuestras*
your (pl.)	*vuestros*	*vuestras*
their	*sus*	

Los verbos

Reflexive verbs

There are several reflexive verbs in Spanish, more than in English. A reflexive verb is one that has a pronoun with it, like 'I enjoy **myself**', or 'he hurt **himself**'. The verb is formed in the normal way, but it needs a pronoun (the '-self' word) with it. You will know which verbs are reflexive because they have *-se* on the end of the infinitive.

This is *llamarse* (to be called) in the present tense.

me *llamo*	I am called (literally 'I call myself')
te *llamas*	you (sing.) are called
se *llama*	he, she, it is called
nos *llamamos*	we are called
os *llamáis*	you (pl.) are called
se *llaman*	they are called

1.2H La familia moderna

OBJECTIVES
- Modern families
- Using linking words
- Common irregular verbs

1 **Read the descriptions and match each one to the correct family picture.**

1

2

3

4

5

6

	Tipo de familia	Descripción
a	Familia homoparental	Una pareja del mismo sexo con hijos biológicos o adoptados.
b	Familia monoparental	Un solo padre (puede ser madre o padre) y los hijos.
c	Familia nuclear	Padre, madre y los hijos; es la familia tradicional.
d	Familia sin hijos	Cuando una pareja no tiene hijos.
e	Familia extendida	Familia con diversos miembros familiares de la misma familia: padres, hijos, abuelos, tíos, primos, etc.
f	Familia reconstituida	Formada por la combinación de dos o más familias diferentes.

2 **Listen to six people describing their family. Match each one to the family types (A–F) in activity 1.**

3 **Listen to the descriptions again and write the Spanish for the following words / phrases:**

a understanding
b love, affection
c typical
d large family
e together
f complicated
g they are separated
h we help our dad at home

4 **Complete the sentences with the correct form of the verbs in brackets.**

a Los sábados, yo ___ (*dar*) un paseo con mi padre y el perro.
b Mi tía ___ (*decir*) que no quiere tener hijos.
c Visitamos a mis abuelos los domingos y yo siempre ___ (*traer*) caramelos.
d Yo ___ (*proteger*) a mi hermana en el instituto porque es muy pequeña.
e Me llevo bien con mi madrastra y a veces ___ (*salir*) de tiendas con ella.
f Yo me ___ (*parecer*) mucho a mi hermano.
g Ayudo a mis madres en casa y ___ (*hacer*) las comidas con ellas.
h Yo me ___ (*poner*) muy nerviosa cuando mis hermanos se pelean.
i Hay una familia numerosa en mi calle; ___ (*conocer*) al hijo mayor.
j Hijos, ___ (*ir*) a visitar a vuestro padre este fin de semana.

5 **Join these phrases together with either *que*, *donde* or *cuando* as appropriate. Write out the full sentence in each case.**

a Hago deporte con mis primos. Voy de vacaciones con ellos.
b Me llevo bien con mis abuelos. Me quedo en su casa.
c Siempre mando mensajes a mis primos. Viven en Argentina.
d Tengo un dormitorio bonito. Hago los deberes.
e Tengo una hermana mayor. Se parece mucho a mi madre.
f Vivo en un pueblo grande. Hay muchas tiendas.
g Conozco a una chica cubana. Vive en Madrid ahora.
h Me peleo con mi hermana. Vemos la tele juntos.

6 **Work with a partner. Cover up the descriptions in activity 1 and take turns to describe the families in the picture. Also, use the categories from the *Tipo de familia* column of the table.**

Es una familia	homoparental. monoparental. nuclear. sin hijos. extendida. reconstituida. tradicional.	Hay	el padre / dos padres la madre / dos madres el abuelo la abuela	y	un hijo / dos hijos una hija / dos hijas

Los verbos

Common irregular verbs

- These verbs are irregular in the 1st person singular **only**: *salir – salgo, hacer – hago, dar – doy, poner – pongo.*
- Verbs whose infinitives end in *-cer* change to *-zco* in the 1st person singular: *conocer – conozco, parecer – parezco.*
- Verbs whose infinitives end in *-aer* change to *-aigo* in the 1st person singular: *caer – caigo, traer – traigo.*
- Verbs whose infinitives end in *-ger* change to *-jo* in the 1st person singular: *coger – cojo, escoger – escojo, proteger – protejo.*
- The present tense of *ir* is: *voy, vas, va, vamos, vais, van.*
- The present tense of *decir* is: *digo, dices, dice, decimos, decís, dicen.*

Gramática

Using linking words

When you want to extend your sentences, you can use *que* (that, who), *cuando* (when) and *donde* (where) to link two phrases together.

Tengo un perro grande. Se llama Tobi. →
*Tengo un perro grande **que** se llama Tobi.*

Esta es mi casa. Vivo aquí con mis padres. →
*Esta es la casa **donde** vivo con mis padres.*

Visito a mi padre los fines de semana. Comparto el dormitorio con mi hermanastro. →
*Comparto el dormitorio con mi hermanastro **cuando** visito a mi padre los fines de semana.*

7 **Translate these sentences into Spanish.**

a I look like my brother.
b She gets on well with her stepfather.
c I argue with my mother.
d I fight with my brother when we share a room.
e I protect my sister when we go out.

8 **Write around 60 words about your family.**

2.1F ¿Estás en forma?

OBJECTIVES
- Keeping fit
- *al* and *del*
- Radical-changing verbs
- Pronunciation *ll*

1 **Who said what? Match the statements to the correct person.**

Darío

La actividad que prefiero es el baile hip hop. Voy a clases en un estudio con otros jóvenes. Tienes que ser muy fuerte y es muy rápido. Pienso que tengo una dieta equilibrada y evito comer mucha grasa. Por supuesto, nunca fumo.

Olivia

Me encanta nadar y soy miembro de un club de natación. Me entreno en la piscina cuatro veces a la semana. Llevo una dieta sana – pescado, pollo y todo tipo de fruta. Evito la comida rápida (pero a veces me gusta comer patatas fritas).

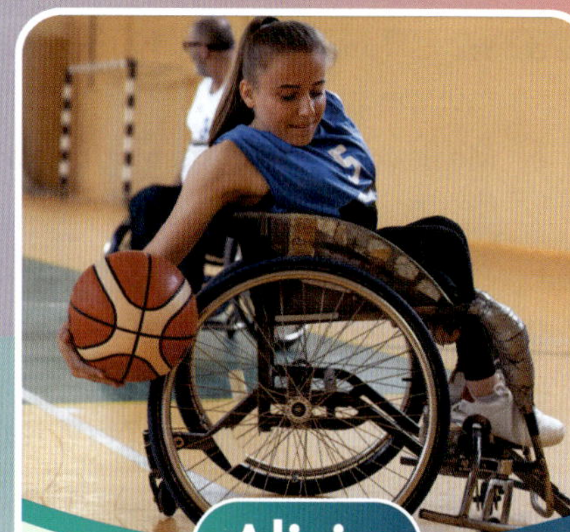

Alicia

Yo juego en un equipo de baloncesto. Entrenamos los sábados y hay partidos los domingos. Este año esperamos ganar la copa. Como muchos platos vegetarianos y un montón de verduras. Los fines de semana me permito una hamburguesa.

a I go training several times a week.
b I take part in competitive sport on Sundays.
c Occasionally I might have some chips.
d It's a really fast activity.
e I love all types of fruit.
f Smoking? No way!
g I keep off meat a lot of the time.
h This needs good body strength.
i Our team should do well this season.
j I avoid fatty food.

2 **Listen to five people talking. For each person (1–5), write down the exercise they do and the food or meal that they mention.**

Cultura

The two most popular sports in Spain are football and basketball. Among the top ten are also tennis, golf, cycling and swimming. A fast-growing sport is 'pádel' or 'paddle tennis'. This has around 2 million players and is similar to tennis, but is played with four people and uses different shaped rackets.

In South America, football is by far the most popular sport. In Central America, baseball has a large following due to the influence of their neighbour, the United States.

Los verbos

Radical-changing verbs

A number of Spanish verbs have a spelling change in the stem of certain persons of the verb. The endings follow the usual rules. This is how the three verb types behave.

	'e' changes to 'ie' *pensar* (to think)	'o' changes to 'ue' *volver* (to return)	'e' changes to 'i' *pedir* (to ask for)
I	*p**ie**nso*	*v**ue**lvo*	*p**i**do*
you (sing.)	*p**ie**nsas*	*v**ue**lves*	*p**i**des*
he/she/it	*p**ie**nsa*	*v**ue**lve*	*p**i**de*
we	*pensamos*	*volvemos*	*pedimos*
you (pl.)	*pensáis*	*volvéis*	*pedís*
they	*p**ie**nsan*	*v**ue**lven*	*p**i**den*

Other 'e' > 'ie' verbs: *divertirse, entender, querer, cerrar, empezar, perder*

Other 'o' > 'ue' verbs: *poder, contar, dormir, costar, encontrar, mostrar, probar*

Other 'e' > 'i' verbs: *repetir, vestir(se)*

3 Complete the sentences with the correct form of the verbs in brackets.

a Mi hermano ___ (*volver*) de jugar al fútbol con el equipo de su instituto.

b ¿Tú ___ (*pensar*) que tienes una dieta sana?

c La chica normalmente ___ (*pedir*) agua con las comidas.

d ¿___ (*volver*) ahora del partido de baloncesto con tus amigos?

e Yo evito la grasa y ___ (*pedir*) hamburguesas bajas en grasa.

f Yo ___ (*pensar*) que es importante tener una dieta equilibrada.

g ¿Por qué ___ (*pedir, tú*) patatas fritas? Tienen mucha sal.

h Chicos, ¿qué ___ (*pensar, vosotros*) de la comida rápida?

i Mi hermano y yo ___ (*volver*) del colegio con nuestro padre.

j Los niños siempre ___ (*pedir*) caramelos en el supermercado.

4 Complete the sentences with the correct words from the box.

al (x2) a la a los del (x2) de la de las

a No hago mucho ejercicio, pero voy ___ instituto en bicicleta.

b Mañana vamos ___ piscina.

c Los beneficios ___ deporte son muy claros.

d El agua ___ piscina está muy fría.

e Los miembros ___ club se entrenan para ganar.

f No me gusta hacer deporte, pero voy ___ estadio para ver el fútbol.

g ¿Vas ___ partidos cuando tu equipo juega en casa?

h El precio ___ hamburguesas es muy caro.

5 Work with a partner. Student A reads aloud Darío's text in activity 1. Student B suggests any corrections needed in pronunciation and then asks these questions for Student A to answer.

¿Qué actividad prefiere Darío?

¿Cómo describe el baile?

¿Cómo es su dieta?

Student B now reads aloud Olivia's text and answers the questions.

¿Cuál es su deporte favorito?

¿Cuándo entrena?

¿Qué más come?

6 Write a paragraph about your exercise, what you eat and what you avoid.

Example: La actividad que prefiero es…
Tengo una dieta (bastante) sana porque como… Evito…

Pronunciación

ll

The double *l* is pronounced like the 'li' in 'million'. Examples are: *pollo, me llamo.*

In some parts of Spain 'll' can be pronounced like a 'y' or even like the English 'j'.

Gramática

al* and *del

When *de* (of, from) and *a* (at, to) are followed by *el* (the masculine singular 'the'), they form one word, like this:

*Soy miembro **del** club de baloncesto.* (*de + el*)

*Vamos **al** estadio cuando juega nuestro equipo.* (*a + el*)

2.1H Cuidar de tu salud

OBJECTIVES
- Looking after your health
- Question words
- Expressions using *tener*

1 **Read the comments made by three young people. Then answer the questions.**

Yo hago ejercicio porque me gusta, pero también porque es importante cuidar del cuerpo. Cuando estás en forma, tu corazón se siente más sano, tienes más energía y hay menor riesgo de enfermedad.

Tenemos que recordar que la salud mental es tan importante como la salud física. Para mí, lo más importante es evitar el estrés y tener tiempo para reflexionar. Por eso, me gusta pasar tiempo en el campo respirando aire puro.

El cuerpo tiene que descansar y es importante dormir bien, idealmente unas ocho horas cada noche. También tienes que cuidar la piel; por ejemplo, usando una crema cuando estás al sol.

a Why does Guillermo exercise? Give **two** reasons.
b What does he say are the **three** benefits of being fit?
c What does Andrea say about mental health?
d What is most important to Andrea?
e What does Andrea like to do? Give full details.
f What does Natalia say about the body?
g How do we achieve this?
h What else does she say we need to do?
i What does she recommend as an example?

2 **Listen to six people (1–6) giving advice and match them to the topic in the grid. There are two topics you don't need.**

A	changing your lifestyle
B	drinking water
C	finding ways to avoid stress
D	getting a good night's sleep
E	getting out into the fresh air
F	having a healthy breakfast
G	switching to a vegan diet
H	taking care in the sun

Los verbos

Phrases with *tener*

These useful expressions all contain the verb *tener*:

tener calor	to be hot (of a person)
tener frío	to be cold (of a person)
tener hambre	to be hungry
tener sed	to be thirsty
tener suerte	to be lucky
tener razón	to be right
tener cuidado	to be careful, to take care
tener que + infinitive	to have (got) to …

3 **Match the statements (a–g) to the reactions (1–7).**

a Recomiendan seis a ocho vasos de agua por día, ¿verdad?
b Señor, ¿puedo abrir la ventana?
c Tengo que tomar algo, no puedo esperar hasta la cena.
d Mis padres me compran una bicicleta nueva mañana.
e Hace mucho sol; voy a quedarme con los niños en casa.
f Voy a poner la calefacción.
g No quiero café; necesito agua.

1 ¿Tienes calor?
2 ¡Qué bien! Tienes suerte.
3 ¿Tienes frío?
4 Sí, tienes razón.
5 Es lo mejor cuando tienes sed.
6 ¿Tienes hambre?
7 Sí, mejor tener cuidado.

4 **Translate these sentences into Spanish.**

a You (sing.) have to take care when the sun is strong.
b I have to drink more water.
c He has got to eat more fruit and vegetables.
d We have to look after our health.
e They have to do more exercise.

5 **Complete each sentence with the correct question word.**

a ¿___ vasos de agua bebes por día?
b ¿___ es esta manzana? Es de Ana.
c ¿___ quieres? ¿El grande o el pequeño?
d ¿___ vive en esta casa?
e ¿___ vas de vacaciones, a la playa o al campo?
f ¿___ tiempo pasas viendo la tele?
g ¿___ está el jamón? Está en el frigo.
h ¿___ estás hoy? ¿Mejor?
i ¿___ es tu cumpleaños?
j ¿___ quieres para la cena?
k ¿___ evitas la sal?
l ¿___ hablas? Con David.

Gramática

Question words

It is very important to learn these question words:

¿qué?	what?
¿cómo?	how?
¿cuándo?	when?
¿dónde?	where?
¿adónde?	where to?
¿por qué?	why?

¿quién, quiénes?	who?
¿a quién, a quiénes?	to whom?
¿de quién, de quiénes?	whose?
¿cuál, cuáles?	which (one, ones)?
¿cuánto, -a?	how much?
¿cuántos, -as?	how many?

6 **Look back at the vocabulary on these two pages and work with a partner to give health advice.**

This grid will give you some ideas for starting your recommendations.

Para estar en forma,	*tienes que*	*cuidar …* *hacer …*
Para llevar una vida sana,	*es importante*	*beber …* *comer …*
Para mejorar tu dieta,	*lo ideal es*	*dormir …* *participar …* *evitar …*

7 **Choose to be either Paco or Pepe and imagine their lifestyle. Write a few sentences to describe how he spends his day.**

Paco

Pepe

2.2F Tipos de dietas

OBJECTIVES
- Different types of diet
- Subject pronouns
- The immediate future tense
- Pronunciation *gue, gui*

1 Read what three young people say about their diet. Complete the text with the correct words from the box.

sur	falta	producto	carne	veterinaria
plantas	larga	corazón	medio ambiente	roja

Pronunciación

gue, gui

When the letter *g* is followed by *ue* or *ui*, the *g* is hard, like the 'g' in 'garden'. The *u* is not pronounced, just like the 'u' in the English word 'guess' is not pronounced.

Examples: *hambur**gue**sa, se**gui**r, **gui**tarra, al**gui**en*

Valeria

Yo soy vegetariana – no como ni (**a**) ___ ni pescado. Me gustan mucho los animales y en el futuro voy a ser (**b**) ___. Como huevos y bebo leche. En general, es una dieta muy sana y no hay una (**c**) ___ de proteína porque puedes sacar proteína de muchos otros tipos de comida.

Marcos

Yo soy vegano. No como ningún (**d**) ___ de origen animal, toda mi comida viene de las (**e**) ___. Es una dieta buena para el (**f**) ___ y me ayuda a mantenerme sano. Lo más importante es que es bueno para el (**g**) ___.

Emma

Aquí en España, y en otras regiones del (**h**) ___ de Europa, seguimos la dieta mediterránea. Esta consiste en mucha verdura y fruta, bastante pescado y poca carne (**i**) ___. Es una dieta muy sana y los médicos dicen que, si sigues esta dieta, puedes vivir una vida más (**j**) ___ y más sana.

2 Listen to six people talking about different eating habits and answer the questions.

a
1 What does he think about the diets he sees online and in magazines?
2 What two things does he recommend for a healthy lifestyle?

b
1 What is her mother trying to do?
2 What does she do during the week?
3 What does she do at weekends?

c
1 What is most important to him?
2 How does he achieve this?

d
1 Where does her sister work?
2 What has she been having for lunches?
3 What does she plan to take for lunch in the future?

e
1 What does his little brother like?
2 What are his parents worried about?

f
1 What sort of diet does she have?
2 Now transcribe (write in Spanish) the two sentences that the girl says.

3 Translate these sentences into English.

a Va a beber más agua.

b Voy a tomar el desayuno.

c ¿Vas a ser veterinario?

d Vamos a dormir.

e Van a seguir una dieta sana.

4 Translate these sentences into Spanish.

a I am going to eat a sandwich.

b She is going to try the fish.

c Are you (sing.) going to serve the food?

d We are going to drink water.

e They are going to avoid the chips.

5 Write out the sentences with the correct subject pronoun. The verb ending or adjectives will tell you which one you need.

a Mi hermano come mucha carne, pero ___ prefiero el pescado.

b Yo tomo el café con leche, ¿cómo lo tomas ___?

c Estos son mis hermanos, José y Eva. ___ es vegetariano y ___ es vegana.

d Salgo a cenar con mis amigos. Yo quiero comida china, pero ___ prefieren mexicana.

e Vamos al restaurante francés. ¿Adónde vais ___?

6 Work with a partner. Student A reads Valeria's text out loud from activity 1 and then Student B asks these questions.

¿Qué no come Valeria?

¿Qué va a ser Valeria en el futuro?

¿Qué come y bebe Valeria?

¿Por qué no hay una falta de proteína?

Now reverse the roles and Student B reads and answers questions on Emma's text.

¿Qué tipo de dieta hay en España?

¿En qué otras regiones tienen una dieta mediterránea?

¿En qué consiste la dieta mediterránea?

¿Cómo afecta a tu vida esta dieta?

Los verbos

The immediate future

To talk about what is **going to** happen, use the verb *ir* (to go), add *a* and then the infinitive of the verb:

ir	*a*	infinitive	
voy	*a*	*comer*	I am going to eat
vas		*beber*	you (sing.) are going to drink
va		*ayudar*	he, she, it is going to help
vamos		*probar*	we are going to try
vais		*descansar*	you (pl.) are going to rest
van		*dormir*	they are going to sleep

Gramática

Subject pronouns

Spanish verbs don't usually need the subject pronoun (I, you, he, we, they, etc). This is because all the verb endings are different from each other, so it is usually clear who is doing the action of the verb. If you need to emphasise the subject of the verb, you can add the subject pronoun:

I	*yo*
you (sing.)	*tú*
he	*él*
she	*ella*
you (polite, sing.)	*usted*

we	*nosotros, -as*
you (pl.)	*vosotros, -as*
they (masc.)	*ellos*
they (fem.)	*ellas*
you (polite, pl.)	*ustedes*

Notice the polite forms of 'you': *usted* and *ustedes*. These go with the third persons singular and plural of the verb (*usted* + third person singular, *ustedes* + third person plural) and are used when you wish to show extra respect to the person you are talking to.

Cultura

The Mediterranean diet has come about because of the foods that are plentiful in southern Europe. It consists of plenty of fruit, vegetables, healthy fats like olive oil and nuts, moderate amounts of fish and seafood and low amounts of meat and dairy products.

2.2H La vida en España

OBJECTIVES
- Spanish lifestyle
- Adjectives of nationality
- Useful verbs

1 Read the texts and answer the questions.

El desayuno

El 80% de los españoles toma el desayuno todos los días. Los adultos prefieren café y los niños beben leche, zumos de fruta o *ColaCao*™ (una bebida de chocolate servida fría o caliente). Algunos toman pan tostado, con tomate y aceite; otros prefieren fruta o algo dulce. Los niños toman pan tostado o cereales o un sándwich de jamón y queso.

ColaCao

La comida

Para evitar tener hambre, muchos jóvenes toman un bocadillo sobre las once o doce de la mañana porque la comida principal del día se toma a las dos o tres de la tarde. La comida típica española es bastante tradicional, preparada con productos frescos de la región.

Un bocadillo

La merienda y la cena

Una tortilla

Los niños y los mayores muchas veces toman una merienda sobre las cinco o seis de la tarde: un bocadillo pequeño y algo de beber. La cena es sobre las nueve de la noche. Es menos grande que la comida, por ejemplo, sopa o una tortilla.

merienda afternoon snack

a What do 80% of Spanish people do?

b What do adults drink at breakfast?

c How is *ColaCao*™ described?

d What do people often put on toast?

e How do young people keep going until lunch?

f When is the main meal of the day?

g How is typical Spanish food described? Give full details.

h When do some people have an afternoon snack?

i At what time is the evening meal?

j How is the evening meal described?

2 Listen to three people talking about aspects of Spanish lifestyle. Choose the correct option to answer the questions.

a The clothes shop opens at **9.00 / 9.30 / 10.00**.

b It closes for lunch at **midday / 1.00 / 1.30**.

c Afternoon hours are **4.30–8.00 / 4.30–8.30 / 5.00–8.00**.

d Who are most likely to have an afternoon nap? **children / the elderly / both**

e How does the woman describe her siesta?
half an hour in bed / a quick nap on the sofa / a short rest before lunch

f What type of festival does the girl not mention? **religious / historical / musical**

g What is 'un puente'? **a sort of festival / an extra pay day / like a bank holiday**

3 Complete the sentences with the equivalent forms of the verbs in brackets. Then translate them into English.

- a ___ (*You have to*) probar los platos vegetarianos.
- b ___ (*I must*) comer más verduras.
- c ___ (*She cannot*) beber leche.
- d Para llevar una vida sana ___ (*it is necessary to*) tener una dieta equilibrada. ___
- e En el campo ___ (*I can*) respirar aire puro.
- f Los niños ___ (*must*) evitar la comida procesada.
- g Esta noche ___ (*we have to*) preparar la cena. ___
- h Para tener una dieta sana, ___ (*one must*) evitar la comida con mucha grasa.

4 Write the correct form of the adjective in brackets for each phrase.

- a la carne (*argentino*)
- b el desayuno (*inglés*)
- c los dulces (*francés*)
- d las tapas (*español*)
- e las tortillas (*mexicano*)
- f los vinos (*chileno*)
- g los platos (*alemán*)
- h las ensaladas (*andaluz*)
- i la dieta (*europeo*)
- j los bocadillos (*inglés*)
- k las patatas fritas (*francés*)
- l la cocina (*alemán*)

5 Translate the following sentences into Spanish.

- a You (sing.) must try the Spanish tapas.
- b The children have to eat a healthy breakfast.
- c I can make a very good paella.
- d One must have a balanced diet.
- e We have to go to a Mexican festival.
- f You (pl.) must not eat sweets before the meal.
- g I have to prepare lunch today.
- h We must try the typical Andalusian dishes.

6 Look back at the vocabulary on these two pages. Then take turns to talk to your partner about the following:

- a breakfast – times and what you have
- b lunch – times and typical meals
- c evening meal – times
- d what one has to do to have a healthy lifestyle

Los verbos

Useful verbs

The following verbs are really useful and are all followed by the infinitive.

These verbs are conjugated (put into the appropriate tense and person).

	Examples
poder (to be able to)	*No puedo dormir.* (I can't sleep.)
deber (must)	*Debes descansar.* (You must rest.)
tener que (to have to)	*Tiene que salir.* (He / She has to go out.)

These verbs do not change and do not have a subject.

	Examples
hay que (it is necessary to / one must)	*Hay que relajarse.* (One must rest.)
se debe (one must)	*Nunca se debe fumar.* (One must never smoke.)

Gramática

Adjectives of nationality

Adjectives of nationality that end in *-o*, like *cuban**o***, *europe**o*** and *mexican**o***, follow the same pattern as *-o* type adjectives. Others behave differently. Here is how they all agree with the noun they describe:

masc. sing.	fem. sing.
chino	*chin**a***
*españo**l***	*español**a***
*ingl**és***	*ingles**a***
*alem**án***	*aleman**a***
*andalu**z******	*andaluz**a***

masc. pl.	fem. pl.
*chin**os***	*chin**as***
*españo**les***	*español**as***
*ingles**es***	*ingles**as***
*aleman**es***	*aleman**as***
*andalu**ces***	*andaluz**as***

*Andalusian – from the Spanish community of Andalusia (*Andalucía*).

3.1F En el instituto

OBJECTIVES
- School facilities and rules
- Comparative adjectives
- Making sentences negative
- Pronunciation *que, qui*

1 **Read what these three young people say about their schools and answer the questions.**

Antonio

Mi instituto es bastante grande y el edificio es viejo. Sin embargo, tenemos un gimnasio nuevo que me encanta porque mi clase favorita es educación física. También los campos de deporte son muy buenos. Los profesores explican bien y nos ayudan mucho. ¡Pero hay demasiados deberes!

Alejandro

Voy a un instituto privado con unas excelentes instalaciones. El edificio es moderno y la biblioteca tiene todo lo que necesitas para tus estudios. Los profesores son estrictos, pero nos apoyan mucho y trabajan duro. Tenemos deberes todos los días, excepto los fines de semana.

Amira

Mi instituto no es muy grande y el ambiente es muy agradable. En general, las instalaciones son buenas – especialmente las de informática. Hay un montón de ordenadores. El patio al que vamos durante el recreo es bonito, con mesas y sillas al aire libre. Confío en los profesores y los respeto.

a Whose school has the following facilities? Write their name.
   1 library
   2 sports fields
   3 computers
   4 gym
   5 outside seating

b Who attends a private school?

c Who complains about the amount of homework?

d Who likes the atmosphere in their school?

e Whose favourite subject is P.E.?

f What does each person say about their teachers?

2 **Listen to these school rules. Match them to the correct letter from the table.**

A	bringing the correct books and equipment
B	raising your hand in class when you want to speak
C	running in the corridors
D	talking while the teacher is speaking
E	treating the people and the school with respect
F	using your mobile
G	wearing the correct uniform

Cultura

Pupils in most Spanish state high schools do not wear a uniform; however, some schools are beginning to introduce uniforms after discussion with parents and the school council. Students in private schools almost always wear a uniform.

In general, pupils call their teachers by their first names.

Pronunciación

que, qui

You will often see the combination of letters *qui* and *que*. These are pronounced like 'key' and 'kay' – the 'u' is not pronounced (so it is never pronounced 'kw').

Examples: *que, quien, equipo, querer, parque, quince*

3 Complete the sentences with the correct negative form (in Spanish) of the words in brackets. Then translate the sentences into English.

a ___ (*not*) tenemos muchos ordenadores en mi instituto.
b Carlos ___ (*never*) habla cuando el profesor está hablando.
c Hoy no tengo ___ (*any*) de los libros correctos.
d Los alumnos son muy buenos. ___ (*nobody*) corre por los pasillos.
e No debes hablar ___ (*without*) levantar primero la mano.
f No hay ___ (*no one*) en la biblioteca.
g Yo ___ (*never*) uso el móvil en clase.
h No hay ___ (*nothing*) útil en Internet para ayudarme con los deberes.

4 Complete the sentences with the correct form (in Spanish) of the words in brackets.

a Me gusta el francés, pero el inglés es ___ (*more useful*).
b Prefiero los deberes de informática porque son ___ (*less difficult*).
c En mi horario, el lunes es ___ (*worse than*) el viernes.
d En mi opinión, ___ (*the best*) clase es la de informática.
e Necesitamos un gimnasio ___ (*bigger*).
f Yo creo que la historia es ___ (*easier than*) la geografía.
g Esta clase es interesante, pero las clases de dibujo son ___ (*more fun*).
h La película no es ___ (*as good as*) el libro.
i Para mí, los idiomas son ___ (*more interesting than*) las ciencias.
j Prefiero las asignaturas ___ (*more practical*).

¡Atención!

With comparative adjectives, the adjective will still agree with what it describes. Work out which noun the adjective is describing before you put it into Spanish.

5 Take turns to say what your school rules are. Use the verbs below, the ideas and vocabulary in activity 3 and the negative words from the grammar box.

Debes… / No debes… / Tienes que… / No puedes…

Gramática

Making sentences negative

Spanish	English	Examples
no	no, not	***No**, **no** tengo deberes.* **No**, I do **not** have homework.
nunca	never	***Nunca** corro por los pasillos.* I **never** run in the corridors.
nadie	nobody, no one	***Nadie** usa el móvil en clase.* **No one** uses their mobile in class.
nada	nothing	***No** hay **nada** en mi mochila.* There is **nothing** in my rucksack.
ninguno, -a, -os, -as	none, not … any, no	***Ninguno** de los alumnos habla en clase.* **No** students talk in class.
sin	without	*Nunca voy a clase **sin** mis libros.* I never go to class **without** my books.

Gramática

Comparative adjectives

Spanish	English	Examples
más … que	more … than	*La biblioteca es **más** grande **que** el gimnasio.*
menos … que	less … than	*La profesora de dibujo es **menos** estricta **que** la profesora de inglés.*
tan … como	as … as	*La informática es **tan** útil **como** la geografía.*
mejor que, el/la/los/las mejor(es)	better than, the best	*Este instituto es **mejor que** mi antiguo instituto. Es **el mejor** de la región.*
peor que, el/la/los/las peor(es)	worse than, the worst	*Este uniforme es **peor que** el anterior. La chaqueta es **la peor**.*

6 Write around 60 words about your school, its facilities and your favourite subjects.

3.1H Lo bueno y lo malo del instituto

OBJECTIVES
- Positive and negative aspects of school
- More negative expressions
- *gustar* and verbs like *gustar*

1 **Read what these young people say about their school and answer the questions.**

En mi instituto hay problemas como el acoso, pero para mí, lo peor es la presión por tener éxito y sacar buenas notas. Cada vez que tenemos una prueba o un examen me pongo enferma por el estrés. Me parece que me paso todo el tiempo estudiando y repasando. **Lucía**

A mí lo que me gusta es la oportunidad de probar cosas nuevas. Por ejemplo, después de las clases, hay clubs para estudiar música, para construir un ordenador o para escribir un periódico. Yo participo en un proyecto para crear una página para los estudiantes en el sitio web del instituto. **Pablo**

Tenemos mucha suerte porque el instituto organiza muchos viajes interesantes, algunos al extranjero y otros a diferentes partes de España. Este año vamos a Galicia, en el norte de España, para conocer la región y participar en actividades al aire libre. **Julia**

Soy bastante ambicioso y necesito aprobar todos los exámenes con las mejores notas posibles. Por eso, me enfado cuando algunos estudiantes hablan en clase y no puedo oír al profesor. A veces el mal comportamiento de unos pocos arruina la experiencia de los demás. **Álvaro**

- **a** Which students are talking about a positive aspect and which are talking about a negative aspect?
- **b** Using no more than three words for each, summarise what aspect of school life each student is talking about.
- **c** What does Lucía feel pressured to do?
- **d** How does she react to stress?
- **e** Where does the school organise trips to?
- **f** What will the students do in Galicia?
- **g** What opportunity does Pablo enjoy?
- **h** Apart from music, what other clubs does he mention?
- **i** What is Pablo helping to create?
- **j** What does Alvaro say he needs to do?
- **k** What makes him angry?
- **l** Translate Álvaro's last sentence into English.

2 **Listen to six students (1–6) talking. Decide whether their opinions are positive (P), negative (N) or both positive and negative (P+N).**

Los verbos

gustar and verbs like *gustar*

These verbs behave differently to the verbs we have covered so far.

- Use *gus**ta*** if what follows is singular or an infinitive: *Me gus**ta** el español, Me gus**ta** leer.*
- Use *gust**an*** if what follows is plural: *Me gust**an** los idiomas.*
- Change the pronoun for different people: ***te** gusta(n)* – you (sing.) like, ***le** gusta(n)* – he/she likes, ***nos** gusta(n)* – we like, ***os** gusta(n)* – you (pl.) like, ***les** gusta(n)* – they like
- Add *no* first to make it negative: ***No** me gusta el uniforme.*

Other verbs that behave in the same way are:

me interesa(n) – I'm interested in, *me falta(n)* – I'm short of, *me encanta(n)* – I love, *me fascina(n)* – I'm fascinated by, *no me importa(n)* – I don't mind.

3 Complete the sentences with the correct verbs and pronouns (in Spanish). Look at the phrases in brackets.

a ___ (*I am fascinated by*) la historia de la región.
b ___ (*They are short of*) ordenadores.
c ___ (*I love*) asistir a las clases de teatro.
d ___ (*He is interested in*) hacer un proyecto sobre el arte español.
e ___ (*We like*) la nueva profesora de ciencias.
f ___ ¿(*Are you, sing., short of*) papel para tomar notas?
g ___ (*She loves*) las instalaciones en su nuevo instituto.
h ___ (*They are interested in*) las matemáticas y las ciencias.
i ___ (*I don't mind*) ayudar a mis compañeros de clase.
j ___ ¿(*Do you, pl., like*) las clases de informática?

Gramática

More negative expressions

Spanish	English	Examples
ya no	no longer, not any more	*Ya no estudio religión.* I don't study R.E. anymore.
tampoco	neither, not … either	*¿Vas al cine? No, yo tampoco.* Are you going to the cinema? No, me neither.
ni … ni	either … or, neither … nor …	*No me gusta ni el color ni el estilo.* I don't like either the colour or the style. (I like neither the colour nor the style.)
jamás	never (stronger, more final than *nunca*)	*Mi hermano no me ayuda jamás.* My brother never helps me.

4 Choose the correct translation of the following sentences. Write down the correct letter.

1 No tengo ni papel ni libros.

a	I've never got the right books.
b	I haven't got paper or books.
c	I've got books but not paper.

2 Ya no hacemos traducción en clase.

a	We hardly ever do translation in class.
b	He makes us do translation in class.
c	We don't do translation in class anymore.

3 El uniforme no es cómodo; tampoco es barato.

a	The uniform isn't comfortable, neither is it cheap.
b	The uniform isn't comfortable, but it is cheap.
c	The uniform is comfortable and cheap as well.

4 Va a suspender el examen; no repasa jamás.

a	He will not pass the exam, nor will he do any revision.
b	He is going to fail the exam; he never revises.
c	He fails the exams because he doesn't revise any more.

5 Work with a partner to ask and answer these questions.

¿Cuál es tu asignatura favorita?
¿Qué asignatura no te gusta?
¿Qué horario tienes en el instituto?
¿Qué tal son los profesores del instituto?
¿Cuál es tu opinión del uniforme?
¿Qué instalaciones hay en tu instituto?
¿Qué piensas de las reglas del instituto?
¿Cuáles son los aspectos positivos de tu instituto?
¿Cuáles son los aspectos negativos de tu instituto?

6 Translate the text into Spanish.

My favourite subject is Geography because I like learning about the world. We don't study R.E. anymore – we now have a lesson when we can study in the library. I have confidence in the teachers because they explain well and help us a lot. I love Fridays because I have History and Art in the afternoon.

3.2F Los trabajos

OBJECTIVES
- Jobs and descriptions
- *lo* + adjective
- Uses of the infinitive
- Pronunciation *cu* + vowel

1 **Read what these young people say and match their names to the most suitable job. What do they want to be?**

¿Cuál sería tu trabajo ideal?

Martín Me gustaría enseñar a los niños para ayudarles a tener éxito en sus estudios y en la vida.

Olivia Lo que más me gusta hacer es **contar** historias. Mi sueño es escribir una novela.

Javier Me gustaría trabajar en un equipo para proteger a la gente y hacer las calles más seguras.

Irene Me interesaría escribir artículos para una revista o presentar las noticias en la tele.

Izan Para mí, lo mejor sería representar papeles en **obras de teatro**, en series en la tele o en películas.

Ana Se **me dan bien** las ciencias y me gusta diseñar. ¿En qué trabajo puedo hacer las dos cosas?

Samuel Yo quiero cuidar a las personas si están enfermas o han tenido un accidente.

Mia Quiero llevar ropa que está de moda y salir en las revistas. Y que me hagan fotos todo el tiempo.

contar	to tell
la obra de teatro	theatre play
darse bien	to be good at

a Martín **nurse** / **teacher** / **painter**
b Olivia **theatre director** / **cook** / **author**
c Javier **police officer** / **bank employee** / **lawyer**
d Irene **doctor** / **journalist** / **actor**
e Izan **actor** / **writer** / **artist**
f Ana **hairdresser** / **nurse** / **engineer**
g Samuel **nurse** / **police officer** / **lawyer**
h Mia **journalist** / **model** / **secretary**

2 **Listen to five people (1–5) talking about their work. Where do they work? Write the correct letter from the table. Also, decide whether they are positive (P) about their work, negative (N) about it, or feel both positive and negative (P+N).**

A	airport
B	bank
C	factory
D	restaurant

E	supermarket
F	theatre
G	tourist office

Cultura

According to one employment agency, 42% of jobs advertised in Spain require vocational training whereas only 38.5% require a degree. The vacancies that companies find it hardest to fill include engineers, cybersecurity experts and experts in artificial intelligence.

3 Translate these sentences into English.

a Para ser enfermero, tienes que escuchar y ser muy comprensivo.

b No debes escoger una profesión sin estudiar todas las opciones.

c Encontrar trabajo en el mundo del deporte puede ser muy difícil.

d Quiero saber qué notas necesito para hacer la carrera de medicina.

e Para mí, viajar es un aspecto importante del trabajo.

4 Translate these sentences into Spanish.

a To be an engineer, you have to study physics.

b You must not accept a job without asking questions.

c Working in the museum is very interesting.

d I want to know what course I need to do to be a journalist.

e Solving problems is an aspect of the job that I like.

aceptar	to accept
hacer preguntas	to ask questions
resolver	to solve

5 Listen to three people (1–3) talking about their jobs. Choose one good thing and one bad thing that each one mentions. Write the correct letter (A–H).

A	amount of responsibility	**E**	journey to work
B	boss	**F**	pay
C	breaks	**G**	working hours
D	colleagues	**H**	working from home

6 Look at this photo. Work with a partner to ask and answer the questions below.

- Describe al camarero.
- ¿Qué están comiendo los clientes?
- ¿Qué es lo bueno de ser camarero?
- ¿Qué trabajo quieres hacer tú en el futuro?
- Para ti, ¿qué aspectos son importantes en un trabajo?

Los verbos

Uses of the infinitive

Use the infinitive after *para* when you want to say 'in order to' do something.

Para ser *abogado, hay que ir a la universidad.* – (In order) to be a lawyer, you must go to university.

Use the infinitive after *sin* when you want to say 'without …-ing'.

El jefe se fue ***sin pagarme****.* – The boss left without paying me.

Use the infinitive on its own, as a noun, when the English ends in '…-ing'.

Trabajar *en un banco fue aburrido.* – Working in a bank was boring.

Pronunciación

cu + vowel

You have met the word *cuidar* in the text in activity 1.

When *cu* is followed by a vowel, it is always pronounced 'kw'. So, when you hear this sound, you will know to spell it 'cu' and not 'qu'.

Examples: *cuando, cuatro, cincuenta, cuerpo, escuela*

Gramática

lo + adjective

To say 'the good thing' or 'the difficult thing', use *lo* + adjective. If you need to say 'about', use *de*.

lo bueno – the good thing

lo difícil – the difficult thing

3.2H Buscando trabajo

OBJECTIVES
- Looking for work
- Verbs for giving advice
- The future tense

1 Read this article about looking for work and find these words and phrases.

Consejos para los que buscan trabajo

Buscar empleo es un trabajo en sí y debes dedicarle, no solo tiempo, sino también planificación y organización. Vale la pena preparar un horario de tus actividades para cada día.

Hay que ser proactivo y buscar en todos los sitios posibles – empresas de recursos humanos, redes sociales, los contactos que ya tienes. También hace falta estudiar los tipos de trabajos que buscan empleados. Podrías hacer algún curso de formación para tener el perfil ideal para esos puestos.

Necesitas escribir un buen currículum para destacar tus conocimientos, tu experiencia y los aspectos positivos de tu personalidad. Nunca se debe mentir ni dar información falsa en el currículum; esto puede tener consecuencias muy graves.

Al solicitar un empleo, además de mandar el currículum, es buena idea acompañarlo con una carta personalizada para explicar por qué te consideras el candidato perfecto para ese trabajo.

- **a** planning
- **b** it is worthwhile
- **c** proactive
- **d** human resources
- **e** the ideal profile
- **f** a good CV
- **g** to emphasise
- **h** personalised letter
- **i** perfect candidate

2 Read the text again and answer the questions.

- a What three things must you dedicate to the task?
- b What should you plan for each day?
- c Where should you start your search? Mention **three** possible sources.
- d What information should you study?
- e What should you emphasise in your CV?
- f What could have serious consequences?
- g What should you send off with your CV?

3 Listen to four people (1–4) giving advice about how to do a successful interview. Complete the sentences with the correct phrases.

Speaker 1

- a An important part of interview success is your **body language** / **preparation beforehand** / **letter of application**.
- b If you research the company, you will be able to **fit in better** / **be more enthusiastic** / **ask better questions**.

Speaker 2

- a You should think of examples you can give to **show your strengths** / **demonstrate work experience** / **provide references**.
- b These examples should **back up your CV** / **avoid focusing on problems** / **relate to the new job**.

Speaker 3

- a The question that is **not** mentioned is **how will you get there?** / **how long will the journey take?** / **what will you wear?**
- b You are advised to arrive with time to spare so that you **give a good impression** / **don't arrive flustered** / **allow for delays**.

Speaker 4

- a The first piece of advice is **smile** / **don't be nervous** / **be yourself**.
- b You should aim to be **friendly and interested** / **lively and enthusiastic** / **responsible and serious**.

4 Translate these sentences into Spanish.

a I will organise a schedule.
b You (sing.) will start at half past eight.
c They will research the company.
d I will apply for the job.
e We will send you (sing.) the information.
f He will ask some questions.
g You (sing.) will know if you are successful.
h She will have a week to prepare.
i You (sing.) will receive the offer next week.
j I will buy a suit to wear to the interview.

Los verbos

The future tense

To form the future tense ('will …', 'shall …'), follow these steps.

Take the infinitive (*trabajar, aprender, escribir*) and add the following endings:

Person	Ending	Examples	English
I	*-é*	*trabajaré*	I will work
you (sing.)	*-ás*	*ayudarás*	you will help
he/she/it	*-á*	*aprenderá*	he, she, it will learn
we	*-emos*	*leeremos*	we will read
you (pl.)	*-éis*	*escribiréis*	you will write
they	*-án*	*vivirán*	they will live

Here you can see the irregular stem of some common verbs in the 1st person singular:

add a 'd'	
venir	*ven**d**ré*
poner	*pon**d**ré*
salir	*sal**d**ré*
tener	*ten**d**ré*
valer	*val**d**ré*

lose an 'e'	
*pod**e**r*	*podré*
*sab**e**r*	*sabré*
*quer**e**r*	*querré*

others	
hacer	*haré*
decir	*diré*

habrá – there will be

5 Translate these sentences into English.

a Nunca se debe llegar tarde para una entrevista.
b Hay que buscar información sobre la empresa antes de asistir a la entrevista.
c Hace falta presentar un buen currículum.
d Se necesita preparar algunas preguntas para demostrar interés por el trabajo.
e Se puede enviar una carta personalizada además del currículum.
f Vale la pena buscar en Internet las preguntas típicas que se hacen en las entrevistas.
g Hay que llevar ropa apropiada para el tipo de trabajo.
h No se debe mentir o exagerar durante la entrevista.

Los verbos

Verbs for giving advice

These words and phrases are followed by the infinitive and are very useful for giving advice and developing your language.

se debe – one/you must
hay que – one/you must
hace falta – it is necessary
se necesita – one needs / you need
se puede – one/you can
vale la pena – it is worthwhile

Note that these verbs cannot be used with a subject. The subject is already 'built in' ('one' or 'it').

6 Work with a partner and talk about how the underlined letters and syllables are pronounced. Then read this short passage out loud to each other.

Jorge decidió seguir una carrera en administración de empresas y, a los treinta años, llegó a comenzar su propio negocio. Ahora tiene un equipo de empleados y va a recibir un premio por sus éxitos en la industria.

Cultura

Aspectos de la vida hispánica

1 **Read this text about the custom of *la siesta* and the village of Ador in the Valencian community. Answer the questions below.**

- **a** Why did the mayor of Aldor become famous?
- **b** What did he say should happen between 2 pm and 5 pm?
- **c** What percentage of Spaniards never have a nap after lunch?
- **d** Describe the traditional working day.
- **e** Why did this schedule for the working day come about?

En 2015, el **alcalde** de Ador se hizo famoso por pedir a los vecinos que durmieran la siesta. Anunció que desde las dos hasta las cinco de la tarde se debía mantener un ambiente tranquilo y sin ruido en el pueblo y que los padres debían mantener a sus hijos en casa.

Sin embargo, casi el 60% de españoles nunca duerme la siesta y solo un 18% lo hace a veces. Tradicionalmente, el día laboral estaba dividido en dos partes; la gente trabajaba de las nueve a las dos, tenía un descanso de dos horas para comer y volvía al trabajo desde las cuatro hasta las ocho. Muchas personas tenían dos trabajos para mantener a sus familias, uno por la mañana y otro por la tarde. Durante las dos horas de la comida les daba tiempo a descansar o volver a casa después de terminar el empleo de la mañana.

el alcalde	mayor

2 **Read the information about the top four sports in South America. Then research the four famous sportsmen and women in the photos. Find which of the four sports each one is famous for and write a sentence about their achievements.**

el béisbol	baseball
cualquier	any

LOS CUATRO DEPORTES MÁS POPULARES EN SUDAMÉRICA

EL FÚTBOL es el deporte más popular y tiene seguidores entre los jóvenes y los mayores, los ricos y los pobres. La Copa América es unos de los torneos más antiguos del mundo.

EL BÉISBOL vuelve loca a la gente de Cuba y la República Dominicana y para ellos, el béisbol es tan importante como el fútbol. Muchos jugadores profesionales de estos países juegan en los Estados Unidos.

EL BOXEO se practica en muchos países de Sudamérica, pero es especialmente popular en México. En este país hay más campeones de boxeo que en **cualquier** otro país, aparte de los Estados Unidos.

EL BALONCESTO es muy popular en Argentina y el equipo nacional ha tenido mucho éxito. Ha ganado cinco de los títulos más importantes en este deporte.

Christiane Endler

Juan Marichal

Anabel Ortiz

Manu Ginobili

3 Read the text. Work with a partner to talk through a translation of the passage.

4 Discuss with your partner why you think this is a common occurrence in Spain. Do you think it would work in your country? Why (not)?

5 Listen to these facts about women in Spain today. Are the statements true (T) or false (F)?

1 a There were eleven women and seven men in the 2018 Spanish government.
  b It was the government with the highest female representation in the world.

2 a In the 2020 list of the most influential Spaniards, all were women.
  b Queen Letizia chose the women on the list.
  c Queen Letizia was a journalist before she married.

3 a The majority of Pedro Sánchez's 2023 government were women.
  b The top jobs of deputy presidents, however, were given to men.

6 Read the text. Which of the facts (a–i) are mentioned?

a which South American countries have *tunas*
b what they wear
c what they play
d where they play
e when the custom started
f how to join a *tuna*
g its original purpose
h serenading a loved one
i why the students take part today

Los vecinos

En las ciudades y pueblos españoles, no es raro ver a un grupo de personas llevar sus sillas a la calle y sentarse allí para charlar con los vecinos. Es algo que se hace sobre las siete u ocho de la tarde cuando no hace tanto calor. Todos creen que es una actividad muy positiva ya que les ofrece un descanso de sus tareas y les permite tomar el fresco de la tarde. Además, es una forma sana y barata de relacionarse con los vecinos y crear un sentido de comunidad.

LA TUNA

En España, Portugal y países de Sudamérica, la 'tuna' es un grupo de estudiantes de la universidad que se viste con ropa tradicional y canta canciones populares, acompañándolas con sus guitarras y otros instrumentos musicales. La costumbre empezó en el siglo trece cuando los estudiantes querían ganar dinero o comida. También en el pasado un novio podía alquilar a la tuna para que cantara bajo la ventana de su novia. Hoy en día, los estudiantes forman parte de la tuna para mantener la tradición y para divertirse.

Grammar practice

Using *hay*, *ser*, *tener*

1 Complete the sentences with *hay* or the correct present form of *ser* or *tener*.

a Pedro y yo ___ hermanos.
b Mi madre ___ el pelo corto y negro.
c En mi familia ___ cinco personas.
d Mi hermana es mayor que yo, pero yo ___ más alta.
e Los españoles ___ una dieta bastante sana, en general.
f En mi clase de español, ___ unos veinte estudiantes.
g No sé qué hacer en el futuro; no ___ ni idea.
h Hablas español muy bien: ¿___ español?
i Sevilla, Granada y Córdoba ___ ciudades importantes del sur de España.
j ___ un buen restaurante vegetariano cerca de donde vivo.

Plural nouns

2 Put the nouns and their articles into the plural.

Examples: la casa → las casas, un lugar → unos lugares, el tema → los temas, una acción → unas acciones

a la mujer	f el periodista	k un color
b un momento	g un animal	l la asignatura
c el hombre	h una clase	m el trabajo
d una ciudad	i el programa	n el artista
e la luz	j la actividad	o una situación

The present tense

3 Complete the sentences with the correct present form of the verbs in brackets.

a Mi padre ___ (*viajar*) mucho por trabajo.
b Los españoles ___ (*comer*) más pescado que los ingleses.
c ¿___ (*salir, tú*) con tus amigos este sábado?
d Mis compañeros y yo ___ (*estudiar*) matemáticas el lunes por la mañana.
e Normalmente yo ___ (*beber*) agua con las comidas.
f Chicos, ¿en qué parte de España ___ (*vivir*)?
g Para la cena, yo ___ (*preparar*) platos sanos.
h Cuando mi amiga viene a mi casa, ___ (*ver*) películas en Netflix.
i Nuestra casa es pequeña y yo ___ (*compartir*) un dormitorio con mi hermano.

Adjectives

4 Choose the correct form of the adjectives to complete the sentences.

a Para mí, las matemáticas son muy **difícil** / **difíciles**.
b Mi prima tiene el pelo **rubio** / **rubia** / **rubios** / **rubias**.
c Tienen los ojos **azul** / **azules**.
d Mis padres son muy **simpático** / **simpática** / **simpáticos** / **simpáticas**.
e Los platos **principal** / **principales** de este restaurante están muy ricos.
f Unos estudiantes **inglés** / **inglesa** / **ingleses** / **inglesas** van a visitar el colegio.
g Conocí a unas chicas **español** / **española** / **españoles** / **españolas** en Londres.

Using *ser* and *estar*

5 Complete the sentences with the correct present form of *ser* or *estar*.

a Mi clase de español ___ bastante pequeña.
b No podemos ir allí hoy porque ___ en Madrid.
c Las tapas de este restaurante ___ muy caras.
d ¿Qué pasa, Carmen? ¿Por qué ___ triste?
e Sí, hablo español, pero ___ inglés.
f Mis padres ___ en el jardín.
g ¿Tú crees que ___ una persona responsable?
h Me quedo en casa porque ___ enfermo.
i No ___ muy religiosos, pero vamos a la iglesia a veces.
j Tu mochila ___ detrás de la silla.

6 **Translate these phrases into Spanish.**

a your bedroom (you, sing.)
b my country
c your books (you, pl.)
d her family
e his ideas
f our custom
g their dogs
h your homework (you, sing.)
i your house (you, pl.)
j our garden

Reflexive verbs

7 **Complete the sentences with the correct present form of the verbs in brackets and the correct reflexive pronoun (*me*, *te*, *se*, *nos* or *os*).**

a Yo ___ (*parecerse*) mucho a mi padre.
b Mi tía ___ (*divorciarse*) de mi tío.
c Juan y yo ___ (*quedarse*) aquí para estudiar.
d Mis perros ___ (*llamarse*) Tobi y Luna.
e El museo ___ (*abrirse*) a las siete.
f Tú siempre ___ (*caerse*) cuando llevas esos zapatos.
g ¿A qué hora ___ (*levantarse*) vosotros normalmente?
h Luisa y yo ___ (*casarse*) en junio del año que viene.
i Mis padres siempre ___ (*preocuparse*) por mí.

Los verbos

Reflexive verbs

There are several reflexive verbs in Spanish, more than in English. A reflexive verb is one that has a pronoun with it, like 'I enjoy **myself**', or 'he hurt **himself**'. The verb is formed in the normal way, but it needs a pronoun (the '-self' word) with it. You will know which verbs are reflexive because they have *-se* on the end of the infinitive.

This is *llamar**se*** (to be called) in the present tense.

me *llamo*	I am called (literally 'I call myself')
te *llamas*	you (sing.) are called
se *llama*	he, she, it is called
nos *llamamos*	we are called
os *llamáis*	you (pl.) are called
se *llaman*	they are called

Interrogatives

8 **Complete the questions with the correct question words from the box.**

adónde cómo cuáles cuándo cuánto cuántos dónde por qué (x2) qué (x2) quién (x3) quiénes

a ¿___ está el gimnasio?
b ¿___ estás hoy? ¿Mejor?
c Está lloviendo… ¿___ no vamos al cine?
d ¿___ haces los fines de semana?
e ¿___ vive en esa casa vieja?
f ¿___ vienes a visitarme a Valencia?
g ¿___ vas de vacaciones? ¿A Barcelona o a Málaga?
h ¿___ quieres hacer el sábado?
i ¿De ___ son estas gafas?
j ¿___ son las mejores películas del año?
k ¿A ___ kilómetros vives de Madrid?
l ¿___ dinero te queda?
m ¿A ___ mandas ese mensaje?
n ¿___ son tus artistas favoritas?
o ¿___ no te gusta hacer deporte?

9 **Match the questions (A–J) to the answers (1–10).**

	Questions		Answers
A	¿Quieres unas tapas?	1	Sí, hoy tengo sueño.
B	¿Vas a dormir la siesta?	2	Sí, tienes razón. A las ocho.
C	¿Quieres agua?	3	No, yo también tengo calor.
D	¿Estás andando por las montañas?	4	Sí, no tengo frío.
E	¿Quieres ir al cine?	5	No, gracias. No tengo hambre.
F	¿Te importa si abro la ventana?	6	Sí, en verano. ¡Tengo mucha suerte!
G	¿Vas a ir a Nueva York?	7	Sí, tiene mucho éxito en YouTube.
H	Tenemos geografía primero ¿verdad?	8	Sí, por favor. Tengo mucha sed.
I	¿Vas a salir en camiseta?	9	Sí, pero no te preocupes; voy a tener cuidado.
J	No la conozco. ¿Es famosa?	10	No, tengo que hacer los deberes.

Grammar practice

Using *que, donde, cuando*

10 **Complete the sentences with *que, donde* or *cuando*. Then translate the sentences into English.**

a Solo duermo la siesta ___ no tengo trabajo por la tarde.

b Me gusta mi dormitorio porque es el sitio ___ puedo relajarme.

c Mi hermana mayor, ___ se llama Susana, estudia en la universidad de Barcelona.

d Este es el bar ___ todos los empleados vienen a tomar café.

e ___ voy al gimnasio a las siete, hay muy poca gente allí.

f A los dieciséis años, estas son las dos opciones ___ los jóvenes pueden escoger.

Irregular present tense verbs

11 **Complete the sentences with the correct present form of the verbs in brackets. (These are all verbs with spelling changes in the singular and 3rd person plural forms of the present.)**

a Ya no ___ (*jugar, nosotros*) al baloncesto los jueves.

b Los niños no ___ (*querer*) comer las verduras.

c La clase ___ (*empezar*) a las dos hoy.

d Tú nunca ___ (*dormir*) bien el día antes de un examen.

e Chicos, ¿___ (*poder*) ayudarme en la cocina, por favor?

f Yo no ___ (*entender*) esta pregunta.

Using *a* and *de*

12 **Complete the sentences with *al, a la, a los, a las, del, de la, de los* or *de las*.**

a Los lunes voy ___ clases de baile en el instituto.

b Voy ___ ciudad los sábados.

c El señor Sánchez es un amigo ___ familia.

d Las casas ___ pueblo son blancas y muy bonitas.

e Vamos ___ puerto para ver los barcos.

f Muchos ___ jóvenes de hoy no beben alcohol.

g Siempre vamos ___ partidos si nuestro equipo juega en casa.

h La biología es una ___ asignaturas más difíciles para mí.

Modal verbs

13 **Translate these sentences into Spanish. Use the appropriate forms of *deber, tener que, poder* or the phrases *se debe / hay que*.**

a You (pl.) must not run in the playground.

b One must always arrive early for an interview.

c I cannot go to the match on Saturday.

d We have to improve our diet.

e We must eat less meat in the future.

f Can you (sing.) solve the problem?

g One must wear the correct uniform.

h I have got to finish my homework.

gustar and verbs like *gustar*

14 **Complete the sentences with the correct pronoun and the correct present form of the verbs in brackets.**

a A mi amiga ___ ___ (*encantar*) jugar al fútbol.

b A mí ___ ___ (*fascinar*) los libros de ciencia ficción.

c A mi marido y a mí ___ ___ (*interesar*) comprar esta casa.

d A mis padres ___ ___ (*faltar*) tiempo para cuidar el jardín.

e ¿A ti ___ ___ (*gustar*) los deportes de equipo?

Los verbos

gustar* and verbs like *gustar

These verbs behave differently to the verbs we have covered so far.

- Use *gusta* if what follows is singular or an infinitive: *Me gust**a** el español, Me gust**a** leer.*
- Use *gust**an*** if what follows is plural: *Me gust**an** los idiomas.*
- Change the pronoun for different people: ***te** gusta(n)* – you (sing.) like, ***le** gusta(n)* –
- he/she likes, ***nos** gusta(n)* – we like, ***os** gusta(n)* – you (pl.) like, ***les** gusta(n)* – they like
- Add *no* first to make it negative: ***No** me gusta el uniforme.*

Negation

15 Choose the correct words/phrases to complete the sentences.

a Hoy no tengo deberes de **jamás** / **nada** / **ninguna** asignatura. ¡Qué bien!

b Cuando llego temprano, no hay **nadie** / **sin** / **nunca** en casa.

c No debes ir al colegio **ya no** / **ninguno** / **sin** tomar el desayuno.

d El restaurante era malísimo; **ningunos** / **ni** / **nunca** más vamos a volver allí.

e Papá, tengo hambre y no hay **nadie** / **nada** / **ningunas** de comer en la cocina.

f Voy a dejar la historia al final del año. **Jamás** / **Ya no** / **Nada** me interesa.

g No me gusta el fútbol; **nadie** / **sin** / **tampoco** me gusta el baloncesto.

h Mi hermana no come ni carne **nada** / **ninguno** / **ni** pescado.

The future tense

16 Translate these sentences into Spanish.

a I am going to study languages in the future.

b Ana is going to play basketball.

c Are you (sing.) going to do your homework?

d The classes are going to start at ten on Friday.

e You (pl.) are going to do a project.

f We are going to prepare the evening meal.

g I am going to eat vegetarian meals during the week.

h The new diet is going to be very healthy.

Comparatives

17 Complete the sentences with the Spanish translation of the words in brackets.

Madrid es (*bigger than*) Granada.

Example: Madrid es más grande que Granada.

a Mi hermana es (*taller than*) mi madre.

b Las matemáticas son (*more difficult than*) la biología.

c El nuevo uniforme es (*worse than*) el uniforme de antes.

d Las naranjas son (*cheaper than*) las manzanas en esta región.

e La película no es (*as good as*) el libro.

f Las tapas de aquí son (*better than*) las tapas del restaurante mexicano.

The simple future

18 Complete the sentences with the correct simple future form of the verbs in brackets.

a ___ (*ir, nosotros*) al instituto en autobús porque está lloviendo.

b Mis hijos no se ___ (*comer*) toda esa carne.

c Yo ___ (*hacer*) un proyecto sobre la historia del pueblo.

d Creo que os ___ (*llevar*) bien con vuestra madrastra.

e Para su cumpleaños ___ (*haber – there will be*) una fiesta en la casa familiar.

f Ya tenemos las cosas de la compra; las ___ (*poner, nosotros*) en la nevera.

g El nuevo jefe ___ (*llegar*) mañana.

h Si no tomas el desayuno, ___ (*tener*) hambre a mediodía.

Translating infinitives

19 Translate these sentences into English.

a Fumar es muy malo para la salud.

b Para mantenerme en forma, voy al gimnasio.

c Para mí, trabajar en una oficina parece muy aburrido.

d Es mejor estudiar sin escuchar música.

e Vivir en el campo es ideal si quieres una vida tranquila.

Using *lo + adjective*

20 Translate these sentences into Spanish.

a The good thing is that I do not have to share a bedroom.

b The important thing is to do the subjects that you prefer.

c The bad thing is that the classes start at eight.

d The worst thing is that my friend is ill.

e The first thing is to choose your subjects.

f The interesting thing is that José is going out with Sara.

Higher Vocabulary

Words that are highlighted in grey in this list are words that may be useful, but you won't need to know them for the exam.

1.1F ¿Qué tipo de persona eres?

alegre cheerful
el/la amigo/a friend
animal animal
artístico/a artistic
bueno/a good
el/la chico/a boy/girl
las ciencias science
cinco five
la clase class
cuando when
deportivo/a (of) sports
difícil difficult
divertido/a fun, enjoyable
especialmente especially
estar to be
el/la estudiante student
fácil easy
feliz happy
fuerte strong
general general
gracioso/a funny
el grupo group
gustar to like (lit. to please)
hoy today
independiente independent
el instituto secondary school
listo/a clever
muy very
nervioso/a nervous
otro/a other, another
pensar to think
perezoso/a lazy
pero but
la persona person
la personalidad personality
poco/a little, bit
porque because
práctico/a practical
responsable responsible
ser to be
serio/a serious
simpático/a nice, friendly
la situación situation
trabajador(a) hard-working
tranquilo/a quiet, peaceful

1.1H Personalidad y aspecto físico

el/la abuelo/a grandfather/grandmother
la actitud attitude
el/la actor/actriz actor/actress
agradable pleasant
alto/a tall
ambicioso/a ambitious
animado/a lively
el aspecto aspect
azul blue
bajo/a short
bonito/a pretty, lovely
buscar to look for, search for
capaz capable
la cara face
el carácter carácter
cómo how
la confianza confidence, trust
contento/a happy, pleased, glad
corto/a short
de momento at the moment
deber to owe (must)
delgado/a slim, thin
la diferencia difference
distinto/a different
dónde where
enojado/a angry
este/esta this
físico/a physical
las gafas glasses
gris grey
guapo/a good-looking
hacer to do, make
el/la hermanastro/a stepbrother/stepsister
el hombre man
interesante interesting
la isla island
largo/a long
llamarse to be called
la madrastra stepmother
la mañana morning
marrón brown
moreno/a brown, dark
la mujer woman/wife
negro/a black
el/la niño/a child, (little) boy/girl
nuevo/a new
el ojo eye
optimista optimistic
orgulloso/a proud
el padrastro stepfather
el papel role, paper
parecer to seem
el pelo hair
pequeño/a small
el/la perro/a dog
el personaje character (ie. In book, film)
popular popular
positivo/a positive
principal principal, main
el programa programme
rubio/a fair, blond(e)
Sudamérica South America
el tatuaje tattoo
tener to have
triste sad
verde green

1.2F Los amigos

a veces sometimes
algo something
allí there
el año year
bien well
casarse to get married
el/la compañero/a colleague, (school) friend
común common
el contacto contact
creer to think, believe
la definición definition
el día day
diferente different
divorciarse to get divorced
escuchar to listen (to)
el estadio stadium
fatal terrible
la frecuencia frequency
genial great
guardar to keep
hablar to speak, talk
hay there is, there are
la idea idea
levantarse to get up
llevarse bien/mal con to get on well/badly with
mejor better, best
la opinión opinion
paciente patient
parecerse a to look like
pasar to pass, spend
pelear(se) to fight
poner(se) to put on, to become
preocupar(se) to worry
el problema problem
próximo/a next
qué what
raramente rarely
raro/a strange, odd, rare
la relación relationship
el sábado Saturday
el secreto secret
siempre always
tarde late
temprano early
el texto text
el tiempo time, weather
todo/a all, every

1.2H La familia moderna

activo/a active
adoptado/a adopted
ahora now
ayudar to help
biológico/a biological
caer to fall
la calle street
el caramel o sweet
el cariño affection
la casa house
claro clear, of course
coger to catch
la combinación combination
la comida food, meal
compartir to share

completo/a complete
complicado/a complicated
comprensivo/a understanding
conocer to know, to get to know
cubano/a Cuban
dar to give
decidir to decide
el deporte sport
diverso/a various
divorciado/a divorced
el domingo Sunday
el dormitorio bedroom
dos two
escoger to choose
estricto/a strict
extendido/a extended
la familia family
la familia reconstituida step family
familiar (of the) family
el fin de semana weekend
grande big
el/la hijo/a son/daughter
juntos/as together
la madre mother
mandar to send
el marido husband
mayor older, bigger, main
el mensaje message
el miembro member
mismo/a same
moderno/a modern
monoparental single parent
nosotros/as we, us
nuclear nuclear
numeroso/a numerous, large
el padre father
la pareja couple, partner
pasarlo bien to have a good time
el paseo walk, stroll
poder to be able
poner to put
el/la primo/a cousin
proteger to protect
el pueblo village, town
querer to want, love
salir to leave, go out
separado/a separated
el sexo sex
sin without
solo/a only, alone
la tele TV, telly
la tienda shop, tent
el/la tío/a uncle/aunt
típico/a typical
tradicional traditional
traer to bring
las vacaciones holidays
ver to see, watch
vez time, occasion
visitar to visit

2.1F ¿Estás en forma?

a pie on foot
la actividad activity
el (fem.) agua water
andar to walk
el baile dance
el beneficio benefit
la bicicleta bicycle
el bocadillo sandwich
el caballo horse
la carne meat
caro/a expensive, dear
cerrar to close, shut
el club club
comer to eat
contar to tell, count
la copa cup, wine glass, trophy
correr to run
costar to cost
cuatro four
el desayuno breakfast
el diente tooth
la dieta diet
divertirse to enjoy oneself, to have fun
dormir(se) to sleep
el ejercicio exercise
empezar to start, begin
encantar to love (lit. to delight)
encontrar to find
entender to understand
entrenarse to train
equilibrado/a balanced
el equipo team, equipment
esperar to wait, hope, expect
el estudio study, studio
evitar to avoid
favorito/a favourite
frío/a cold
la fruta fruit
fumar to smoke
ganar to earn, win
el gimnasio gym
la grasa grease, fat
la hamburguesa burger
el jamón ham
joven young
jugar to play
el kilómetro kilometre
llevar to take, carry, wear, lead
malo/a bad
mental mental
montar to ride, set up
el montón load, lot
mostrar to show
la natación swimming
normalmente normally
nunca never
el parque park
el partido match, game
las patatas fritas chips, fries
pedir to ask for, order
perder to lose
permitir to permit, allow
el pescado fish
el pollo chicken
el precio price
preferir to prefer
probar to try, test, sample
rápido/a fast, quick
la sal salt
la salud health
sano/a healthy
la semana week
el supermercado supermarket
tener que to have to
terrible terrible
la variedad variety
vegetariano/a vegetarian
la(s) verdura(s) vegetables
volver to return, go back

2.1H Cuidar de tu salud

¿a quién/quiénes? whom, to whom?
abrir to open
acostarse to go to bed
adaptarse to adapt
¿adónde? where to?
el aire air
antes (de) before
así like this, like that
beber to drink
la cabeza head
cada each, every
la calefacción heating
el calor heat
la cama bed
cambiar to change
el cambio change
la cena dinner, tea, evening meal
como as, like
¿cómo? how?
comprar to buy
el corazón heart
la crema cream
¿cuál/cuáles? which (ones)?
¿cuándo? when?
¿cuánto/a/os/as? how much?, how many?
cubrir to cover
el cuerpo body
el cuidado care
cuidar to care for, look after
de quién/quiénes? whose?
descansar to rest
diario daily
disfrutar to enjoy
dónde? where?
la energía energy
la enfermedad illness, disease
estar en forma to be fit
el estrés stress
el (fem.) hambre hunger
hasta until, up to
la hora hour, time
el huevo egg
ideal ideal
igual equal, same
importante important
ir to go
la leche milk
leer to read
el libro book
la manzana apple
menos less, least
necesitar to need

la noche night
ocho eight
olvidar to forget
el pan bread
la piel skin
por eso so, therefore
¿por qué? why?
primero/a first
puro/a pure
quedarse to stay
¿quién/quiénes? who?
el rato time, while
la razón reason
recomendar to recommend
recordar to remember
el régimen diet
relajante relaxing
respirar to breathe
el riesgo risk
la sed thirst
el sol sun
la sombra shadow, shade
la suerte luck
también also, as well
tan …como as … as
usar to use
vegano/a vegan
la ventana window
la vida life

2.2F Tipos de dietas

aquí here
el azúcar sugar
bastante quite
consistir to consist
durante during
la ensalada salad
España Spain
Europa Europe
la falta lack, shortage
fresco/a cool, fresh
frito/a fried
el futuro future
el/la hermano/a brother/sister
intentar to try
el/la Internet
lo que what
luego then
más more, most
el/la médico/a doctor
el medio ambiente environment
mediterráneo Mediterranean
menor younger, smaller
natural natural
ninguno/a none, not any
la oficina office
el peso weight
la planta plant
preparar to prepare
el producto product
la proteína protein
la región region
la revista magazine
sacar to take out, (get)
seguir to follow
servir to serve
el sur south
el tipo type
tonto/a silly, stupid
trabajar to work
venir to come
el/la veterinario/a vet

2.2H La vida en España

el aceite oil
el/la adulto/a adult
alemán/alemana German
alguno/a some
andaluz(a) Andalusian
argentino/a Argentinian
la bebida drink
el café coffee
caliente hot
los cereales cereals
cerrado/a closed, shut
chileno/a Chilean
chino/a Chinese
el chocolate chocolate
decir to say, tell
declarar to declare
demasiado too, too much
después after, afterwards
doce twelve
el/la dueño/a owner
dulce sweet
el ejemplo example
la escuela school
español(a) Spanish
europeo/a European
la fiesta festival, party
francés/francesa (adj.) French
la gente people
hay que you/one must, it is necessary to
histórico/a historic
el horario timetable, schedule
inglés/inglesa (adj.) English
el lunes Monday
la manera manner, way
el martes Tuesday
medio/a half
la merienda afternoon snack
mexicano/a Mexican
nuestro/a our
nueve nine
once eleven
la paella paella (rice and seafood dish)
el plato dish, plate
por for
procesado/a processed
el puente bridge, Bank holiday
el queso cheese
quince fifteen
religioso/a religious
la ropa clothes
el sándwich sandwich
seis six
sentarse to sit (down)
la siesta siesta, afternoon nap
sobre on, about
el sofá sofa, settee
la sopa soup
la tarde afternoon, evening
todavía still
tomar to take, have, drink, eat
el tomate tomato
la tortilla Spanish omelette
tostado/a toasted
el trabajo work, job
treinta thirty
tres three
el zumo juice

3.1F En el instituto

el/la alumno/a pupil
el ambiente atmosphere
anterior previous
apoyar to support
la asignatura subject
la biblioteca library
la chaqueta jacket
correcto/a correct
los deberes homework
el dibujo art, drawing
donde where
duro/a hard
el edificio building
la educación education
explicar to expla in
la geografía geography
la historia history
el idioma language
la informática ICT
el inglés (n.) English (language)
la instalación facility
levantar to raise
la mano hand
la mesa table, desk
el móvil mobile (phone)
nada nothing
el ordenador computer, PC
el pasillo corridor
el patio yard, patio, playground
peor worse, worst
privado/a private
el/la profesor(a) teacher
el recreo break, break time
respetar to respect
la silla chair
sin embargo however
el uniforme uniform
útil useful
el viernes Friday

3.1H Lo bueno y lo malo del instituto

el acoso bullying
el aire libre in the open air, outdoors
apreciar to appreciate
aprender to learn
aprobar to pass (eg. exam)
arruinar to ruin
el arte art
asistir (a) to attend
barato/a cheap
casi almost, nearly
el color colour

cómodo/a comfortable

el comportamiento behaviour

construir to build

la cosa thing

crear to create

describir to describe

el diccionario dictionary

enfermo/a ill, sick

escribir to write

estudiar to study

el examen exam

el éxito success

la experiencia experience

extra extra

el extranjero abroad

faltar to be lacking, missing

fascinar to fascinate

feo/a ugly

el francés (n.) French (language)

importar to matter

interesar to interest

jamás never

lento/a slow

libre free, unoccupied

los/las demás the others, the rest

mal badly

matemáticas Maths

mejorar to improve

el mundo world

la música music

negativo/a negative

ni neither, nor

normal normal

el norte north

la nota grade, mark

oír to hear

online online

la oportunidad opportunity

organizar to organise

la página page

la palabra word

para to, for

la parte part

participar to participate, take part

el periódico newspaper

pocos/as a few, few, not many

posible possible

la presión pressure

el proyecto project

la prueba test, exam

¿Qué tal ...? How is/was ..., how are/were ...?

el recurso resource

la regla rule, ruler

la religión religion

repasar to revise

el resto rest

el resultado result

sentirse to feel

el sitio web website

suspender to fail (ie. exam)

tampoco neither, either

el teatro theatre, drama

terminar to finish

la traducción translation

la ventaja advantage

el viaje journey

viejo/a old

ya no no longer, not ... any more

3.2F Los trabajos

aburrido/a boring

el/la abogado/a lawyer

el accidente accident

aceptar to accept

el aeropuerto airport

el artículo article

el banco bank

la caja box, till

el/la camarero/a waiter/waitress

la carrera career, degree course, race

el centro centre

cerca de near to

la ciudad city

el/la cliente customer

de moda fashionable

la desventaja disadvantage

diseñar to design

el/la empleado/a employee

el/la enfermero/a nurse

enseñar to teach, show

estupendo/a great, brilliant

el euro euro

la experiencia laboral work experience

la física physics

gritar to shout

hacer preguntas to ask questions

hermoso/a beautiful

la información information

el/la ingeniero/a engineer

el/la jefe/jefa boss

la medicina medicine

mil thousand

el museo museum

las noticias news

la novela novel

la obra work (of art, literature)

la opción option

pagar to pay

la película film

el/la periodista journalist

presentar to present, introduce

la profesión profession

resolver to solve

el restaurante restaurant

saber to know

el salario salary

seguro/a safe, sure, secure

la serie series

tener éxito to be successful

el traje suit, costume

la universidad university

viajar to travel

el vuelo flight

3.2H Buscando trabajo

acompañar to accompany

además de as well as

la administración administration

apropiado/a appropriate

el/la candidato/a candidate

la carta letter

cierto/a certain

comenzar to begin, start

el conocimiento knowledge

la consecuencia consequence

considerar to consider

el currículum CV

dedicar to dedicate, devote

demostrar to show, demonstrate

depender to depend

destacar to highlight, emphasise

el detalle detail

el empleo work, employment

la empresa firm, company

en sí mismo/a in itself

la entrevista interview

enviar to send

exagerar to exaggerate

falso/a false

la formación training

funcionar to work, function

grave serious

hace falta it is necessary, you must

la historia story

humano/a human

la imagen image

la industria industry

el interés interest

investigar to research

llegar to arrive

lograr to manage

mentir to lie, tell a lie

el minuto minute

nadie no one, nobody

el negocio business

la organización organisation

perfecto/a perfect

el perfil profile

personalizado/a personalised

planear to plan

la planificación planning

la pregunta question

el premio prize

la preparación preparation

proactivo/a proactive

el puesto job, post

el punto point

recibir to receive

la red social social network

relajado/a relaxed

sino but

el sitio place

solicitar to apply for

tal y como just as, exactly as

tardar to take (time)

tú mismo/a yourself

vale la pena it is worthwhile

Test and revise: Higher Listening

1 Listen to these people talking about members of their family. Answer the questions in English.

a What does the girl say about her older sister? **1 mark**

b What does the boy think is going to happen? **1 mark**

c What does the woman say about her two sons? **1 mark**

d What does the boy do if he is worried? **1 mark**

Consejo

Make sure you include *all* the information you think may be needed to answer a question. For example, in question 1d, you need to mention who the boy talks to *and* what he asks for.

2 Listen to these people talking about a problem they have had with a friend.

Write **A** if only statement A is correct
B if only statement B is correct
A+B if both statements A and B are correct.

a Sara

A	Sara lent Carla a T-shirt.
B	Carla lost the T-shirt.

1 mark

b Jaime

A	Jaime finds Álvaro unreliable.
B	They need Álvaro on the team.

1 mark

c Ángela

A	Lucía helps Ángela in Biology.
B	Lucía wants help with homework.

1 mark

d David

A	José betrayed David's trust.
B	David has managed to forgive José.

1 mark

3 Silvia is talking about aspects of her lifestyle.

Write **P** for a **positive** opinion.
N for a **negative** opinion.
P+N for a **positive** and **negative** opinion.

a Diet **1 mark**

b Exercise **1 mark**

c Sleep **1 mark**

d Work / life balance **1 mark**

4 These people are talking about the good and bad aspects of their meal in a restaurant. Write down the correct letter for each aspect.

A	Cost
B	Food
C	Menu
D	Restaurant
E	Service
F	Wine

a Eric: Good aspect Bad aspect **2 marks**

b Lorena: Good aspect Bad aspect **2 marks**

5 Listen to the head teacher talking in assembly at a Spanish school. When does each event take place?

Write **P** for something that happened **in the past**
N for something that is happening **now**
F for something that is going to happen **in the future**.

a the final exam **1 mark**
b the football competition **1 mark**
c the visit by English students **1 mark**
d non-uniform day **1 mark**

Consejo

For this type of question, you need to listen out for clues to the time frame. To start with, listen to the verbs and decide whether they are past, present or future. Secondly, listen out for time phrases like *mañana por la tarde* or *el mes pasado*.

6 Listen to these questions that an interviewer asks. What is the focus of each of her questions? Write the correct letter.

a A relationship with others
B job suitability
C appropriate qualifications **1 mark**

b A exam results
B working away from home
C training **1 mark**

c A managing people
B organising work events
C learning from mistakes **1 mark**

d A work experience
B reason for application
C knowledge of the company **1 mark**

Dictation A

You will now hear 5 short sentences.

- Listen carefully and using your knowledge of Spanish sounds, write down in **Spanish** exactly what you hear for each sentence.
- You will hear each sentence **three** times: the first time as a full sentence, the second time in short sections and the third time again as a full sentence.
- Use your knowledge of Spanish sounds and grammar to make sure that what you have written makes sense. Check carefully that your spelling is accurate.

10 marks

Consejo

In the dictation, there are about 30 words in total so there will be about 5–7 words per sentence. Remember tips like: there are no double letters with f, s, p; there is no 'ph' in Spanish, it is always 'f'; and bear in mind there may be a silent 'h' somewhere – but in a word that you will know and recognise.

Dictation B

You will now hear 5 short sentences.

- Listen carefully and using your knowledge of Spanish sounds, write down in **Spanish** exactly what you hear for each sentence.
- You will hear each sentence **three** times: the first time as a full sentence, the second time in short sections and the third time again as a full sentence.
- Use your knowledge of Spanish sounds and grammar to make sure that what you have written makes sense. Check carefully that your spelling is accurate.

10 marks

Test and revise: Higher Speaking

Role Play

You are talking to your Mexican friend.

Your teacher (or partner) will play the part of your friend and will speak first.

You should address your friend as *tú*.

When you see this – ? – you will have to ask a question.

In order to score full marks, you must include a verb in your response to each task.

1. Say what you think about your school and give one reason why. (Give **one** opinion and **one** reason.)
2. Say what you are going to do at school tomorrow. (Give **two** details.)
3. Say what is a disadvantage of the school timetable. (Give **one** disadvantage.)
4. Say why homework is important. (Give **one** detail).
5. **?** Ask your friend a question about the subjects they study.

Consejo

When you plan the role play during the preparation time, remember that each question in the role play is marked individually. You won't be penalised for repeating information twice.

Reading aloud task

When your teacher (or partner) asks you, read aloud the following text in **Spanish**.

Hace cuatro meses, cuando fui a España por primera vez, viajé a algunas ciudades del sur del país.

Creo que la vida allí es bastante tranquila.

La gente pasa más tiempo en la calle al aire libre porque el clima es agradable. La comida es muy rica y siempre usan productos regionales.

You will then be asked four questions in **Spanish** that relate to the topic of **Healthy living and lifestyle**. Make sure you answer **all four questions as fully as you can**.

Consejo

In the reading aloud task, do not think that speaking very fast makes you sound authentic and impressive. Examiners need to hear the accuracy of your pronunciation, so speak at a normal, steady pace and speak up loud and clear.

Photo card

- During your preparation time, look at the two photos. You may make as many notes as you wish on an Additional Answer Sheet and use these notes during the test.
- Your teacher (or partner) will ask you to talk about the content of these photos. The recommended time is approximately **one and a half minutes. You must say at least one thing about each photo.**
- After you have spoken about the content of the photos, your teacher (or partner) will then ask you questions related to **any** of the topics within the theme of **People and lifestyle.**

Consejo

When talking about the photo card, there are no quality of language marks, so descriptions can be simple. You can make assumptions when talking about the photo, for example, in Photo 2 below, you could say you think the boy is explaining to his grandfather how to use his new phone.

Photo 1

Photo 2

Test and revise: Higher Reading

1 Some young people have uploaded these posts to a blog about school. What does each person complain about?

El gobierno tiene que dedicar más dinero al sistema educativo. En nuestro instituto, el edificio es viejo y frío. Y ¿cómo podemos aprender informática si nos faltan ordenadores? **Daniel**

Hoy en día, el nivel de presión es difícil de aguantar. Hay que estudiar horas y horas cada noche. Además, si suspendemos las pruebas, nuestros padres nos pueden castigar. **Chloe**

Lo peor del colegio es cómo tratan a los pequeños los estudiantes mayores. A veces, les quitan los libros y los tiran a la basura o les roban el dinero para comprar la comida. **Sergio**

Lo que necesitamos es más apoyo **a la hora** de escoger qué vamos a hacer en el futuro. Por ejemplo, no sabemos lo suficiente sobre las diferencias entre el bachillerato y la formación profesional. **Claudia**

A	Bullying	**D**	Help with homework
B	Choosing a course	**E**	Parents' evenings
C	Facilities	**F**	Stress

a Daniel **1 mark**
b Chloe **1 mark**
c Sergio **1 mark**
d Claudia **1 mark**

e Read the last paragraph carefully.
What do you think *a la hora de* means?

A	when it comes to
B	early
C	because we can't

1 mark

Consejo

Question 1e above requires you to **work out the general meaning of a word or phrase from the context**. You will need to read around it and use all the clues in the rest of the sentence or paragraph. There will be two questions like this on the reading exam.

2 Two young people have posted these comments about how a friend has helped them.

For each question, write **A** if only statement A is correct
B if only statement B is correct
A+B if both statements A and B are correct.

Mi amiga Mónica

El año pasado me peleé con mis padres y decidí escaparme de casa. Cogí mi mochila y me fui a la ciudad. Mi madre llamó a mi amiga, llorando, y cuando Mónica entendió lo que pasaba, me siguió a la ciudad y me encontró dormida en la calle. Insistió en llevarme a casa. No sé qué me habría pasado sin ella. **Victoria**

a **A** Victoria ran away from home.
B Victoria phoned her friend for help. **1 mark**

b **A** Victoria's mother was very upset.
B Mónica went in search of Victoria. **1 mark**

Mi amigo Rodrigo

A mí me cuesta mucho entender las matemáticas cuando el profesor explica en clase y, sin duda, no iba a aprobar el examen. Mi amigo, Rodrigo, se ofreció para venir a mi casa para darme unas clases. Es muy listo y además es muy paciente; con él, he logrado superar mis dificultades y tengo confianza para el examen de este jueves. **Nicolás**

c **A** Nicolás struggles with Maths.
B Nicolás failed the Maths exam. **1 mark**

d **A** Rodrigo gave Nicolás extra help.
B Nicolás finally passed the exam. **1 mark**

3 **Some people have been posting their comments on a healthy living website. Answer the questions in English.**

Yo antes comía demasiada carne, normalmente con todas las comidas. Desde hace dos semanas he intentado cambiar la carne por platos vegetarianos o por pescado. Me siento mucho mejor.
Mateo

Cuando era niña, hacía muchas actividades físicas como baloncesto y baile. Hoy en día no puedo encontrar tiempo para nada y no me gusta cómo soy. Necesito perder peso.
Daniela

Mis compañeros toman mucho café durante la mañana en la oficina y se comen los caramelos que guardan en la mesa. Para no hacer lo mismo, yo compro un montón de naranjas y manzanas para llevar al trabajo y solo bebo agua.
Valeria

- **a** Why did Mateo feel he should change his diet? **1 mark**
- **b** Why is Mateo feeling much better now? **1 mark**
- **c** How do we know that Daniela was an active child? **1 mark**
- **d** What is Daniela unhappy about now? **1 mark**
- **e** What unhealthy habits have Valeria's colleagues got into? **1 mark**
- **f** What does Valeria do instead? **1 mark**

Consejo

Make sure you give all the relevant information that might be required in an answer. For instance, in question 3c, we are told of two activities that Daniela used to do when younger. They are both relevant to the question, so both must be included in the answer.

4 **Translate these sentences into English.**

- **a** María preparará el arroz que van a tomar para la cena.
- **b** Estudio alemán desde hace diez meses.
- **c** Acabamos de terminar nuestro examen de dibujo.
- **d** Les preguntaré si pueden hacerme una ensalada sin aceite.
- **e** Lo mejor de mi familia es que nunca discutimos. **10 marks**

5 **Translate these sentences into English.**

- **a** Hay que tomar un desayuno saludable antes de ir al instituto.
- **b** Jamás fumo y nunca voy a empezar.
- **c** No vale la pena intentar repasar durante el recreo.
- **d** El colegio se cerrará porque va a haber una huelga de profesores.
- **e** El horario típico de un instituto español comienza a las ocho y termina a las dos y media. **10 marks**

Test and revise: Higher Writing

1 Translate the following sentences into Spanish.

a I have to do my homework in the evenings.

b It is important to study foreign languages.

c Next month, my brother is going to play in a basketball tournament.

d In order to have a healthy life, you need to eat a balanced diet.

e Tonight my friends and I will see a very good film in the cinema.

10 marks

Consejo

Don't leave out a whole sentence if you are finding it hard. Marks will be awarded for the sections that are completed so always do the parts that you can and then go back to the text and make a considered guess for any gaps you may have.

Either Question 2.1 *or* Question 2.2

2.1 You are writing to a new penfriend about your family and friends.
Write approximately 90 words in Spanish.
You must write something about each bullet point.

Mention:

- what your best friend is like
- where you went with friends last weekend
- activities that you will do with your family.

15 marks

2.2 You are writing an article about healthy living.
Write approximately 90 words in Spanish.
You must write something about each bullet point.

Mention:

- what you do to keep fit
- something you used to eat that was not very healthy.
- what healthy things you will do in the future.

15 marks

Consejo

Use the list of bullet points as a check list and tick each topic off once you have mentioned it. Also, pay attention to the time frame of each bullet point. Is it asking about the past, present or future?

Either Question 3.1 *or* Question 3.2

3.1 You are writing a post for a Spanish website on health and lifestyle.
Write approximately 150 words in Spanish.
You must write something about both bullet points.

Mention:

- how to have a healthy and active lifestyle
- how this lifestyle will improve your health and well-being in the future.

25 marks

3.2 You are writing an article about education.
Write approximately 150 words in Spanish.
You must write something about both bullet points.

Describe:

- subjects you think should be taught in schools and why
- how you will prepare for getting a job in the future.

25 marks

Consejo

If you think you can say a lot more about one of the bullet points than the other, this is not a problem. You will not be marked down if you write more about one aspect than the other, but **you must cover both bullet points**.

Theme 2
Popular culture

Free-time activities

1 **Listen to these young people talking about what they do in their free time. Match each statement to the correct image (a–f).**

a

b

c

d

e

f

la app	app
aprender	to learn
el atletismo	athletics
el deporte	sport
el instrumento	instrument
ir de compras	to go shopping
jugar (a)	to play
leer	to read
la lengua	language
el libro	book
practicar	to practise
el tiempo libre	free time
tocar	to play (an instrument)
ver	to watch
el videojuego	videogame

2 **Match each question to its most likely answer.**

1 ¿Vas a salir con tus amigos esta tarde?
2 ¿Te gusta nadar en el mar?
3 ¿Cuál es tu deporte preferido?
4 ¿Eres muy activa los fines de semana?
5 ¿Cuál es tu opinión sobre cocinar?
6 ¿Te interesan las redes sociales?

a El fútbol porque es un deporte rápido. Mi jugador favorito es Gavi.
b No, es peligroso. Prefiero ir a la piscina.
c Un montón – me encanta subir fotos a mi cuenta de Instagram.
d Sí, voy a salir con Mario y Alicia a las tres.
e Me gusta mucho preparar platos sencillos para mi familia.
f No mucho. Los sábados normalmente descanso en casa.

cocinar	to cook	*la piscina*	swimming pool
la cuenta	account	*rápido/a*	fast
descansar	to rest/relax	*la red social*	social network
el fin de semana	weekend	*salir*	to go out
el/la jugador/a	player	*sencillo/a*	simple
nadar	to swim	*subir fotos*	to upload photos
peligroso/a	dangerous		

3 **Match the adjectives to the correct antonym (opposite word) from the box.**

barato/a · divertido/a · útil · bueno/a · fácil · lento/a · peligroso/a

aburrido/a · caro/a · seguro/a · inútil · difícil · rápido/a · malo/a

la ciencia ficción	science fiction
el concierto	concert
el documental	documentary
encantar	to love
en vivo	live
guay	cool
aburrir	to be boring
la película	film
pensar	to think
raro/a	odd
la serie	series

4 **Listen to six people (1–6) discussing TV and film. Decide whether their statements are positive (P), negative (N) or positive and negative (P+N).**

Customs, festivals and celebrations

5 **Read this blog entry and answer the questions. Then translate the text into English.**

El blog de Miguel

Vivo en San Sebastián, también conocida como Donostia. Es una ciudad en el norte de España y tiene muchas costumbres y tradiciones únicas.

Tenemos un Festival Internacional de Cine anual muy importante, con premios y visitas de actores y actrices famosos.

El año que viene va a venir el actor chileno Pedro Pascal. ¡Qué emocionante! Me encantan sus series y películas.

Además de las películas y los videojuegos, también me encanta ir a la playa de mi ciudad, que se llama 'La Concha'. ¡Es hermosa!

¡Qué suerte tengo de vivir aquí!

además de	as well as
anual	annual, yearly
el cine	cinema
conocido/a	known
la costumbre	custom
emocionante	exciting
hermoso/a	beautiful
el premio	prize
la suerte	luck
único/a	unique
venir	to come

a What is San Sebastián also known as?

b Where is it located?

c How often does the San Sebastián film festival take place?

d How do we know Miguel is a fan of Pedro Pascal? (two details)

e What is 'La Concha' and how does Miguel describe it?

6 Read Amaia's description of Christmas festivities at home. Complete each sentence with the correct word from the box.

familia rojo hermano celebraciones árbol abuelos

¡Me llamo Amaia y me encantan las [1] ___! En la foto...

Soy la niña sonriente con el vestido [2] ___ .

Koldo, mi [3] ___ pequeño lleva un jersey.

Mis padres y mis [4] ___ también están en esta foto.

Hay un [5] ___ de Navidad muy bonito con luces.

Me gustan los regalos, pero lo mejor de todo es pasar tiempo con mi [6] ___ ¡Qué divertido!

los abuelos	grandparents
el árbol	tree
la celebración	celebration
sonriente	smiley
llevar	to wear
las luces	lights
lo mejor	the best thing
la Navidad	Christmas
el/la niño/a	child
los padres	parents
pasar (tiempo)	to spend (time)
el regalo	present, gift
el vestido	dress

7 Listen to Amaia's friend, Ester, describe another traditional festival. Complete the fact file with the correct information.

Fact File

Name: *Ester*

Age: 1 ___

Home city: 2 ___

Location: 3 ___

Date of festival: 4 ___

Name of festival: 5 ___

Why it is important: 6 ___

Where many young people celebrate it: 7 ___

Why they celebrate it there: 8 ___

allí	there
celebrar	to celebrate
la ciudad	city
corto/a	short
la fiesta	party, festival
el/la joven	teenager, young person
largo/a	long
la noche	night
la playa	beach

8 **Match the items of clothing (1–6) to the correct picture (a–f).**

1 una camisa de flores
2 un vestido largo
3 unos zapatos negros
4 un reloj inteligente
5 unas zapatillas de marca
6 una camiseta roja

a

b

c

d

e

f

una camisa shirt
una camiseta T-shirt
un reloj watch
un vestido dress
unas zapatillas trainers
unos zapatos shoes

Celebrity culture

9 **Listen to five young people discussing their favourite celebrities. Complete the sentences with the words from the box. Then translate them into English.**

subir perfiles videojuegos activa siempre
favorito lleva habla famoso ver

1 El tenista Carlos Alcaraz es mi deportista **a** ___. Siempre **b** ___ con sus seguidores.
2 Selena Gómez no es muy **a** ___ en Instagram. ¿Va a **b** ___ alguna foto interesante?
3 El actor Manu Ríos es divertido y **a** ___ ropa que está de moda. Me gusta **b** ___ sus series en Netflix.
4 No sigo a ningún **a** ___ en TikTok. Prefiero los **b** ___ sobre comida o viajes.
5 Mi streamer favorita se llama Espe; **a** ___ juega a **b** ___ en Twitch.

de moda fashionable
el/la famoso/a celebrity
hablar to talk
la ropa clothes
el/la seguidor/a follower
seguir to follow
subir to upload
ver to watch

10 **Read Leonardo's daily routine and complete the table with the missing information.**

La rutina de Leonardo, un actor mexicano
Leonardo trabaja en varias series de televisión. Su rutina por la mañana es sencilla. Se levanta a las siete, desayuna a las siete y cuarto y se viste a las siete y media. Antes de salir de casa a las ocho, se lava los dientes. Trabaja hasta las seis y vuelve a casa a las seis y media. Cena con su familia a las nueve.

Activity	Time
gets up	**1** ___
2 ___	7:15 am
gets dressed	**3** ___
4 ___	8:00 am
finishes work	**5** ___
6 ___	6:30 pm
has dinner	**7** ___

cenar to have dinner
desayunar to have breakfast
lavarse los dientes to brush one's teeth
levantarse to get up
la mañana morning
la rutina routine
salir to go out
sencillo/a simple
vestirse to get dressed
volver to return

4.1F ¡Nos gusta el riesgo!

OBJECTIVES
- Extreme sports
- The personal *a*
- The present continuous (including irregular gerunds)
- Pronunciation *g*

1 **Read the adverts promoting summer camps. Match the adverts (1–4) to the photos (a–d).**

1 Este verano puedes hacer kayak con tus amigos. Aquí, los chicos y las chicas siempre están subiendo y bajando las aguas rápidas en el río.

2 Durante el mes de septiembre tienes clases de submarinismo en la costa. ¡Los peces están nadando cerca de ti!

3 Hay dos visitas al día a la ciudad de Bilbao donde los jóvenes están haciendo parkour entre las casas y los edificios del barrio antiguo.

4 ¿Te gustan las montañas? Tenemos dos actividades emocionantes: alpinismo y escalada. Puedes ver los pájaros mientras estás respirando aire puro.

Gramática

The present continuous

The present continuous is used to describe an action that is in progress. It is formed by using the verb *estar* ('to be') in the present tense and the present participle (the *-ing* form of a verb).

To form the present participle – also known as 'the gerund' – remove the *-ar* ending from the infinitive and add *-ando*.

jugar – to play

estoy jugando – I am playing

For *-er* and *-ir* verbs, remove the *-er* or *-ir* and add *-iendo*.

hacer – to do

está haciendo – he / she is doing

a

b

c

d

2 **Find four examples of the present continuous in activity 1 and translate them into English.**

3 **Complete each sentence with the present participle of the verbs in brackets.**

a Mi hermano está ___ (*practicar*) natación al aire libre.
b Los jóvenes están ___ (*subir*) la montaña.
c Yo estoy ___ (*leer*) un libro sobre la historia del deporte en México.
d Los jugadores están ___ (*entrenar*) muy duro en el gimnasio.
e ¡El chico se está ___ (*caer*) de la bicicleta!

Gramática

Irregular gerunds

Be careful! There are several irregular present participles in Spanish. Some examples of these are:

leer – *le**y**endo* (reading)

traer – *tra**y**endo* (bringing)

caer – *ca**y**endo* (falling)

ir – ***y**endo* (going)

preferir – *pref**i**riendo* (preferring)

vestir – *v**i**stiendo* (dressing)

seguir – *s**i**guiendo* (following, continuing)

morir – *m**u**riendo* (dying)

dormir – *d**u**rmiendo* (sleeping)

4 **Listen to Elias talk about skydiving, his favourite extreme sport. Complete the sentences in English.**

a You jump out when the plane reaches a height of ___.
b My step mum thinks it is ___, but I am not ___.
c Normally, I do this sport ___.
d It's best when the weather is ___ and ___.
e The only problem is that ___ because ___.

5 **With a partner, take turns to read aloud the following sentences in Spanish.**

a Ayer vi a mi tío Pedro en el estadio de fútbol.
b Visito a mis abuelos los domingos.
c Isabel, ¿conoces a Miguel?
d Creo que Óscar está llamando a David.

Pronunciación

g

When it comes directly before the vowels 'a', 'o' and 'u', the 'g' makes a hard sound, just as it does in English.

Examples: *jugando, gobierno, gustar*

Gramática

The personal *a*

The personal *a* is used when the direct object of a sentence is a person. For example:

*Veo **a** Marta.* – I see Marta.

*Voy a ver **a** mi primo.* – I am going to see my cousin.

But:

Veo la casa. – I see the house.

Visito Italia. – I visit Italy.

6 **Translate the sentences in activity 5 into English.**

7 **Look at the photo and write at least <u>five</u> sentences in Spanish to describe it.**

From a photo, you can describe location, people, objects or animals, and you can also give justified opinions. You can use the following expressions to help structure a description of any photo:

en la foto hay – in the photo there is / are
se puede ver – you can see
que yo vea – as far as I can see
a mi modo de ver – in my opinion
creo que – I think that
además – furthermore
a la izquierda / a la derecha / en el centro hay – on the left / right / in the centre there is / are
en primer plano hay – in the foreground there is / are
al fondo hay – in the background there is / are

You can also use the present continuous tense:

está hablando – he / she is talking
está sonriendo – he / she is smiling
está mirando – he / she is looking at
está haciendo – he / she is doing

8 **Read aloud your sentences from activity 7 to a partner.**

4.1H ¡Mi tiempo libre es infinito!

OBJECTIVES
- A wide range of hobbies
- Verbs with prepositions
- Demonstrative adjectives *this, that, these* and *those*

1 Read the online profiles. Complete the texts with the correct word from the box below. Be careful! There are some words you don't need.

aire   carreras   casa   deporte   ropa   tiempo

Raúl @raumiau
Soy muy aficionado a los videojuegos. Tengo dos **consolas** en casa y siempre que puedo, después del insti, juego una hora al día. Prefiero los juegos de aventuras y las **1** ___ de coches, aunque también disfruto mucho con los juegos clásicos como el Tetris o el ***Comecocos***.

Nuria @lanuri26
La moda es muy importante para mí, y por eso me gusta ir de compras con mis amigos. Desafortunadamente, hay que ahorrar mucho dinero si quieres comprar **2** ___ de marca. Por eso prefiero ir a tiendas de segunda mano.

Pascual @paskirisas
A pesar de ser una actividad lenta y sin riesgo, los domingos me gusta mucho pasear al **3** ___ libre. No me importa hacerlo solo o en compañía. Me interesa andar por el campo o cerca del mar.

Lola y Juana @lasmellis
Somos dos hermanas y nuestra actividad favorita es entrenar en el gimnasio. El beneficio es para nuestra salud física y mental. Si no tenemos **4** ___ para ir al gimnasio, entrenamos en el salón de casa o en el jardín. Nos gusta ver vídeos de **gimnastas** famosos en línea e intentar copiarlos.

la consola	games console
Comecocos	Pac-Man
a pesar de	despite
el / la gimnasta	gymnast
copiar	to copy

2 Read the texts again and answer the following questions in English.

a What two types of videogames does Raúl prefer?
b According to Nuria, what is the disadvantage of being interested in fashion?
c Which two areas does Pascual like to walk in?
d What do Lola and Juana do if they can't make it to the gym?

3 Translate these sentences into Spanish. For each sentence, choose the correct conjugated verb with preposition from the box below.

aprendí a   empezaron a   estás esperando a
hablarás con   me olvidé de   voy a dejar de

a Will you talk to Luis in the car?
b I am going to stop playing videogames.
c They started to dance salsa at the party.
d I learnt to cook paella with my friend in Valencia.
e Are you waiting for your sister?
f I forgot to buy a present for my cousin's birthday.

Los verbos

Verbs with prepositions

There are many common verbs in Spanish which are followed by a preposition you may not expect so they just have to be learnt. They include:

acordarse de – to remember
aprender a (+ infinitive) – to learn to
comenzar a (+ infinitive) – to start
consistir en – to consist of
dejar de (+ infinitive) – to stop / quit
empezar a (+ infinitive) – to start
esperar a – to wait for (a person)
hablar con – to speak to
olvidarse de – to forget about
pensar en – to think about
soñar con – to dream about / of
tardar en (+ infinitive) – to take a while to

4 Listen to this news item from a podcast about hobbies. Read the summary and complete each gap with the correct percentage according to what you hear.

According to a study by the University of Lima in Peru, **1** ___ % of young people prefer videogames to other activities. **2** ___% prefer classic videogames such as Super Mario. **3** Just ___% go out for a walk during the week and only **4** ___% cook at home. With regard to sports, **5** ___% prefer football above all, although **6** ___% say working out is important to them.

5 Complete the sentences with the correct form of the demonstrative adjectives in brackets.

a Voy a comprar ___ (*this*) videojuego.

b Quiero leer ___ (*those*) novelas.

c En mi opinión, ___ (*these*) zapatillas son cómodas.

d ___ (*That over there*) estadio es muy moderno.

e Me gusta mucho ___ (*that*) camiseta del Real Madrid.

Gramática

Demonstrative adjectives *this, that, these* and *those*

These adjectives change according to the gender and number of the noun they describe.

	masculine	feminine
this	*este*	*esta*
these	*estos*	*estas*
that	*ese*	*esa*
those	*esos*	*esas*
that (over there)	*aquel*	*aquella*
those (over there)	*aquellos*	*aquellas*

este videojuego – this videogame (masculine singular)

esa actividad – that activity (feminine singular)

estos deportes – these sports (masculine plural)

aquellas jóvenes – those young women (over there) (feminine plural)

6 Answer the following questions in Spanish in as much detail as possible. Use the tables to help you structure your answers. Then ask and answer the questions with a partner.

a ¿Qué te gusta hacer en tu tiempo libre?

b ¿Qué actividades te gustaría hacer en el futuro?

a	a / b	a / b	a / b	a / b	a / b	a / b
Me apasiona Me encanta Me gusta (mucho) Me interesa Prefiero Suelo **b** Me gustaría Pienso en Sueño con Voy a aprender a Voy a empezar / comenzar a	bailar… cantar… cocinar… escuchar… entrenar… hacer… jugar… leer… pasear / caminar… pintar… practicar… tocar… ver…	porque / ya que / dado que pienso que / creo que que yo sepa a mi modo de ver es…	bastante demasiado muy súper tan un poco	bueno / a divertido / a económico / a emocionante fácil genial guay increíble interesante maravilloso rápido / a útil	y también además aunque pero es…	bueno / a divertido / a económico / a emocionante fácil genial guay increíble interesante maravilloso rápido / a útil

4.2F Veo, veo... ¿Qué ves?

OBJECTIVES
- Television and film
- Adverbs of frequency
- The preterite for regular verbs, plus irregular *ver* and *ir*

1 **Look at the list of types of TV programme in Spanish and match them to the pictures (a–h).**

un documental sobre el Amazonas
el tiempo
una serie de aventuras
las noticias
un programa de cocina
una telenovela colombiana
un programa de entrevistas
un concurso cultural

2 **Listen to six people talking about what they watch on television. For each person (1–6), write in Spanish the type of programme from activity 1 that they describe.**

3 **Listen again to the people in activity 2 and write down seven adverbs or expressions of frequency you hear.**

4 **Complete the sentences with the correct form of the preterite tense of the verbs in brackets. Watch out for irregular verbs *ir* and *ver*.**

a Ayer yo ___ (*ver*) una película muy buena.
b Anoche, Carmen ___ (*ver*) un documental sobre animales.
c En Madrid tú ___ (*escuchar*) música en vivo.
d La semana pasada yo ___ (*escribir*) sobre mi serie favorita.
e El fin de semana pasado mi amiga y yo ___ (*ir*) al parque.
f En Alicante, mis amigos ___ (*disfrutar*) del buen tiempo.

Gramática

The preterite tense for regular verbs, plus irregular *ver* and *ir*

This past tense is used to describe actions completed at a fixed point in time or during a specific period of time. It is formed by removing the *-ar*, *-er* or *-ir* of the infinitive, then adding the following endings:

pronoun	-ar	-er / -ir
yo	*-é*	*-í*
tú	*-aste*	*-iste*
él / ella / usted	*-ó*	*-ió*
nosotros / as	*-amos*	*-imos*
vosotros / as	*-asteis*	*-isteis*
ellos / ellas / ustedes	*-aron*	*-ieron*

comprar – to buy   *compr**é*** – I bought
salir – to go out   *sal**iste*** – you went out

There are many irregular verbs in the preterite tense. Some of these verbs are highly irregular, like the verb *ir*, whereas others only have minor changes, such as *ver*, which does not include any accents.

ir – to go: *fui, fuiste, fue, fuimos, fuisteis, fueron*

ver – to see: *vi, viste, vio, vimos, visteis, vieron*

5 **Read Rocío and Pascual's opinions on cinema. Then match statements (a–f) to the correct person, Rocío (R), Pascual (P) or both (R+P).**

Rocío

Prefiero ver las películas en casa, porque tengo una televisión muy grande. El cine me parece muy caro. Entre mis preferencias están las películas del oeste, las de dibujos animados y las musicales, aunque me gusta todo tipo de películas. La semana pasada vi una peli en Netflix con mi primo Luis. Quiero ver una película en otro idioma, pero es difícil leer rápidamente en español.

Pascual

Me gusta un montón ir al cine solo. Allí el ambiente es genial porque es tranquilo, cómodo y la pantalla es grande. Ayer vi una peli romántica en el cine y no estuvo nada mal. Además, me interesan las películas antiguas en blanco y negro, aunque a veces las pelis de historia son difíciles de entender. ¿Mis favoritas? Sin duda, las películas extranjeras.

Who…

- **a** has a negative opinion of the cinema?
- **b** watches films alone?
- **c** is interested in foreign films?
- **d** watches films on a big screen?
- **e** likes any type of film?
- **f** finds subtitles hard to read?

6 **Describe the last time you went to the cinema. Mention the following points:**

- when and where you went
- what film you saw and what type of film it is
- your opinion of both the film and the cinema
- how often you go to the cinema
- whether you prefer to watch films at home or in the cinema
- what film you would like to watch next

Use the following language to help you structure your answer:

fui – I went

vi – I saw

fue – it was

prefiero… – I prefer…

me gustaría ver… – I would like to see…

7 **Present your answer to your class or to a small group.**

Gramática

Adverbs of frequency

They are words that explain how often something is done. Some common examples are:

a veces – sometimes | *siempre* – always

nunca – never | *normalmente* – normally

Other common ways of expressing frequency are:

una vez / dos veces – once / twice

al día / mes / año – a day / month / year

a la semana – a week

una vez al día – once a day

cada – every

cada lunes – every Monday

todos los días – every day

4.2H Mi tiempo es oro

OBJECTIVES
- Unusual hobbies
- The superlative
- First-person spelling changes in the preterite tense

1 **Read the advertisements from a TV producer looking for young people with unusual hobbies. Complete the texts using the words from the box below. There are two words you don't need.**

cosa cuidado mano miedo objetos pasado ríos tiempo

trasladarse	transport (oneself)
los enseres	goods
el/la cuidador/a de animales	animal keeper/handler
abstracto	abstract
expresivo/a	expressive

Diseñador de "estilo *vintage*"

¿Te gustan los juguetes, libros u **1** ___ antiguos? ¿Vas a cafés decorados con muebles de segunda **2** ___ donde te **trasladas** al pasado? ¿Eres el más aficionado a la combinación de **enseres** reciclados, diseño nórdico e industrial y decoraciones pasadas de moda? ¡Queremos conocerte!

Cuidador de animales

¿Tienes animales en casa? Buscamos a alguien con las mascotas menos comunes. Si no te importa el peligro y no tienes **3** ___, eres la persona ideal para nosotros, sobre todo si ya tienes experiencia en el **4** ___ de animales exóticos.

Pintores abstractos

Si tienes una actitud artística y pintas mucho en tu **5** ___ libre, eres la persona que buscamos. ¿Pintas con colores vivos, formas nuevas y diferentes? ¿O dibujas paisajes, montañas o **6** ___ de una manera artística o **expresiva**? ¿Piensas que eres el Picasso del futuro? Te esperamos.

2 **Translate the text on abstract painters into English.**

Cultura

Pablo Picasso is one of the most famous and acclaimed artists of the twentieth century. As well as a painter, he was also a sculptor and ceramicist. He co-founded a new artistic movement known as Cubism and became a highly influential figure in modern art.

3 **Listen to three young people giving their opinion on Pablo Picasso. For each person (1–3), decide if their opinions are positive (P), negative (N) or positive and negative (P+N).**

Gramática

The superlative

When talking about 'the most' or 'the least' of something, use *el/la/los/las* + *más/menos* + adjective.

David es ***el más*** *alto.* – David is the tallest.

Note the following superlatives are irregular:

mejor(es) – best

peor(es) – worst

mayor(es) – oldest/biggest

menor(es) – youngest/smallest

Mi madre es la mayor de sus hermanas.
My mum is the eldest of her sisters.

4 Complete the sentences with the most appropriate adjective from the box below.

deliciosa | hermosa | inteligente | mayor | mejor | peor

a Raúl es **el estudiante más** ___ de la clase.
b Ese restaurante español es maravilloso. Tiene **la paella más** ___ de la ciudad.
c La playa que visité en México era **la más** ___ del mundo.
d En mi pueblo, la contaminación es **el** ___ **problema** que tenemos.
e Para mí, *Guernica*, de Pablo Picasso, es **la** ___ **obra de arte** de todos los tiempos.
f No me gustó nada aquel viaje a las montañas. Fue **la** ___ **experiencia** de mi vida.

5 Translate the sentences from activity 4 into English.

6 Read the following list of common verbs that undergo a spelling change in the first person of the preterite tense. Write each verb in the first person of the preterite tense and then translate into English.

Example: pagar > pagué – I paid for

a tocar
b alcanzar
c practicar
d castigar
e comenzar
f cruzar
g organizar
h negar

Gramática

First-person spelling changes in the preterite tense

The first-person singular endings of verbs which end in *-car*, *-gar* and *-zar* (like *buscar*, *llegar* and *empezar*) have a spelling change in the preterite tense.

Verb ending	First-person change	Example
-car	c > qu	*busqué* – I looked for
-gar	g > gu	*llegué* – I arrived
-zar	z > c	*empecé* – I started

Note that these verbs follow a regular pattern in all other persons of the preterite tense.

Mi diario

Me interesa la astronomía. Sigo a Sara García, una astronauta y científica en la **Agencia Espacial Europea**. Ella es un modelo a seguir para mí. Empecé a mirar las estrellas hace diez años desde la ventana de mi dormitorio. Antes tuve otros pasatiempos también: toqué la guitarra y busqué **fósiles** en las rocas de cerca de la playa. ¡Pero ahora estoy seguro de que este pasatiempo es el más divertido! La semana pasada compré mi primer **telescopio**. Fue bastante caro, pero valió la pena porque mi sueño es trabajar en la NASA y viajar a la **Luna**.

Sara García

la astronomía	astronomy
la Agencia Espacial Europea	European Space Agency
el fósil	fossil
el telescopio	telescope
la Luna	the Moon

7 Read about Jorge's diary. Complete the sentences with the correct information.

a Jorge started to look at the stars…
b He looked for fossils…
c His telescope was quite expensive, but…

8 With a partner, ask and answer the following questions.

a ¿Cuál es tu pasatiempo favorito?
b ¿Cuándo lo empezaste?
c ¿Con quién lo haces?
d ¿Cuáles son las ventajas y desventajas de este pasatiempo?

5.1F Nuestras tradiciones de siempre

OBJECTIVES
- Religious celebrations
- Past-tense time phrases
- Irregular verbs in the preterite tense
- Pronunciation *r*

1 **Rodrigo and Elisa are describing how they celebrate Christmas, New Year or Hanukkah at home. Listen carefully and decide who makes the following statements (a–g), Rodrigo (R), Elisa (E) or both (R+E).**

a Last year I got a bike!
b You have to eat twelve grapes!
c I like to spend time with family.
d My grandparents come to visit.
e My mum is a single parent.
f Lights are important.
g My sister is vegan.

La Nochebuena

La Nochevieja

Los Reyes Magos

La Janucá

2 **Translate these sentences into Spanish. Use the past tense verbs from the box.**

anduviste dije dijo hizo pude supo tuve

a I had a problem yesterday.
b Last night I told the truth.
c Last week, Sonia did her homework.
d Did you walk to the party?
e I couldn't speak to my mum.
f Two days ago, he said that he knew.

Pronunciación

r

The softer Spanish 'r' is found in the middle of a word. It is not rolled like the 'rr', or 'r' at the start of a word, but is still not at all like the English 'r'. The sound is closer to an English 'dd'.

Examples: *favorito, durante, traer*

Gramática

Past-tense time phrases

Some common time phrases you can use to refer to past events are:

ayer – yesterday
anoche – last night
pasado/a – last
el lunes pasado – last Monday
la semana pasada – last week
hace… – ago…
hace diez minutos – ten minutes ago
hace tres días – three days ago
durante – for
durante dos horas – for two hours
durante un año – for a year

3 **Read about three traditions in the cities of Seville, Madrid and Barcelona. Find a synonym for words (a–f). They appear in the order of the text and there are two in each paragraph.**

- **a** hermosas
- **b** el grupo
- **c** diferente
- **d** feliz
- **e** termina
- **f** enseñar

sacar una foto	take a photo
el barrio	neighbourhood
el desfile	parade
el ayuno	fasting
subir	upload

LA PASCUA

La semana antes del Domingo de Pascua en España se llama Semana Santa. Hay muchas celebraciones católicas en las calles de las ciudades, normalmente en el mes de abril. Para Adrián Téllez, un estudiante de Sevilla, 'es la mejor semana del año. Es una fiesta religiosa, pero no importa si eres religioso o no, las imágenes son tan bonitas. El martes pasado **saqué** varias **fotos** y después pude ir a escuchar la música de la banda local cerca de la Plaza de Curtidores'.

¡FELIZ AÑO NUEVO CHINO!

Esta celebración normalmente tiene lugar a principios del mes de febrero. Cada año un animal distinto tiene mucha importancia, por ejemplo, 2030 será 'el Año del Perro'. Hao, un hombre que vive en el **barrio** de Usera en Madrid, donde hay una comunidad china de más de 6.000 personas dice, 'hoy vine a esta plaza con mi mujer a celebrar el año nuevo chino. Además, hace dos horas fui al **desfile** y fue una experiencia muy alegre'.

¡FELIZ EID!

El día de Eid al-Fitr es la fiesta que pone fin a un mes de **ayuno** y es un día muy importante en la cultura musulmana. En Barcelona el año pasado, hubo muchas celebraciones familiares, con amigos y vecinos. Según Ramia Schannel, una influencer en YouTube, 'lo más importante es disfrutar de toda la comida en buena compañía después de un mes de esfuerzo'. Ramia **subió** una foto a su Instagram ayer para mostrar su desayuno la mañana del día de Eid.

4 **Translate the second paragraph describing the Chinese New Year into English.**

5 **Read aloud the last two sentences from the paragraph about Easter (from *Es una fiesta religiosa*) and ask your partner for feedback on your accent and intonation.**

6 **Answer the following questions in a short paragraph.**

- ¿Cuál es tu fiesta favorita?
- ¿Cuándo tiene lugar esta fiesta?
- ¿Con quién la celebras?
- ¿Cuál es tu opinión sobre esta fiesta?
- Describe lo que hiciste la última vez que celebraste esta fiesta.

5.1H ¡Un año más!

OBJECTIVES
- Unique family traditions
- Prepositional pronouns
- Stem changes in the preterite tense

1 **Listen to the descriptions of four different Hispanic birthday traditions. Match each description (1–4) to the correct image (A–D).**

la oreja	ear
la videoconsola	videogames console
la mordida	bite
el pastel	cake

a

b

c

d

2 **Listen to the descriptions again and write phrases a–d in Spanish to match what you hear.**

a They say it is funny.
b I usually invite my school friends.
c I always ask my family.
d then someone pushes you.

3 **Read the sentences in English and complete the Spanish with the correct preposition and prepositional pronoun.**

a The gift is for her. | El regalo es…
b Are you going to come with me? | ¿Vas a venir…
c David works for us. | David trabaja…
d We went without them. | Fuimos…
e She is next to you (sing.). | Ella está…
f I want to go with him. | Quiero ir…

Gramática

Prepositional pronouns

These pronouns are used to replace a noun after prepositions such as *para* (for), *con* (with), *sin* (without), *de* (of, about, from), and prepositions of place such as *delante de* (in front of), *detrás de* (behind) and *al lado de* (next to).

mí (me)
ti (you, sing.)
él (him)
ella (her)
nosotros / nosotras (us)
vosotros / vosotras (you, pl.)
ellos / ellas (them)

*Adela habla mucho **de mí**.* – Adela talks a lot about me.
*¿Quieres ir a la fiesta **con nosotros**?* – Do you want to go to the party with us?

Note that *con* (with) has irregular forms:
conmigo – with me
contigo – with you

4 Read Eréndira's blog about her special 15th birthday celebrations. Choose the five correct statements from the options a–h.

- a Eréndira's 15th birthday party took place last month.
- b The day before the ceremony Eréndira went to church.
- c Eréndira visited the hairdresser's with her mum and two cousins.
- d Eréndira's elder sister couldn't come to the family meal.
- e On the day of her 15th birthday, Eréndira could not sleep well.
- f Eréndira says the occasion is similar to a wedding.
- g Eréndira took lots of photos.
- h Eréndira's parents embarrassed her at the end of the party.

BLOG ABOUT CONTACT

Siempre voy a recordar la increíble fiesta que tuve el mes pasado.

Soy de Puebla, en México y la tradición de las fiestas de **quinceañera** aquí en mi país es algo muy importante, con muchos momentos profundos. Primero, el día antes de la ceremonia en la iglesia, mi madre, mis primas Irene y Sofía y yo visitamos a nuestra peluquera. Después, fuimos a la tienda a recoger mi vestido rojo. ¡Qué precioso!

Por la noche, mi familia prefirió cenar en casa. Fue muy especial para mí porque vino mi hermana mayor. Actualmente vive en Guadalajara y no nos vemos con frecuencia.

El día de mi quinceañera, no pude dormir bien. Me levanté muy temprano para preparar todo. Mi madre, mis tías y mi hermana me ayudaron a vestirme. Después, fuimos a la iglesia para la ceremonia religiosa. Cierta gente sugiere que es como una boda, pero no estoy de acuerdo.

Una hora más tarde, tuve mi fiesta privada con mis compañeros de instituto, con baile, regalos y comida. Celebramos de forma muy animada y ¡saqué un montón de fotos, claro! Al final, para sorprenderme, mis padres pusieron un vídeo de mi vida, con fotos y música. ¡Qué vergüenza!

la quinceañera girl's 15th birthday (Latin American cultures)

Gramática

Stem changes in the preterite tense

There are some verbs that have a spelling change in the 'he'/'she' and 'they' forms of the preterite tense.

-*e* > -*i* stem change

Example: *preferir* – to prefer

preferí	*preferiste*	*pref**i**rió*
preferimos	*preferisteis*	*pref**i**rieron*

-*o* > -*u* stem change

Example: *dormir* – to sleep

dormí	*dormiste*	*d**u**rmió*
dormimos	*dormisteis*	*d**u**rmieron*

-*y* stem change

Example: *leer* – to read

leí	*leíste*	*le**y**ó*
leímos	*leísteis*	*le**y**eron*

5 Translate these verbs into Spanish. Use the preterite.

- a they felt
- b she asked for
- c he died
- d they believed
- e she fell
- f they heard

6 Look at the photo of the girl celebrating her *quinceañera* with her family in activity 4 and describe it in as much detail as possible.

5.2F Latinoamérica celebra la vida

OBJECTIVES
- Latin American festivals
- Apocopation of adjectives
- *antes de, después de, al* + infinitive
- Pronunciation *ch*

1 **Listen to the descriptions of *Día de Muertos* and *Feria de las Flores*. Then choose the correct option (a–c) to complete the sentences.**

1 Day of the Dead takes place on the…
- a 12th November.
- b 2nd November.
- c 2nd December.

2 The origins of the tradition are…
- a Catholic.
- b Mexican.
- c both Catholic and Mexican.

3 The atmosphere is full of…
- a sadness and death.
- b joy and life.
- c tension and emotion.

4 The *Feria de las Flores* is celebrated…
- a every August.
- b in all of Colombia's cities.
- c in the east of Colombia.

5 This year, the festival will have more than 4,000…
- a different activities on offer.
- b typical foods to try.
- c foreign tourists in attendance.

2 **Complete the sentences with the correct form of the adjectives in brackets. Apply the rules of apocopation.**

- a No hay desfiles hoy a causa del ___ (*malo*) tiempo.
- b En Colombia, es famosa la ___ (*grande*) Feria de Cali.
- c El ___ (*primero*) día del Carnaval fue increíble.
- d No hay ___ (*ninguno*) supermercado en el pueblo.
- e Voy a ser profesora ___ (*alguno*) día.
- f Mi tío es un ___ (*bueno*) hombre.

Gramática

Apocopation of adjectives

Some adjectives can be placed before a noun. When placed before a masculine noun, they have a shortened form.

bueno > *buen* – good
un buen ambiente – a good atmosphere
malo > *mal* – bad
un mal olor – a bad smell
primero > *primer* – first
en primer lugar – in the first place
tercero > *tercer* – third
el tercer día – the third day
alguno > *algún* – some, any
en algún momento – at some point
ninguno > *ningún* – not a single, no
ningún problema – no problem

Grande is shortened to *gran* when placed before a masculine **or** feminine noun, and means 'great'.

una gran fiesta – a great party
un gran amigo – a great friend

3 **Read this tourist leaflet from the historic city of Cusco, Peru. Complete the text with the words from the box below.**

gran aprender entre teatro antes bebe

Este año **1** ___ el 20 y 23 de junio, Cusco se viste de alegría para celebrar el *Inti Raymi*, una fiesta que en lengua quechua significa 'fiesta del sol'. Hay carnavales, música y **2** ___ en las calles de la ciudad.

Consejos para turistas:

- ¡**3** ___ mucha agua! Hará calor y estarás mucho tiempo en la calle.
- Es importante ponerse zapatos cómodos **4** ___ de salir del hotel.
- Después de ver las celebraciones, puedes visitar los museos de la ciudad para **5** ___ más sobre nuestra cultura.
- ¡Trae tu móvil o una cámara! Al llegar a esta **6** ___ fiesta, vas a sacar muchas fotos desde el primer día.

4 **Translate the four pieces of advice from activity 3 into English.**

5 **Translate these sentences into Spanish.**

a Before going to Mexico, I am going to buy a suitcase.

b I went to the party with a good friend.

c After studying the great history of Peru, I visited Cusco.

d On entering the kitchen, I saw a lot of delicious food.

e The first hotel is very clean and modern.

6 **Research one of the following Latin American festivals online and present five or more facts in Spanish about it to your class.**

- La Fiesta de la Vendimia in Mendoza, Argentina
- Mistura, in Lima, Peru
- Tapati Rapa Nui, Isla de Pascua, Chile

Example: · *Se celebra en...*
· *Las principales características de esta fiesta son...*
· *La fiesta es popular por su...*
· *En mi opinión, esta fiesta es interesante porque...*

Mention:

- when it takes place
- its main features
- the number of visitors
- why it is popular
- your opinion of it.

Gramática

***antes de, después de, al* + infinitive**

When translating the sentences in activity 4, make sure you use the gerund form of the verb with the following constructions:

al… – on / upon…

antes de – before…

después de – after…

al llegar – on arriving

antes de ir – before going

después de comer – after eating

Pronunciación

ch

The 'ch' sound is an easy one to master as it is the same as the English 'ch' found in 'church' and 'cheese'. Whereas in English, 'chef' is much softer, in Spanish it always retains the harder sound.

Examples: *Quechua, Chile, coche*

Cultura

Quechua is an official language of Perú and Bolivia. It has approximately 10 million speakers and was the main language of the Inca Empire for more than four centuries.

5.2H Bailando al ritmo hispano

OBJECTIVES
- Traditional Hispanic music and dance
- Interrogatives with prepositions
- *seguir* and *continuar* with the present participle

1 **Listen to some descriptions of the tango and flamenco. Choose the five correct statements from a–h.**

The tango…

a first appeared in the 18th century.

b is a mixture of Afroamerican and European styles.

c is also famous in Uruguay.

d is not a difficult dance to learn.

Flamenco…

e originated in southern Spain.

f first appeared in the 8th century.

g awakens deep feelings.

h is not easy to dance.

2 **Read statements a–e carefully. Write a suitable question for each statement using the correct preposition and an interrogative phrase from the box below.**

¿De qué…? ¿De quién…? ¿Con quién…? ¿A quién…? ¿Para qué…?

a Ayer vi un espectáculo de tango con Aurora.

b Uso la falda roja para bailar flamenco.

c Ese coche azul es de tu tío Luis.

d Voy a visitar a mi primo.

e Estamos hablando de los bailes populares de Colombia.

Gramática

Interrogatives with prepositions

You have already come across a range of interrogatives (question words) in Spanish, such as *¿qué?* (what?). When we need to ask a question using a verb that is followed by a preposition, such as *de*, *a*, *para* or *con*, the preposition must be placed at the beginning of the question, before the question word.

¿De qué…?

¿De qué hablas? – What are you talking about?

¿De quién…?

¿De quién es ese libro? – Whose is that book?

¿Con quién…?

¿Con quién fuiste? – Who did you go with?

¿A quién…?

¿A quién viste? – Who did you see?

¿Para qué?

¿Para qué es eso? – What is that for?

¿En qué…?

¿En qué consiste? – What does it consist of?

¡Bailando con las Estrellas!

En el programa en vivo de *Bailando con las Estrellas* de la semana que viene, nuestras parejas intentarán ganar la semifinal con bailes latinos.

Bruno García y Simona del Río bailarán salsa. La salsa es un baile con influencia **caribeña** con pasos rápidos a la derecha y la izquierda. Aunque ya lo hacen muy bien, la pareja sigue practicando seis horas al día para ganar.

David López y Rosita Sánchez traen los **ritmos** más calientes con una rumba. La rumba empezó en Cuba como un baile individual y más tarde, en pareja o en grupo. A David le duele la pierna y si no puede seguir bailando, la pareja tendrá que abandonar el concurso.

Ramón Comares y Silvia Téllez tienen una sorpresa: esta semana bailarán un bolero muy romántico y también una bachata en el último minuto. La bachata es un tipo de baile cada vez más popular, que todo el mundo conoce. ¡Seguro que gran parte del público les votará!

El año que viene, el programa espera continuar teniendo representación de otros bailes latinos como el Cha Cha Cha o el Mambo. ¡Hay tantos bailes latinos y son todos verdaderos espectáculos!

caribeño / a	Caribbean
el ritmo	rhythm

3 **Read the preview of the next episode of the dance programme *Bailando con las Estrellas* and answer the questions in English.**

a When will the next episode be shown?

b How is the salsa dance described?

c How do we know Bruno García and Simona Del Río are eager to win?

d Why might David López and Rosita Sánchez have to leave the competition?

e Why is it likely that Ramón Comares and Silvia Téllez will receive a lot of votes?

f What do the producers hope will happen next year?

4 **Read the text again to find and translate into English the three examples of *seguir / continuar* + present participle.**

5 **Read aloud this passage in Spanish. Then answer the following questions about yourself, extending your answers as much as possible.**

Hay tantos bailes latinos y la mayoría me parecen bastante rápidos. Actualmente, sigo leyendo un libro sobre la rumba que empecé la semana pasada. Tengo intención de aprender este baile en una escuela cerca de mi casa. ¿Con quién bailaré? Con mi mejor amiga Sara, ¡claro!

- ¿Te gusta la música latina?
- ¿Cuál es tu estilo de música favorito?
- ¿Tienes algún cantante o grupo preferido?
- ¿Tocas algún instrumento?
- ¿Te gustaría ir a un concierto?

Los verbos

***seguir* and *continuar* with the present participle**

The verbs *seguir* and *continuar* must be followed with the present participle of a verb to express the idea of 'to continue / keep on doing something'.

Seguimos practicando los bailes tradicionales. – We keep on practising traditional dances.

Es importante continuar respetando otras culturas. – It is important to continue respecting other cultures.

6 **Write a 90-word paragraph in Spanish describing your musical preferences. Use your responses to the questions in activity 5 to help structure your answer.**

6.1F Lola y Rosalía, ayer y hoy

OBJECTIVES
- Comparing and contrasting two female icons
- Suffixes *-ísimo* and *-ito*
- The imperfect tense in full
- Pronunciation *a, e, i*

1 Read the texts on Lola Flores and Rosalía and decide whether each phrase (a–f) refers to Lola (L), Rosalía (R) or both (R+L).

ROSALÍA

Rosalía es una de las estrellas de la música más importantes del mundo. Nació en 1992 y su **estilo** moderno tiene muchas **influencias**, como el flamenco, la música **urbana** y el hip hop. A veces canta con otros artistas famosos como Ozuna, The Weeknd o Billie Eilish.

Cuando era más joven, Rosalía estudiaba música todos los días porque quería ser cantante profesional. Ahora, gana muchos premios en Europa y Estados Unidos, y sus vídeos en YouTube tienen millones de visitas.

LOLA FLORES

Lola nació en el año 1923 y murió en el 1995. Fue una cantante, actriz y artista única en España. Era, y todavía es, un **icono** de la cultura popular porque siempre tenía muchísima energía y su personalidad era fuerte y animada.

Lola tuvo mucha **fama** internacional en la televisión y en el cine. Siempre bailaba y cantaba flamenco de una **forma** muy personal. En 1951 viajó a América por primera vez y tuvo mucho éxito en México y en Estados Unidos.

el estilo	style
la influencia	influence
urbano/a	urban
el icono	icon
la fama	fame
la forma	way

a an actress and movie star
b a fan of flamenco music
c a strong character
d a student of music in her childhood
e an online star
f a success in the USA

2 Listen to two short statements. Write one word in Spanish in each gap according to what you hear. Check carefully that your spelling is accurate.

Lola Flores

Sus fotos, ___ y ___ siguen ___ muy ___. Me ___ que nunca ___ a pasar de ___.

Rosalía

El ___ pasado, la ___ ___ en ___ de ___ conciertos en ___.

3 Read the texts in activity 1 again. Find six examples of different verbs in the imperfect tense and translate them into English.

4 **Complete each sentence with the correct imperfect tense form of the verbs in brackets. Then translate the sentences into English.**

a Tú siempre ___ (*escuchar*) música pop.
b Mi hermana ___ (*llevar*) gafas.
c De niña, mi madrastra ___ (*vivir*) en Barcelona.
d Cada verano, mi familia y yo ___ (*visitar*) a nuestros abuelos.
e Por la mañana, los niños ___ (*beber*) leche en la escuela.
f Mis amigos y yo ___ (*ver*) una película en el cine todos los sábados.
g Los profesores de mi escuela primaria ___ (*ser*) muy simpáticos.
h Cuando yo ___ (*ser*) pequeña, ___ (*jugar*) en el jardín todos los días.

5 **Read these statements about Lola Flores and Rosalía and decide whether each one is positive (P), negative (N) or positive and negative (P+N).**

a Pienso que la música de Rosalía es muy buena. Sus canciones son increíbles.
b Opino que no hay otra artista como Lola Flores. Es la mejor de todos los tiempos.
c Los conciertos de Rosalía son muy emocionantes, aunque ¡las entradas son muy caras!
d Lo siento, pero la música y las películas de Lola Flores me interesan muy poco.
e Es verdad que la música de Rosalía siempre me hace querer bailar.
f Lola Flores es una cantante muy importante. Cantaba y bailaba con mucha pasión.

6 **Read the underlined words in sentences a, c and f in activity 5 again. Rewrite them using the suffixes -*ísimo*, -*ísima*, -*ísimos* or -*ísimas* as required.**

Pronunciación

a, e, i

Spanish vowels are shorter in duration than their English equivalents. The vowels 'a', 'e' and 'i' sound a bit like those taught to young children as part of the English phonetic alphabet ('a' as in 'apple', 'e' as in 'net' and 'i' as in 'meet'.

Examples: **a**ño, **e**s, n**i**ño, **A**m**é**r**i**c**a**

Los verbos

The imperfect tense in full

The imperfect tense is used to describe a past action that does not have a clear beginning or end:

- when saying what people or things used to be like.
  De niño, siempre comía chocolate. – As a child, I always ate / used to eat chocolate.
- when describing what someone or something was like.
  Mi abuelo tenía los ojos verdes. – My grandfather had green eyes.

The imperfect tense is formed by removing the *-ar*, *-er* or *-ir* endings of the infinitive, then adding the following endings:

	***-ar* verbs**	***-er* and *-ir* verbs**
yo	*-aba*	*-ía*
tú	*-abas*	*-ías*
él / ella / usted	*-aba*	*-ía*
nosotros / as	*-ábamos*	*-íamos*
vosotros / as	*-abais*	*-íais*
ellos / ellas / ustedes	*-aban*	*-ían*

There are three irregular verbs in this tense:

	***ser* (to be)**	***ir* (to go)**	***ver* (to see)**
yo	*era*	*iba*	*veía*
tú	*eras*	*ibas*	*veías*
él / ella / usted	*era*	*iba*	*veía*
nosotros / as	*éramos*	*íbamos*	*veíamos*
vosotros / as	*erais*	*ibais*	*veíais*
ellos / ellas / ustedes	*eran*	*iban*	*veían*

Gramática

Suffixes -*ísimo* and -*ito*

You can convey the idea of 'very', 'really' or 'extremely' in Spanish by using the suffixes *-ísimo, -ísima, -ísimos, -ísimas* at the end of an adjective.

es lento > es lentísimo – he is slow; he is really slow

son inteligentes > son inteligentísimos – they are intelligent; they are really intelligent

You can say something is smaller by adding *-ito, -ita, -itos* or *-itas* to the end of a noun or adjective.

la mesa – the table; *la mes**ita*** – the little table

bajo – short; *baj**ito*** – very short

6.1H La nueva cultura de la fama

OBJECTIVES
- Celebrity culture
- Adjectives with *ser* and *estar*
- The preterite and imperfect tenses

¡Salto a la fama!

La historia de Georgina Rodríguez es sin duda una historia interesante, sobre una chica de barrio que llegó a ser famosa mundialmente. Su padre es argentino y su madre española y cuando era pequeña, hacía **danza** y ballet clásico. Pasó varios años trabajando de **niñera** en Inglaterra. Más tarde, cuando vivía en Madrid, trabajó en una tienda de ropa de la marca Gucci donde un día conoció al jugador de fútbol portugués Cristiano Ronaldo, su pareja actual.

Su fama internacional como *influencer* y modelo ya es enorme. Tiene más de cincuenta millones de seguidores en Instagram y su propio programa en Netflix, que muestra su vida diaria sin vergüenza. Georgina tiene un avión privado y va a galas de música o **estrenos** de películas en París, Nueva York, Milán o Barcelona. Sin embargo, intenta mostrar su lado **generoso** con su trabajo en la organización *Nuevo Futuro*, que da apoyo a niños **desfavorecidos**.

1 **Read the article on Georgina Rodríguez and answer the questions in English.**

- a How do we know Georgina is likely to speak English?
- b How did Georgina meet her current partner?
- c How do we know Georgina has an extravagant lifestyle?
- d How does Georgina show her generous side?

la danza	dance
la niñera	nanny / au pair
el estreno	premiere
generoso / a	generous
desfavorecido / a	disadvantaged

2 **Read the report again and find the Spanish for the following words.**

- a became
- b worldwide
- c brand
- d current
- e followers
- f own
- g support

3 **Listen to four young people discussing celebrity lifestyle and fame. Complete the sentences with the correct information.**

- a I'm interested in seeing Georgina's house … (two details)
- b My favourite celebrity is the Venezuelan athlete Yulimar Rojas because … (two details)
- c Joaquín Sánchez shows his great sense of humour on … (two details)
- d As well as being an actor and singer, Franco Masini has … (two details)

Yulimar Rojas

Joaquín Sánchez

Franco Masini

4 **Read the sentences and choose the correct form of *ser* or *estar*. Pay attention to the context.**

- a Georgina Rodríguez tiene mucho dinero. **Es / Está** muy rica.
- b Me gustaría ser famoso en Internet; además, **soy / estoy** interesado en las redes sociales.
- c Ayer comí un pastel de chocolate y **era / estaba** muy rico.
- d **Soy / Estoy** bastante listo y me gustaría ir a la universidad.
- e El jugador Joaquín **es / está** muy orgulloso de su carrera futbolística.
- f Muchos famosos **están / son** malas personas. Solo quieren más fama y dinero.

5 **Use the imperfect tense to describe what you were like when you were younger. Include at least one example of a sentence containing both the imperfect and preterite tenses. To help you, use some of the key verbs and expressions listed below, as well as the examples from the grammar box.**

¿Cómo eras de pequeño? – What were you like as a child?
Recuerdo que… – I remember that …
era – I used to be / I was
tenía – I used to have / I had
llevaba – I used to wear
iba – I used to go
jugaba – I used to play
veía – I used to watch
leía – I used to read
un dia… – one day …
mientras – while
cuando – when

6 **Present your description from activity 5 to your class. Try to narrate it with good expression and pronunciation.**

Gramática

Adjectives with *ser* and *estar*

Some adjectives change their meaning depending on whether they are used with the verb *ser* or *estar*.

Mi hermana Lola es nerviosa. – My sister Lola is a nervous person (by nature).

Mi hermana Lola está nerviosa. – My sister Lola is nervous (at the moment, for a particular reason).

***ser** listo / a:* to be clever
***estar** listo / a:* to be ready

***ser** bueno / a:* to be kind, a good person
***estar** bueno / a:* to taste good

***ser** malo / a:* to be a bad person
***estar** malo / a:* to taste bad **or** to feel ill

***ser** rico / a:* to be rich
***estar** rico / a:* to be tasty, delicious

***ser** orgulloso / a:* to be arrogant
***estar** orgulloso/a:* to be proud

***ser** interesado / a:* to be selfish
***estar** interesado / a*: to be interested

***ser** aburrido / a:* to be boring
***estar** aburrido / a:* to be bored

Gramática

The preterite and imperfect tenses

As well as describing what people or things used to be like, the imperfect tense is used to narrate what was happening when a completed action took place. In such cases, we must use both the imperfect and preterite tenses.

*Anoche me **caí** mientras **corría** por el parque.* – Last night I fell over while I was running in the park.

***Era** ya bastante tarde cuando **llegó** mi amigo.* – It was quite late when my friend arrived.

***No quería** ver a nadie ese día y **me encontré** a mi primo Miguel.* – I didn't want to see anybody that day and bumped into my cousin MIguel.

6.2F Famosos que valen la pena

OBJECTIVES
- Debating celebrities as role models
- Pronunciation *o, u*
- Using three time frames
- Possession with *de*

1 **Read the profiles of two Hispanic actresses and decide if the statements are true (T), false (F) or not mentioned (NM).**

YALITZA APARICIO

Yalitza es una actriz mexicana de Oaxaca, una ciudad al sur de México. Habla español e inglés, pero también habla triqui y mixteco, dos idiomas **indígenas**. Fue la primera actriz indígena en recibir una **nominación** a los premios Oscar y en estos momentos es una de las mujeres más importantes del cine latinoamericano. Yalitza va a continuar hablando de las comunidades indígenas en la televisión, cine e Internet, porque piensa que estas comunidades no tienen voz.

ROSARIO DAWSON

Rosario es una actriz de **ascendencia** cubana y **puertorriqueña**. De niña, vivía en Nueva York. Participó en muchas películas y programas de televisión, y su papel como Ahsoka Tano en *Star Wars* la hizo mucho más famosa. Ella está usando su fama para apoyar a organizaciones como Oxfam y Voto Latino. En Voto Latino, Rosario dará **visibilidad** a los jóvenes latinos en Estados Unidos para animarlos a votar y a tener más participación en la vida social y cultural del país.

indígena	indigenous (native)
la nominación	nomination
la ascendencia	heritage
puertorriqueño / a	Puerto Rican
la visibilidad	visibility

a Yalitza speaks four languages.
b Yalitza has won an Oscar.
c Yalitza thinks that indigenous communities are underrepresented in the media.
d Rosario used to live in Cuba.
e Rosario's highest paid role was in *Star Wars*.
f Rosario wants more young latinos in the USA to be able to vote.

2 **Read the profiles again and complete the table, making a list of verbs that appear in a past, present or future time frame.**

Past time frame	Present time frame	Future time frame

Pronunciación

a, e, i

The Spanish vowels 'a', 'e' and 'i' are shorter in duration than their English equivalents. They sound a bit like those taught to young children as part of the English phonetic alphabet ('a' as in 'apple', 'e' as in 'net' and 'i' as in 'meet'.

Examples: *a**ñ**o, **e**s, ni**ñ**o, Am**é**rica*

o, u

The Spanish vowel sound 'o' is much shorter and less pronounced that the distinct English 'o'. The 'u' is similar to the 'oo' in the English word 'moon', with the lips rounded, almost closed.

Saying the 'o' and the 'u' correctly is essential for a good Spanish accent.

Examples: *s**o**lo, **U**ruguay, m**u**cho*

3 **Listen to the report about a Spanish footballer and answer the questions in English.**

- a Where is Pedri from? (two details)
- b What are the aims of the project Pedri is participating in? (two details)
- c What is Pedri sure about?
- d What does Pedri no longer do on the football pitch?

4 **Complete the sentences by translating the words in brackets into Spanish.**

- a ___ (*Pedri's family*) vive en el norte de Tenerife.
- b ___ (*Zara's clothing*) es muy moderna.
- c ___ (*Rosalía's songs*) son únicas.
- d ___ (*Real Madrid's stadium*) es muy grande.
- e ___ (*Pedro Almodóvar's films*) son muy emocionantes.
- f ___ (*Frida Kahlo's house*) es un museo.
- g ___ (*My brother's car*) es blanco.
- h ___ (*My friend's father*) está enfermo.

Gramática

Possession with *de*

In Spanish, the preposition *de* is used to express possession:

la hermana ***de*** *David* – David's sister

el dormitorio ***de*** *mi primo* – my cousin's bedroom

5 **Translate this paragraph into English.**

Las organizaciones españolas con más seguidores en X (Twitter) son: Fundación Internacional de Derechos Humanos, Greenpeace España, Médicos sin Fronteras, Amigos de la Tierra y Unicef España. ¿Apoyarás su trabajo este año? Puedes encontrar más información sobre estas conocidas organizaciones en sus páginas web y en las redes sociales.

6 **Choose a celebrity and explain whether you think they are a good role model or not, justifying your opinion with details. Use the box below to structure your answer.**

un modelo a seguir – role model

En mi opinión, *Que yo sepa,* *A mi modo de ver,*	___ *es un buen modelo a seguir porque es…*	*comprensivo / a* *educado / a* *generoso / a* *simpático / a* *inteligente* *humilde* *sincero / a* *trabajador / a* *optimista*	*y* *también* *pero* *aunque*	*me inspira mucho.* *apoya a organizaciones como…* *usa su fama para ayudar a…* *dona dinero a…* *da visibilidad a…* *continúa hablando de…*
	___ ***no*** *es un buen modelo a seguir porque es…*	*agresivo / a* *egoísta* *antipático / a* *deshonesto / a* *maleducado / a* *perezoso / a* *pesimista*		

7 **Share your answer to activity 6 with a partner. At first, use your written answer to help you, then try again, speaking from memory.**

6.2H ¡La fama tiene dos caras!

OBJECTIVES
- The pros and cons of fame
- A wide range of tenses
- *soler* + infinitive

1 **Read the article and choose the correct option to complete the sentences.**

1 Shakira has lived in Barcelona for…
   - **a** ten years.
   - **b** twelve years.
   - **c** over a decade.

2 Shakira thinks life in Miami will be…
   - **a** more lively.
   - **b** more quiet.
   - **c** more dangerous.

3 Shakira is leaving Barcelona because…
   - **a** she does not have any privacy there.
   - **b** her two children do not like the city.
   - **c** it has far too much traffic.

¡ADIÓS!

Shakira, la famosa cantante colombiana que vivió en Barcelona durante más de diez años, ayer decidió por fin dejar la ciudad para siempre después de su **separación** del jugador de fútbol Gerard Piqué. La estrella dice que preferiría una vida más tranquila en Miami, lejos de las cámaras de los fotógrafos que la **acosaban** día y noche. Shakira cuenta que la semana pasada, cuando iba conduciendo su coche con sus dos hijos, vio a cuatro ***paparazzi*** escondidos en otro coche y luego hubo una peligrosa **persecución**. En ese momento, ella se dijo que, para proteger a sus dos hijos pequeños, algo tenía que cambiar.

Muchos famosos suelen quejarse de la falta de privacidad cuando salen a un lugar público y del acoso de los periodistas o de las personas con teléfono móvil. ¿Dónde está el límite?

la separación	separation
acosar	to harass
los paparazzi	paparazzi (photographers who pursue celebrities)
la persecución	pursuit, chase

2 **According to the text, what <u>three</u> things do celebrities usually complain about?**

3 **Read the article again and find <u>one</u> example of a verb in the:**
- present tense
- preterite tense
- imperfect tense
- conditional tense

Translate each example into English.

4 Listen to the podcast in which presenters Rodrigo Fernández and Clara Puente discuss the pros and cons of fame. Choose the five correct statements from a–h.

Aitana…

- a is a famous singer.
- b is afraid all the time.
- c lives alone in Madrid.
- d feels a bit sad.
- e takes lots of photos.
- f is visited by people she doesn't know.
- g says she has the right to a private life.
- h is going to move house.

5 Match each sentence to the correct ending. Then translate the complete sentences into English.

1. Mi hermano…
2. En julio, nosotros…
3. Marcos, tú…
4. En las redes sociales, las estrellas de telerrealidad…
5. En mi tiempo libre…

- a sueles entrenar todos los días, ¿no?
- b suele ir de compras los fines de semana.
- c suelo leer novelas.
- d solemos ir de vacaciones a Málaga.
- e suelen tener muchos seguidores.

6 Translate the following opinions into Spanish, making sure you use the correct tense for each verb.

- a We have the right to a private life.
- b Harassment is very dangerous.
- c I would not like to be famous like Shakira.
- d Celebrities usually complain too much.
- e We are going to protect our family.
- f I used to take lots of photos on my mobile phone.
- g Next year Aitana will earn a lot of money.
- h Last night, I saw a video of a famous singer on TikTok.

7 Would you like to be famous? Ask and answer this question with a partner. Use the sentences in activity 6 to help add detail to your answer.

¿Te gustaría ser famoso / a?

Gramática

***soler* + infinitive**

As an alternative to using adverbs such as *normalmente* (normally), you can use the verb *soler* in the present tense followed by an infinitive:

soler

yo suelo	*nosotros / as solemos*
tú sueles	*vosotros / as soléis*
él / ella / usted suele	*ellos / ellas / ustedes suelen*

Suelo ver películas con mi hermana. – I usually watch films with my sister.

Cultura

In 2023, the Spanish women's national football team won the World Cup for the first time. Players such as Salma Paralluelo and Jenni Hermoso have featured prominently on social media since the win.

Aitana

Cultura

¡Bienvenidos a Viña del Mar!

1 **Read the text. Work with a partner to talk through a translation of the passage.**

El icónico festival de música de Chile

Viña del Mar is an annual music festival that takes place in the city of Viña del Mar, Chile, in February. Established in 1960, it is one of the longest-running music festivals in the world and it continues to attract a range of famous artists. It is broadcast live on Chilean television and YouTube, and some of its iconic performances have millions of views online.

Julián es de Ciudad de México y Marcela vive en Buenos Aires, Argentina. Todos los años viajan a Viña del Mar para ir al festival. Este año van a quedarse en la casa de la tía de Julián. A Marcela le encanta ir a Viña del Mar porque puede descansar, ir a la playa y tomar el sol.

Julián está muy contento porque este año, su cantante favorito, Camilo, canta en vivo en el festival. Camilo es un cantante argentino y es muy popular en Internet. En cambio, Marcela prefiere a Karol G, una cantante colombiana muy famosa que **lanzó** su cuarto álbum *Mañana será bonito* en febrero.

lanzar to release

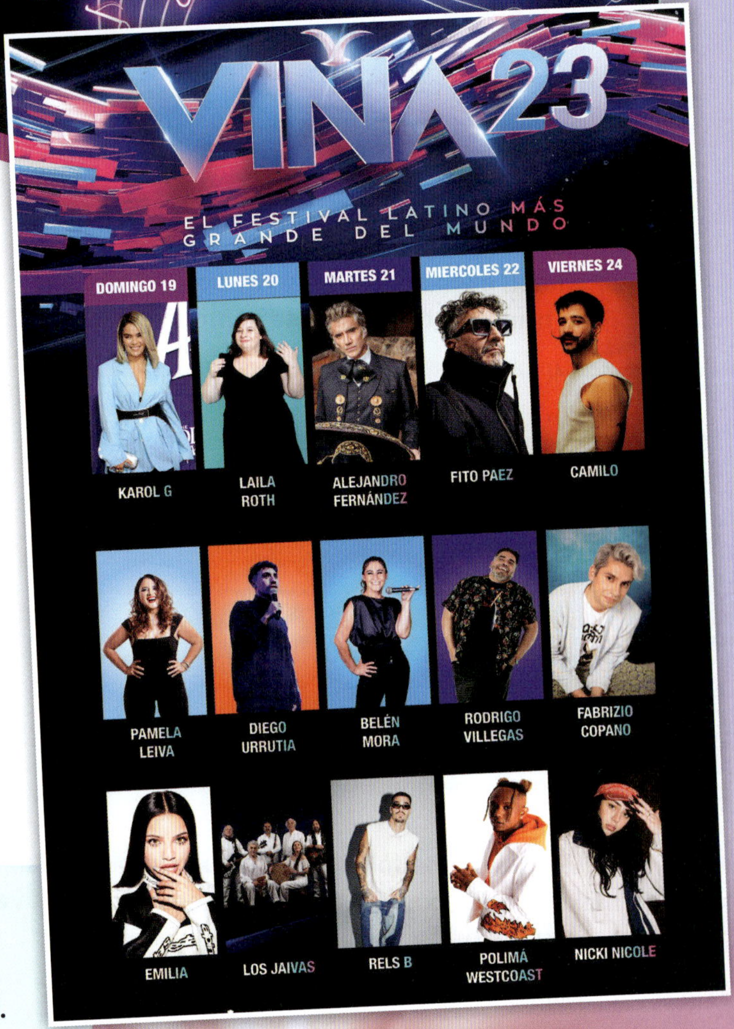

2 **Julián and Marcela are two TikTokers with many followers and they are preparing to go to the Viña del Mar festival this year. Answer the questions in English.**

- **a** Where are Julián and Marcela going to stay this year?
- **b** Why does Marcela love going to Viña del Mar? (three details)
- **c** Why is Julián very happy?
- **d** What did the singer Karol G do in February?

3 **Read Marcela and Julián's itinerary and decide which day (1–3) each statement (a–f) refers to.**

a The influencers will be tourists for the day.
b Marcela would like to buy a souvenir.
c The best song award will be announced.
d Julián and Marcela will upload content to social media.
e Julián will enjoy the architecture.
f The most extraordinary day of all.

4 **Listen to this advert promoting the Viña del Mar festival on Spotify. Complete the table with the correct information.**

Date and time tickets go on sale:	
Special discounts for:	
Examples of free activities during the week:	

a la venta	on sale
a partir de	from
el descuento	discount
el boleto	ticket
la ruta	route
icónico / a	iconic

5 **Read the list of famous music festivals in the Spanish-speaking world. Choose one and research it online. Then describe what you are going to do on Days 1, 2 and 3 of the festival, using the diary of the trip to Viña del Mar to help you.**

- Benicassim
- Primavera Sound
- Festival Mad Cool
- Estéreo picnic
- Cosquín Rock

Día 1

Marcela estará nerviosa porque Karol G va a cantar en un concierto ante más de 15.000 fanáticos. Marcela y Julián van a hacer un vídeo de TikTok desde el estadio Quinta Vergara y subirán varias fotos a Instagram. Marcela llevará una camiseta con la foto de Karol G y espera comprar un póster para su dormitorio.

Julián y Marcela

Día 2

Los *influencers* quieren visitar la ciudad de Viña del Mar y sacar muchas fotos. Marcela va a ir al famoso Reloj de Flores y Julián tiene muchas ganas de ver el Castillo Wulff en realidad. Este castillo es de estilo alemán y tiene más de cien años. ¡Qué guay!

Castillo Wulff

Día 3

Este día podría ser el más especial. En la final, se va a escoger la mejor canción del festival. También hay otros premios. El premio más **prestigioso** del festival es **la Gaviota de Platino**, que hasta el momento solo han recibido tres artistas: el mexicano Luis Miguel, la española Isabel Pantoja y el chileno Lucho Gatica.

Reloj de Flores

prestigioso	prestigious
la Gaviota de Platino	the Platinum Seagull award

Theme 2 Grammar practice

Present continuous tense

1 Complete the sentences. Choose the correct present form of *estar* and add the gerund of the verbs in brackets.

a Rosalía **estoy / estás / está** ___ (*grabar*) su nueva canción.

b Yo **estoy / está / estáis** ___ (*leer*) un libro de Isabel Allende.

c Pedri y Gavi **está / estamos / están** ___ (*jugar*) muy bien.

d Chicos, ¿**estás / estamos / estáis** ___ (*ver*) el concierto de Ozuna?

e Los seguidores de Lupita Nyong'o **está / estás / están** ___ (*esperar*) su nueva película.

f Nosotros **estamos / estáis / están** ___ (*seguir*) a Shakira en Instagram.

Gramática

The present continuous

The present continuous is used to describe an action that is in progress.

It is formed by using the verb *estar* ('to be') in the present tense and the present participle (the *-ing* form of a verb).

To form the present participle – also known as 'the gerund' – remove the *-ar* ending from the infinitive and add *-ando*.

jugar – to play

estoy jugando – I am playing

For *-er* and *-ir* verbs, remove the *-er* or *-ir* and add *-iendo*.

hacer – to do

está haciendo – he / she is doing

Personal *a*

2 Insert the personal *a* into the correct position in each sentence. Then translate the sentences into English.

a Esta mañana vi María y Pepe.

b Vamos a visitar nuestros abuelos en diciembre.

c Encontré mi amigo en el parque.

d Hoy tengo que llamar mi madre.

e Laura quiere invitar su novia a la fiesta.

f Busco mi hermano. ¿Sabes dónde está?

Prepositions

3 Complete the sentences with the correct preposition. Then translate the sentences into English.

a A veces sueño ___ mi fiesta de cumpleaños.

b Lola y Ferrán siempre tardan mucho ___ hacer los deberes.

c ¿___ qué consiste tu trabajo?

d Vosotros dejasteis ___ comer chocolate.

e Luis se olvidó ___ comprar las entradas.

f Voy a empezar ___ jugar a este nuevo videojuego.

Demonstrative pronouns

4 Choose the correct demonstrative pronouns to complete the sentences.

a Prefiero **esos / estos / aquellos** pantalones cortos. (*these*)

b **Estos / Aquellos / Esos** edificios son más antiguos. (*those*)

c **Ese / Este / Aquel** problema es muy grave. (*this*)

d **Este / Aquel / Ese** cine siempre está cerrado. (*that over there*)

e **Esta / Esa / Aquella** piscina es ideal para nadar en verano. (*that*)

f **Aquellas / Esas / Estas** montañas son muy bonitas. (*those over there*)

g ¡No me puedo creer **esto / este / esta**! (*this*)

Preterite tense

5 Complete the sentences with the correct preterite form of the verbs in brackets.

a El pasado julio, mis amigos y yo ___ (*visitar*) Pamplona.

b El sábado, mi equipo de fútbol favorito ___ (*ganar*) el partido.

c Ayer yo ___ (*comer*) mucha fruta.

d Esta mañana mis padres___ (*desayunar*) a las siete.

e ¿Vosotros ___ (*celebrar*) la Semana Santa en Sevilla el pasado abril?

f El verano pasado, yo ___ (*conocer*) a una persona muy especial en una fiesta de cumpleaños.

Preterite tense (translation)

6 Translate these sentences into Spanish. Use the verbs in brackets.

a I crossed the bridge. (*cruzar*)
b Last night, I played tennis with my cousin. (*jugar*)
c I paid a lot a money. (*pagar*)
d Last month, I organised a party. (*organizar*)
e I arrived a bit late. (*llegar*)
f I looked for a hotel. (*buscar*)

Superlatives

7 Complete the sentences with the most appropriate superlative form of the adjectives from the box.

alta caro interesantes mejores
peor pequeño popular

a Pienso que Picasso y Sorolla son los ___ artistas españoles.
b No me gustan estos libros. Son los menos ___ de todos.
c ¿Cuál es la montaña más ___ del mundo?
d El fútbol es el deporte más ___ entre los argentinos.
e ¿Cuál es el transporte menos ___ para ir a Madrid?
f ¡Qué desastre! Es el ___ momento de mi vida.
g Pablo solo tiene tres años. Es el más ___ de todos mis hermanos.

Gramática

The superlative

When talking about 'the most' or 'the least' of something, use *el / la / los / las* + *más / menos* + adjective.

*David es **el más** alto.* – David is the tallest.

Irregular verbs in the preterite tense

8 Complete the sentences with the correct preterite form of the verbs in brackets. (These verbs are irregular in the preterite tense.)

a Mi hermano ___ (*decir*) que su cantante favorita es Rosalía.
b Yo no ___ (*poder*) ir al concierto ayer.
c Mis amigos ___ (*tener*) que comprar dos entradas.
d Tú ___ (*venir*) al festival el año pasado.
e Salma Hayek ___ (*producir*) la película *Frida* en 2002.
f Luis y su novia no ___ (*querer*) viajar a Bilbao en tren.
g ¿___ (*traer*) vosotros la ensalada de frutas a la fiesta?
h Nosotros ___ (*estar*) en casa de Marta el viernes pasado.

Stem changes in the preterite tense

9 Complete the sentences with the correct preterite form of the verbs in brackets. (These verbs have a spelling change in the 'he' / 'she' and 'they' forms of the preterite tense.)

a Juan ___(*dormir*) hasta las once de la mañana.
b Elena y Daniela ___ (*sentir*) mucha alegría.
c Ellos ___(*pedir*) una pizza grande para la fiesta de cumpleaños.
d Raúl ___ (*preferir*) quedarse en casa ayer.
e Los camareros ___ (*servir*) la cena a las nueve y media.
f Maya se ___ (*vestir*) de negro para la fiesta.
g ¿Usted ___ (*leer*) el mensaje de Adela?
h El profesor ___ (*repetir*) la información.

Pronouns after prepositions

10 Complete the sentences with the correct options from the box.

conmigo de ellos de mí para ella sin vosotras

a Mi padre siempre viene ___ al supermercado.
b Es el cumpleaños de mi madrastra. Tengo un regalo ___.
c ¿Esta tableta es de tus primos? – Sí, estoy seguro de que es ___.
d En clase, Lola se sienta delante ___.
e Zahara y María, si no venís a la fiesta ya, iremos ___.

Grammar practice

Using *al*, *antes de* or *después de*

11 Translate the sentence starters into Spanish. Use either *al*, *antes de* or *después de* followed by the correct infinitive form of the verb.

- a On arriving in Peru …
- b Before eating the fruit …
- c After travelling to Cusco …
- d On leaving the house …
- e Before buying a car …
- f After reading the novel …

Apocopation

12 Complete the sentences with the apocopated form of the adjectives in brackets.

- a Mi ___ (*bueno*) amigo Fernando celebra el Día de Muertos en casa.
- b En ___ (*ninguno*) país de Europa celebran el Carnaval como en Canarias.
- c El ___ (*primero*) día vamos al museo.
- d La ___ (*grande*) fiesta empieza a las ocho.
- e El ___ (*tercero*) día de las vacaciones, hay un baile en Caracas.

Present continuous with *seguir* and *continuar*

13 Complete the sentences with *seguir* or *continuar* in the correct present form and the present participle of the verbs in brackets.

- a Yo ___ (*estudiar*) para el examen de mañana.
- b ¿Tú ___ (*trabajar*) en el supermercado?
- c Él ___ (*practicar*) con la guitarra todos los días.
- d Nosotros ___ (*aprender*) inglés.
- e Vosotros ___ (*viajar*) por Latinoamérica.
- f Ellas ___ (*correr*) en el parque todas las mañanas.
- g Ustedes ___ (*ayudar*) en a la comunidad.
- h Los estudiantes ___ (*repasar*) biología.

Interrogatives with prepositions

14 Translate these sentences into English.

- a ¿De quién es este coche?
- b ¿Con quién hablaste ayer?
- c ¿Para qué es este papel?
- d ¿A qué hora terminó el partido?
- e ¿En qué estás pensando?
- f ¿Con quién vas a la fiesta?

Imperfect tense

15 Complete the sentences with the correct imperfect form of the verbs in brackets.

- a Cada viernes, nosotros ___ (*ver*) una película muy emocionante en el cine.
- b Yo siempre ___ (*ser*) el primero en llegar a la fiesta.
- c Los domingos, mis amigos y yo ___ (*tomar*) helado en el parque.
- d Cada verano, mis padres ___ (*ir*) de vacaciones a Gran Canaria.
- e De pequeño, mi abuela me ___ (*comprar*) muchos juguetes.
- f Durante el invierno, tú ___ (*hacer*) esquí en los Pirineos.
- g Mi hermana siempre ___ (*leer*) antes de dormir.
- h Los fines de semana, vosotros ___ (*disfrutar*) del buen ambiente de Barcelona.

Suffixes

16 Translate these words into English. Make sure you convey the meaning of the *-ísimo* or *-ito* suffix.

- a lentísima
- b un zapatito
- c un gatito
- d limpísimo
- e divertidísima
- f un papelito
- g rapidísimo
- h unas casitas

Preterite or imperfect?

17 Choose the correct verb tense to complete the paragraph.

Cuando yo (a) **era / fui** niña, (b) **vivía / viví** en una casa de un pueblo pequeño en el norte de Colombia. Un día, mi padre me (c) **compraba / compró** una entrada para el concierto de Shakira, mi artista favorita. (d) ¡**Era / Fue** una sorpresa enorme! El día del concierto, mi padre (e) **conducía / condujo** el coche hacia la capital, Bogotá, mientras yo (f) **escuchaba / escuché** varias canciones de Shakira. A las dos de la tarde, (g) **veía / vi** el estadio por primera vez. ¡Qué enorme! El concierto me (h) **encantaba / encantó**. Siempre lo voy a recordar.

Gramática

The preterite and imperfect tenses

As well as describing what people or things used to be like, the imperfect tense is used to narrate what was happening when a completed action took place. In such cases, we must use both the imperfect and preterite tenses.

*Anoche me **caí** mientras **corría** por el parque.* – Last night I fell over while I was running in the park.

Using *ser* and *estar*

18 Choose the correct form of *ser* or *estar* to complete the sentences and convey the appropriate meaning.

a Hoy tengo un examen. **Estoy / Soy** nervioso.

b ¡Esta paella **está / es** riquísima!

c Mis abuelos **están / son** muy orgullosos de nosotros.

d Yusuf aprobó todos los exámenes. **Es / Está** muy listo.

e Quiero ser científico porque **estoy / soy** interesado en las ciencias.

f No me gusta nada este concierto. **Es / está** aburrido.

Adjectival agreement

19 Translate these sentences into Spanish.

a My friend's dog is small.

b Barcelona's beach is clean.

c Rosalía's sister lives in Barcelona.

d Rosario's Spanish is excellent.

e Your uncle's house is modern.

f My brother's bedroom is small.

g Colombia's dishes are delicious.

h Yalitza's films are entertaining.

All tenses translation

20 Translate these sentences into English. Pay close attention to the tense of the verbs.

a La cantante Aitana tiene tres conciertos este mes.

b Ayer, mi hermana y yo vimos a dos famosos en un restaurante.

c Cuando era pequeña, Gloria escuchaba música rock en el jardín.

d Yo sería mucho más feliz sin tanto trabajo.

e Los obreros construyeron el palacio en siete años.

f No puedes viajar a mi pueblo en tren.

g Rubén saldrá con Isaac esta noche.

h Llovía mucho cuando llegué a Barcelona.

Using *soler*

21 Rewrite the sentences to include the verb *soler* instead of *normalmente*.

a Normalmente, desayuno temprano los fines de semana.

b Normalmente, navegamos por Internet en casa.

c Normalmente, vas al gimnasio por la tarde.

d Normalmente, los jóvenes quedan en la plaza.

Higher Vocabulary

Words that are highlighted in grey in this list are words that may be useful, but you won't need to know them for the exam.

4.1F ¡Nos gusta el riesgo!

el aire air
el alpinismo mountain climbing
el/la amigo/a friend
antiguo/a old
aquí here
el avión plane
bajar to descend, to go down
el barrio neighbourhood
la bicicleta bicycle
caer(se) to fall
el calor heat
cerca near
la costa coast
creer to believe
el domingo Sunday
duro/a hard
el edificio building
emocionante exciting
entre between, among
la escalada rock climbing
el fondo the end, bottom
el gimnasio gym
el kayak kayak
leer to read
limpio/a clean
llamar to call
la madrastra stepmother
el miedo fear
mientras while
la montaña mountain
morir to die
nadar to swim
el pájaro bird
el paracaidismo skydiving
el parkour parkour
peligroso/a dangerous
el pez fish
el problema problem
puro/a pure
respirar to breathe
el riesgo risk
el río river
sobre about
sonreír to smile
subir to ascend, to go up
el submarinismo scuba diving
tirarse to jump off
ver to see, watch
el verano summer
la visita visit

4.1H ¡Mi tiempo libre es infinito!

la actualidad at present, now
a pesar de despite
aficionado/a enthusiast
ahorrar to save
el aire libre outdoors
andar to walk
la aventura adventure
bailar to dance
bueno/a good
caminar to walk
la camiseta t-shirt, football shirt
el campo countryside
cantar to sing
la carrera race
cocinar to cook
el coche car
el/la cocinero/a cook, chef
Comecocos Pac-Man
comenzar to start
la compañía company
comprar to buy
la consola games console
copiar to copy
de segunda mano second hand
de vez en cuando from time to time
desafortunadamente unfortunately
el desayuno breakfast
el dinero money
divertido/a fun
el/la doctor(a) doctor
económico/a inexpensive
emocionante exciting
empezar to start
entrenar to train
escuchar to listen
fácil easy
el fin de semana weekend
físico/a physical
genial great
el/la gimnasta gymnast
guay cool
increíble incredible
el instituto (insti) secondary school
ir de compras to go shopping
el jardín garden
el juego game
leer to read
maravilloso/a wonderful
la marca brand
la mitad half
la moda fashion
el mundo world
la novela novel
olvidar(se) to forget
pasear to go for a walk
pintar to paint
por ciento percent
preparar to prepare
rápido/a fast, quick
el regalo present
el riesgo risk
la ropa clothing
según according to
siempre que puedo whenever I can
sin without
sobre todo above all
soler to usually do something
soñar (con) to dream (about)
el tiempo time
tocar to play
trabajar to work
útil useful
ver to watch, see
el videojuego video game

4.2F Veo, veo… ¿Qué ves?

el ambiente atmosphere
el amor love
anoche last night
aprender to learn
ayer yesterday
el cine cinema
la cocina cooking, kitchen
el concurso contest, game show
los dibujos animados cartoons
difícil difficult
disfrutar to enjoy
el documental documentary
los efectos especiales special effects
entender to understand
la entrevista interview
en vivo live
escribir to write
extranjero/a foreign
el/la famoso celebrity
finalmente finally
el idioma language
la lluvia rain
un montón a lot
las noticias news
el oeste western (film)
la pantalla screen
la pelea fight
por ejemplo for example
la preferencia preference
el/la primo/a cousin
la película film
la pregunta question
probablemente probably
el programa programme
rápidamente quickly
responder to answer
sin duda without doubt
sobre about
el sol sun
el tiempo weather

la ***telenovela*** soap opera

la ***televisión*** TV

la ***temperatura*** temperature

el ***tiempo*** weather, weather forecast

todos los días every day

un montón a lot

ver to see, watch

4.2H Mi tiempo es oro

abstracto/a abstract

la ***actitud*** attitude

aficionado/a fan, enthusiast

alguien someone

el/la ***anticuario/a*** antique dealer

la ***antigüedad*** antique

el/la ***astronauta*** astronaut

la ***astronomía*** astronomy

el ***automovilismo*** car racing

buscar to search, look for

cambiar to change

la ***carrera*** race

el/la ***científico/a*** scientist

el ***circuito*** circuit

coleccionar to collect

comenzar to start

común common

conducir to drive

la ***contaminación*** pollution

la ***cosa*** thing

cruzar to cross

el/la ***cuidador(a)*** carer

la ***decoración*** decoration

la ***desventaja*** disadvantage

dibujar to draw

en cambio on the other hand

la ***entrada*** ticket

los ***enseres*** goods

la ***época*** era, period

el ***establecimiento*** establishment, shop

estar de acuerdo (con) to agree (with)

la ***estrella*** star

el/la ***estudiante*** student

europeo/a European

exótico/a exotic

la ***experiencia*** experience

expresivo/a expressive

la ***forma*** shape, form

el ***fósil*** fossil

gracioso/a funny

el ***juguete*** toy

el ***libro*** book

la ***luna*** moon

la ***mano*** hand

la ***mascota*** pet

la ***mesa*** table

el ***miedo*** fear

mirar to look at

el/la ***modelo a seguir*** role model

el ***mueble*** furniture

el ***objeto*** object

la ***obra de arte*** artwork

ocupar to occupy

el ***padrastro*** stepfather

el ***paisaje*** landscape

el ***papel*** role

peor worse

el ***peligro*** danger

pintar to paint

la ***playa*** beach

la ***posibilidad*** possibility

profundo/a deep

reconocer to recognize, acknowledge

regalar to gift

la ***regla*** rule

el ***río*** river

la ***roca*** rock

romper to break

el ***siglo*** century

el ***sueño*** dream

tan so

el ***telescopio*** telescope

la ***tienda*** shop

tocar to play (an instrument)

trasladarse to transport oneself

valer la pena to be worth it

la ***velocidad*** speed

la ***ventaja*** advantage

la ***ventana*** window

el ***viaje*** trip, journey

vivo/a vivid

5.1F Nuestras tradiciones de siempre

abril April

los ***abuelos*** grandparents

anoche last night

antes before

ayer yesterday

el ***ayuno*** fasting

la ***banda*** (music) band

católico/a Catholic

la ***bicicleta*** bicycle

la ***carne*** meat

la ***celebración*** celebration

la ***compañía*** company

decir to say

el ***desayuno*** breakfast

el ***desfile*** parade

disfrutar to enjoy

distinto/a different

el ***domingo*** Sunday

durante for, during

el ***esfuerzo*** effort

estar to be

hace… …ago

hacer to do, make

la ***importancia*** importance

importar to matter

la ***Janucá*** Hanukkah

la ***luz*** light

el ***martes*** Tuesday

el ***mes*** month

musulmán/musulmana Muslim

la ***Navidad*** Christmas

nervioso/a nervous

la ***Nochebuena*** Christmas Eve

la ***Nochevieja*** New Year's Eve

el ***ordenador*** computer

pasado/a last

la ***Pascua*** Easter

la ***plaza*** square

poner fin a to bring an end to

por ejemplo for example

el ***principio*** beginning

el ***regalo*** gift

religioso/a religious

saber to know

sacar (fotos) to take (photos)

la ***Semana Santa*** Holy (Easter) Week

soltero/a single

subir to upload

tener lugar to take place

los ***Tres Reyes Magos*** the Three Wise Men

la ***tradición*** tradition

la ***uva*** grape

varios/as several, various

el/la ***vecino/a*** neighbour

5.1H ¡Un año más!

actualmente now, at present

al final at the end

el ***baile*** dance

la ***cara*** face

la ***ceremonia*** ceremony

cierto/a certain

claro of course

conmigo with me

la ***costumbre*** custom, tradition

de acuerdo (estar) to agree

doler to hurt

dormir to sleep

empujar to push

estar de acuerdo (con) to agree (with)

la ***fiesta*** party

la ***frecuencia*** frequency

gracioso/a funny

la ***iglesia*** church

increíble incredible

la ***letra*** lyric

el ***momento*** moment

la ***mordida*** bite

nosotros/as we, us

la ***oreja*** ear

el ***pastel*** cake

el/la ***peluquero/a*** hairdresser

precioso/a beautiful

la Quinceañera girl's 15th birthday (Lat Am.)
recoger to pick up, collect
recordar to remember
soler to usually do something
sorprender to surprise
sugerir to suggest
la tienda shop
tirar to throw, pull
todo all, everything
un montón de lots of
la vergüenza embarrassment
vestirse to get dressed
la vida life
la videoconsola video game console

5.2F Latinoamérica celebra la vida

además furthermore, moreover
la alegría joy
antes before
aprender to learn
bueno/a good
la calle street
el calor heat
la cámara camera
el campo countryside
el carnaval carnival
celebrar to celebrate
consistir en to consist of
desde from, since
el desfile parade
después after
egoísta selfish
entre between, among
esperar to wait, to hope
la feria fair
la flor flower
la influencia influence
la lengua language
llegar to arrive
llenar to fill
el lugar place
el móvil mobile (phone)
muerto/a dead
ninguno/a no, none
el olor smell
poder to be able to
ponerse to put on
primero/a first
el quechua Quechua (indigenous language)
el teatro theater
el tiempo time
traer to bring
triste sad
la variedad variety
ver to watch, see
visitar to visit
el zapato shoe

5.2H Bailando al ritmo hispano

afroamericano/a African American
abandonar to leave
aparecer to appear
ayer yesterday
bailar to dance
caribeño/a Caribbean
el coche car
con with
como like
conocer to know
conocido/a known, familiar
el concurso competition
la derecha right
despertarse to wake up
empezar to start
en vivo live
el espectáculo show, spectacle
esperar to hope
la estrella star
la falda skirt
ganar to win
el grupo group
individual individual
la influencia influence
la izquierda left
latino/a Latin
la mano hand
la mezcla mixture
el minuto minute
nacer to be born
necesario/a necessary
otro/a other
para for, in order to
la pareja couple
el paso step
el pie foot
la pierna leg
practicar to practice
el público public
rápido fast, quick
el ritmo rhythm
romántico/a romantic
seguro/a sure
situarse to be located
la sorpresa surprise
también also
el/la tío/a uncle/aunt
el tipo sort, type
el/la último/a last
usar to use
verdadero/a true
visitar to visit
votar to vote
ya now, already

6.1F Lola y Rosalía, ayer y hoy

animado/a lively
el/la artista artist
bailar to dance
cada each, every
cantar to sing
la canción song
caro/a expensive
el cine cinema
el concierto concert
la cultura culture
emocionante exciting
la energía energy
la entrada ticket
escuchar to listen
el estilo style
la estrella star
Estados Unidos United States
la fama fame
la forma way
hacer to make, do
el icono icon
llevar to wear
mejor better, best
morir to die
nacer to be born
nuestro/a our
opinar to believe, think
otro/a other
pasar de moda to be out of fashion
la pasión passion
la película film
pensar to think
personal personal
la personalidad personality
presentarse to appear, give
seguir to continue, follow
tanto/a so many, so much
el tiempo time
todavía still
único/a only, unique
urbano/a urban
la vez time

6.1H La nueva cultura de la fama

actual current
el apoyo support
argentino/a Argentinian
ayer yesterday
el ballet ballet
caminar to walk
caerse to fall over
clásico/a classical
la danza dance
desfavorecido/a disadvantaged
el/la deportista sportsman/sportswoman, athlete
el dinero money
el/la diseñador(a) designer
la duda doubt
enorme enormous
el equipo team
el esfuerzo effort
el estreno premiere
generoso/a generous
la historia story
el/la influencer influencer
el/la jugador(a) player

el *lado* side
llamar la atención to stand out, be noteworthy
llegar a ser to become
loco/a crazy
la *manera* manner, way
más tarde later
mientras while
mundialmente worldwide
el/la *niñero/a* nanny/au pair
la *organización* organisation
el *pastel* cake
portugués/a Portuguese
el/la *programa* programme
privado/a private
propio/a own
la *red social* social network
rico/a rich
el/la *seguidor(a)* follower
el *sentido del humor* sense of humour
sin without
la *tienda* shop
trabajar to work
la *universidad* university
varios/as several
la *vida* life
ya now, already

6.2F Famosos que valen la pena

a mi modo de ver as I see it
agresivo/a aggressive
antipático/a unpleasant
la *ascendencia* heritage
aunque although
el *cine* cinema
la *ciudad* city
como as
comprensivo/a understanding
la *comunidad* community
de niño/a as a child
deshonesto dishonest
donar to donate
educado/a polite
egoísta selfish
emocionante exciting
enfermo/a ill
la *escuela* (primary) school
Estados Unidos United States
estar seguro/a to be sure
la *fama* fame
hablar to speak
humilde humble
el *idioma* language
importante important
indígena native, indigenous
inspirar to inspire
el/la *joven* young person
latinoamericano/a Latin American
maleducado/a impolite
mexicano/a Mexican
el/la *modelo a seguir* role model
el *norte* north
la *nominación* nomination
Nueva York New York
opinar to think
optimista optimistic
el *país* country
el *papel* role
parecer to seem
la *participación* participation
participar to participate
perezoso/a lazy
pesimista pessimistic
el *premio* award, prize
el *proyecto* project
puertorriqueño/a Puerto Rican
que yo sepa as far as I know
recibir to receive
reducir to reduce
sincero/a honest
el *sur* south
la *televisión* TV
trabajador(a) hard-working
único/a unique
valer la pena to be worth it
la *verdad* truth
la *vida social* social life
la *visibilidad* visibility, awareness
votar to vote
la *voz* voice

6.2H ¡La fama tiene dos caras!

a causa de because of
el *acoso* harassment
acosar to harass
cambiar to change
decir to say
dejar to leave
durante for, during
entrenar to train
esconder to hide
el *espacio* space
estar de acuerdo (con) to agree (with)
la *falta* lack
el *fin de semana* weekend
el *fotógrafo/a* photographer
ir de compras to go shopping
el *jugador(a)* player
la *lástima* pity, shame
lejos de far from
leer to read
el *límite* limit
el *lugar* place
la *novela* novel
la *página* page
paparazzi photographer who follows famous people
para siempre forever
la *pasión* passion
peligroso/a dangerous
el/la *periodista* journalist
la *persecución* pursuit
por fin finally
preferir to prefer
preguntar to ask a question
la *privacidad* privacy
público/a public
quejarse to complain
el *respeto* respect
el/la *seguidor(a)* follower
la *separación* separation
el *teléfono móvil* mobile phone
la *telerrealidad* reality TV
tener derecho a to have the right to
tener miedo to be afraid
el *tiempo libre* free time
las *vacaciones* holidays
ver to see

Test and revise: Higher Listening

1 You hear some Spanish students discussing birthday celebrations. What is their opinion of each celebration they mention?

Write **P** for a **positive** opinion
N for a **negative** opinion
P+N for a **positive** and **negative** opinion.

a Student 1 **1 mark**
b Student 2 **1 mark**
c Student 3 **1 mark**
d Student 4 **1 mark**

Consejo

With all questions, but especially this type, it is essential to listen carefully to the full recording before deciding on your answer. You may hear a positive opinion to start with, but the speaker may then give a negative viewpoint as well. Only answer when you have heard the full utterance.

2 Your Spanish friend, Elena, leaves you a voice message about her favourite TikTokers, Twin Melody. Listen to the message and write down the correct letter.

a Paula and Aitana are…
  A 26 years old.
  B 15 years old.
  C 16 years old. **1 mark**

b They upload videos of themselves…
  A singing.
  B dancing.
  C singing and dancing. **1 mark**

c At Benidorm Fest they…
  A presented a TV show.
  B won a competition.
  C performed a song. **1 mark**

d Elena says that Paula and Aitana…
  A like animated films.
  B are good role models.
  C are very sympathetic. **1 mark**

3 You hear these adverts on the radio. Choose the two correct statements for each advert.

a

A	The painting club needs new members.
B	The focus of the club is landscape painting.
C	No prior experience of painting is required.
D	The painting club has a new website.

1 mark

b

A	This trip is ideal for animal lovers.
B	The trip will be free.
C	The trip will take place this spring.
D	You will need to upload a photo to Instagram.

1 mark

c

A	This role would suit people who like working alone outdoors.
B	The local government urgently needs experts.
C	The role offered is low paid.
D	The local surroundings are in need of improvement.

1 mark

4 Listen to these questions from a teacher about Day of the Dead in Mexico. What is the teacher asking the students? Answer the questions in English.

Question 1 **1 mark**
Question 2 **1 mark**
Question 3 **1 mark**
Question 4 **1 mark**

5 Listen to this profile of the actress Katy Jurado.

Write **A** if only statement A is correct
B if only statement B is correct
A+B if both statements A and B are correct.

a Katy Jurado appeared in…
- A her first film in the 1940s.
- B more than seventy films. **1 mark**

b Katy won…
- A several important awards in Mexico.
- B awards abroad. **1 mark**

c Katy was always…
- A aware that cinema was a demanding industry.
- B loved by the public. **1 mark**

d On social media…
- A she had millions of followers from around the world.
- B she would have been very popular. **1 mark**

6 Listen to this news item about Villano Antillano, a Puerto Rican rapper. Answer the questions in English.

a When did Villano Antillano's interview take place? **1 mark**

b What **two** themes does she talk about in her songs? **2 marks**

c Where will tomorrow's concert take place? **1 mark**

d How do we know Villano is a popular artist? **1 mark**

Consejo

Make sure you read each question carefully to see how much information is needed. For example, you need two themes in part 6b to answer the question fully.

Dictation A

You will now hear 5 short sentences.

- Listen carefully and using your knowledge of Spanish sounds, write down in **Spanish** exactly what you hear for each sentence.
- You will hear each sentence **three** times: the first time as a full sentence, the second time in short sections and the third time again as a full sentence.
- Use your knowledge of Spanish sounds and grammar to make sure that what you have written makes sense. Check carefully that your spelling is accurate.

10 marks

Dictation B

You will now hear 5 short sentences.

- Listen carefully and using your knowledge of Spanish sounds, write down in **Spanish** exactly what you hear for each sentence.
- You will hear each sentence **three** times: the first time as a full sentence, the second time in short sections and the third time again as a full sentence.
- Use your knowledge of Spanish sounds and grammar to make sure that what you have written makes sense. Check carefully that your spelling is accurate.

10 marks

Test and revise: Higher Speaking

Role Play

You are talking to your Costa Rican friend.

Your teacher (or partner) will play the part of your friend and will speak first.

You should address your friend as *tú*.

When you see this – ? – you will have to ask a question.

In order to score full marks, you must include a verb in your response to each task.

1 Say what type of music you like and why. (Give **one** type and **one** reason.)

2 Describe your favourite singer. (Give **two** details.)

3 Say something you are going to do in your free time next weekend. (Give **two** details.)

4 Give **one** advantage about watching films in the cinema.

5 **?** Ask your friend a question about television.

Consejo

When you are preparing for a role play, make sure you've read all details carefully so you know how much you need to prepare. For example, in this role play you need to give two details for tasks 2 and 3, and you need to give both a type of music and a reason in task 1.

Reading aloud task

When your teacher (or partner) asks you, read aloud the following text in **Spanish**.

La semana pasada fui a un concierto en Madrid con mi familia.

Mi hermana compró las entradas porque es muy generosa.

Me encanta pasar mucho tiempo con ella.

Además, a mí me gusta mucho bailar y cantar.

En Latinoamérica hay muchos festivales históricos que son muy divertidos.

You will then be asked four questions in **Spanish** that relate to the topic of **Customs, festivals and celebrations**. Make sure you answer **all four questions as fully as you can**.

Photo card

- During your preparation time, look at the two photos on Popular culture. You may make as many notes as you wish on an Additional Answer Sheet and use these notes during the test.
- Your teacher (or partner) will ask you to talk about the content of these photos. The recommended time is approximately **one and a half minutes. You must say at least one thing about each photo.**
- After you have spoken about the content of the photos, your teacher (or partner) will then ask you questions related to **any** of the topics within the theme of **Popular culture.**

Consejo

When you are given pictures to prepare, don't just think about language connected to the stated topic. The instructions for the second part of the photo card task state 'any topics within the theme of...' so think when you are preparing of other topics that might come up.

Photo 1

Photo 2

Test and revise: Higher Reading

1 **You are reading about festivals on the Internet and come across these opinions in an online forum.**

Gloria
En Puerto Rico celebramos el Día de Acción de Gracias en noviembre. Suele ser muy agradable estar con la familia.

Pedro
La Feria de Sevilla es decepcionante. A causa del ambiente animado, todos los años me cuesta dormir por la noche.

Luisa
Vivo en Pamplona y me parece que la tradición de San Fermín está pasada de moda. Es verdad que hay ventajas económicas gracias a los turistas que vienen a la ciudad.

Lola
¿Tienes ganas de venir a la Tomatina de Buñol este año? Yo cuando pienso en este festival, siempre me hace sonreír.

What do these people think about each festival?

Write **P** for a **positive** opinion
N for a **negative** opinion
P+N for a **positive** and **negative** opinion.

a Gloria **1 mark**
b Luisa **1 mark**
c Pedro **1 mark**
d Lola **1 mark**

2 **You read an email from your friend, describing her idol.**

En estos momentos, sigo con atención a la influencer Eugenia Tenenbaum. Me gusta no solo por su belleza y su estilo, sino también por su inteligencia. Publicó el libro *Las mujeres de Picasso* hace ocho meses, y me parece una obra muy importante. Pronto iré a la biblioteca de mi barrio para leerlo. Vi una entrevista suya en Internet promoviendo el libro y fue muy educativa. Estoy intentando mejorar mi conocimiento de la historia del arte cada día. Además, compré una entrada para la feria del libro.

Esperanza

What does she say about these events?

Write **P** for something that happened **in the past**
N for something that is happening **now**
F for something that will happen **in the future**.

1 Following an influencer **1 mark**
2 Publishing a book **1 mark**
3 Going to the library **1 mark**
4 Watching an interview **1 mark**
5 Improving knowledge of art history **1 mark**
6 Buying a ticket for a book festival **1 mark**

3 Amaia has completed a survey with her classmates as part of a school project on hobbies.

Según mis recientes investigaciones, es evidente que la mayoría de mis compañeros de clase hacen cada vez menos ejercicio. Muchos reconocen que no encuentran la oportunidad de seguir practicando deportes a causa de los deberes escolares y, en mi opinión, debido también a la presión social que aumenta durante la juventud. Más de la mitad de mi clase dice que usan las redes sociales todos los días, y en algunos casos, durante más de ocho horas al día. Muchos juegan a videojuegos violentos en casa, pero no les preocupa que estos videojuegos puedan tener un efecto negativo en ellos. Finalmente, hablando de los deportes de riesgo, todos mis compañeros de clase piensan que son demasiado caros, pero el sesenta y cinco por ciento sueña con viajar a un país tropical. Allí, parece que quieren hacer algún deporte acuático como el buceo.

For each question, write **A** if only statement A is correct
B if only statement B is correct
A+B if both statements A and B are correct.

a **A** Half of Amaia's class use social networks every day.
B Some of Amaia's class use social networks for eight hours a day. **1 mark**

b **A** Many of her classmates play violent videogames at home.
B They are not worried about the possible negative effects of these games on them. **1 mark**

c **A** All of Amaia's classmates think extreme sports are too expensive.
B A minority of her classmates dream of travelling to a tropical country. **1 mark**

d Read the last paragraph again. What do you think *el buceo* is?
A rock climbing **B** scuba diving **C** paragliding **1 mark**

Consejo

Question 4d above requires you to work out the general meaning of a word or phrase from the context. You will need to read around it and use all the clues in the rest of the sentence or paragraph. There will be two questions like this in the reading exam.

4 Translate these sentences into English.

a Desafortunadamente, no voy a tener tiempo para comprar las entradas esta tarde.

b Estoy triste porque no puedo asistir al concierto contigo.

c Antes de hacer los deberes, tuve que llamar a mi novia.

d Esa película me da mucho miedo, pero es de buena calidad.

e Vi un programa sobre la historia musulmana en España. **10 marks**

Consejo

You won't always know all the words in a translation and you will need to use linguistic common sense to make a sensible guess at the meaning of a word. Look at the words around the one you don't know to see if they can give you any clues.

5 Translate these sentences into English.

a Sueño con pasar la Navidad en el extranjero.

b Quizás buscaré un vestido bonito de segunda mano.

c No tengo ganas de ir a la fiesta sin Laura.

d De niña, mi hermana era bastante mala, pero ahora estoy muy orgulloso de ella.

e Ya no me quiero seguir a ese famoso, porque evita pagar impuestos. **10 marks**

Test and revise: Higher Writing

1 Translate the following sentences into Spanish.

a I want to use my new tablet this afternoon.

b It is best to visit Mexico between December and April.

c Next week, my friend is going to celebrate her birthday.

d I don't know if I am going to be famous in the future.

e I will start to follow my favourite actor on social media.

10 marks

Either Question 2.1 *or* Question 2.2

2.1 You are emailing your friend from Paraguay about festivals and celebrations.
Write approximately 90 words in Spanish.
You must write something about each bullet point.

Mention:

- your favourite Spanish or Latin American festival
- a celebration that recently took place
- what you are going to do in the summer holidays.

15 marks

2.2 You are writing an essay about celebrity culture.
Write approximately 90 words in Spanish.
You must write something about each bullet point.

Mention:

- a film or TV programme you enjoy
- a famous person you liked when you were younger
- if you would like to be famous in the future.

15 marks

Consejo

Keep an eye on your word count. It is no advantage at all to write pages and pages – you are given a word guide of approximately 90 words. If you write lots more, you will rush and allow more errors to creep in.

Either Question **3.1** *or* Question **3.2**

3.1 You are writing a social media post about celebrity culture.
Write approximately 150 words in Spanish.
You must write something about both bullet points.

Mention:

- a celebrity you think is a good role model
- whether you would enjoy being famous in the future.

25 marks

3.2 You are writing a blog on Hispanic festivals for a website.
Write approximately 150 words in Spanish.
You must write something about both bullet points.

Mention:

- the importance of festivals in general
- any Hispanic festivals you are going to go to in the future.

25 marks

Consejo

If you think you can say a lot more about one of the bullet points than the other, this is not a problem. You will not be marked down if you write more about one aspect than the other, but you must cover both points.

Theme 3 Communication and the world around us

Travel and tourism

1 **Match the Spanish and English words for different forms of transport.**

1	autobús
2	avión
3	barco
4	bicicleta
5	coche
6	metro
7	tren

A	underground, tube
B	car
C	bus
D	train
E	plane
F	boat
G	bicycle

2 **Listen to Ana's account of her trip to Barcelona. Write down in the correct order the different forms of transport she used.**

alquilar to hire

3 **Look at Martín's plan for his holiday.**

sábado	visitar los sitios de interés del pueblo
domingo	tomar el sol y nadar en la piscina del hotel
lunes	ir a un parque temático
martes	jugar al bádminton en la playa
miércoles	hay fiesta en el pueblo – ver los fuegos artificiales
jueves	ver el espectáculo de baile en el hotel
viernes	ir a las tiendas para comprar recuerdos

el sitio	place
el pueblo	town, village
tomar el sol	to sunbathe
nadar	to swim
la piscina	swimming pool
el parque temático	theme park
jugar	to play
los fuegos artificiales	fireworks
el espectáculo	show
el baile	dance
la tienda	shop
el recuerdo	souvenir

On which day does he plan to do the following?

a see a firework display
b sunbathe by the pool
c shop for souvenirs
d go to a theme park
e play games on the beach
f go for a swim
g watch the show in the hotel
h go sightseeing

4 A Spanish travel magazine is doing a survey to find out what type of holiday people prefer. Which option from the table would each of these people choose?

A	sol y playa		E	en el extranjero
B	deportes de invierno		F	centro ciudad
C	actividades al aire libre		G	actividades para niños
D	visitas culturales		H	descanso en el campo

Carla
Me gusta comer en restaurantes, ver tiendas e ir al teatro.

Jorge
Si mis dos hijos pequeños están contentos, yo también lo estoy.

Luisa
Me encanta estar en las montañas haciendo actividades cuando hace frío y hay nieve.

Enrique
Busco unos días tranquilos en la naturaleza.

Marta
Me interesa ver las iglesias, los edificios históricos y los castillos.

Pablo
Quiero montar a caballo, cocinar sobre un fuego y dar paseos.

Lucía
Quiero explorar el mundo y ver muchos países.

Rafael
Prefiero el calor y pasar tiempo al lado del mar.

el deporte	sport
el invierno	winter
la actividad	activity
al aire libre	outdoors, in the open air
el extranjero	abroad
la ciudad	city
los niños	children
el descanso	rest
el campo	country, countryside
la tienda	shop, tent
el teatro	theatre
montar a caballo	to go horse-riding
cocinar	to cook
el fuego	fire
dar un paseo	to go for a walk
la montaña	mountain
el frío	cold
la nieve	snow
la iglesia	church
el edificio	building
el castillo	castle
tranquilo	quiet, peaceful
la naturaleza	nature
el mundo	world
el país	country
muchos	many
el calor	heat
pasar	to spend (time)
al lado de	next to

Media and technology

5 Listen to six people (1–6) explaining how they use social media. What does each one use social media for?

A	business		E	texting and instant messaging
B	finding old friends		F	uploading photos
C	following celebrities		G	videocalls
D	local events		H	watching music videos

la red social	social network	*la página*	page
el cantante	singer	*la empresa*	company
subir	to upload	*el negocio*	business
seguir	to follow	*las noticias*	news
mandar	to send	*pasar*	to happen, to spend
el mensaje	message	*el pueblo*	town, village

6 **Listen and unscramble the words to write the correct nouns.**

a  el mivól ___

b  el prittloá ___

c  la aplantal ___

d  el docatel ___

e  el dranodeor ___

Where people live

7 **Read what this girl is complaining about in her bedroom and select the correct letter (a–i) to describe each item.**

La cama no es muy cómoda y la luz no funciona muy bien. Las paredes son de un color muy feo y la ventana está sucia. Los **estantes** son demasiado pequeños y no puedo abrir el armario. El **portátil** está roto y la silla es demasiado baja. Sin embargo, la mesa es demasiado alta.

a	broken
b	dirty
c	does not like the colour
d	does not work
e	too high
f	too low
g	too small
h	uncomfortable
i	will not open

1 the bed
2 the light
3 the walls
4 the window
5 the shelves
6 the wardrobe / cupboard
7 the laptop
8 the chair
9 the desk / table

el estante	shelf

8 **Listen to eight people (1–8) talking about where they live. Which two places does each person mention?**

el banco	bank
el bosque	wood, forest
el cine	cinema
el estadio	stadium
el mercado	market
el parque	park
el puerto	port
el supermercado	supermarket
la estación	station
la fábrica	factory
la mezquita	mosque
la montaña	mountain
la playa	beach

The environment

9 **Listen to six people (1–6) talking about environmental issues. Which issue is each one talking about?**

A	endangered species
B	global warming
C	drought
D	poor air quality
E	protecting woodland
F	risk of wildfires
G	saving energy
H	water pollution

ahorrar	to save	*alto/a*	high
el animal	animal	*la energía*	energy
el árbol	tree	*la especie*	species
el calor	heat	*la flor*	flower
el esfuerzo	effort	*la lluvia*	rain
el incendio	fire	*la planta*	plant
el mundo	world	*la temperatura*	temperature
el peligro	danger	*la tierra*	land, earth
el riesgo	risk	*proteger*	to protect
el verano	summer	*seco/a*	dry
el viento	wind		

10 **Read the sentences and complete them with the correct verb from the box.**

separar	apagar	plantar
recoger	reciclar	ahorrar
usar	llevar	

a Tenemos un jardín grande y vamos a ___ dos árboles allí.

b Los alumnos del colegio van a ___ la basura del parque.

c Hay un nuevo contenedor en el patio; es para las botellas de plástico que vamos a ___.

d Para usar menos electricidad, debemos ___ las pantallas al final de la clase.

e Hemos tenido varios años muy secos; tenemos que ___ más agua.

f Es muy importante ___ la basura en casa y ponerla en el contenedor correcto.

g Cuando la gente está en el campo, debería ___ su basura a casa.

h En el instituto vamos a hablar de cómo podemos ___ menos energía.

apagar	to turn off, put out	*llevar*	to take, carry, wear
cómo	how	*plantar*	to plant
el contenedor	bin, container	*reciclar*	to recycle
en casa	at home	*recoger*	to collect, pick up
la basura	rubbish, litter	*separar*	to separate
la energía	energy	*usar*	to use

7.1F ¿Qué haces durante las vacaciones?

OBJECTIVES
- Holiday activities
- Phrases with *ir de*
- The conditional tense
- Pronunciation *j*

1 **Read what these young people say. Write the correct name for each question.**

Durante las vacaciones hago camping con mis amigos. Vamos al campo, con todo nuestro equipo en mochilas, y montamos la tienda al lado de un río. Cocinamos las comidas al fuego. Nos encanta estar al aire libre.

Cuando estamos de vacaciones, vamos de compras en los pueblos y las ciudades que visitamos. Mi madre compra recuerdos y yo miro la ropa. A veces vamos a los mercados que venden de todo y compro regalos para mis amigos.

Yo prefiero estar activo y siempre busco actividades nuevas para probar. El año pasado jugué al baloncesto en la piscina y este verano voy a aprender a montar a caballo. A veces, voy de paseo en bicicleta con un grupo de amigos.

Cuando visito un lugar que no conozco, me gusta mirar el plano de la ciudad y visitar todos los sitios de interés. Me encanta aprender de la historia y ver los edificios históricos. Siempre tengo el móvil y hago fotos todo el tiempo.

Para mí, las vacaciones son para descansar y mi actividad favorita es tomar el sol en la playa. Cuando tengo demasiado calor, nado en el mar o voy al café para tomar una bebida fresca. Si estamos en un hotel, descanso en los jardines cerca de la piscina.

Who…

a likes shopping?
b enjoys photography?
c likes trying different sports?
d likes the outdoor life?
e prefers just to relax?
f likes to learn about places?

2 **Look at the texts again and answer the questions.**

a Where does Paula camp?
b How do they prepare their meals?
c What does Jaime's mother buy?
d What does Jaime do in the markets?
e What did Leo try last year?
f What is he going to learn this year?
g What do he and his friends sometimes do?
h What does Martina always have with her when she visits a town?
i What is Alba's favourite holiday activity?
j What does she do when it gets too hot?

3 **Listen to these people talking about what type of holiday they would like. Write the correct letters from the table.**

A	a beach holiday		**E**	a road trip
B	a boating holiday		**F**	a theme park trip
C	a luxurious stay		**G**	a wildlife experience
D	a peaceful time		**H**	a winter holiday

4 **Complete the sentences with the correct form of the verb in brackets in the conditional tense. Then translate the sentences into English.**

a Decidí que ___ (*ir, yo*) al campo en verano.
b ¿Crees que ___ (*poder, tú*) reservar la excursión hoy?
c Dijeron que me ___ (*comprar, ellos*) un regalo.
d Pensé que el hotel ___ (*tener*) un gimnasio.
e Creímos que la recepción ___ (*estar*) abierta veinticuatro horas.
f La ciudad es muy grande; nos ___ (*perder, nosotros*) sin un plano.
g Decidimos que ___ (*poner, nosotros*) las maletas en un lugar seguro.
h No sé cuánto ___ (*costar*) la excursión a la isla.

5 **Read these sentences and write P if the sentence is in the past, N if it is in the present and F if it will happen in the future.**

a Vamos a ir de vacaciones en agosto.
b Fue de compras el sábado.
c Voy de paseo por el parque.
d Van de compras cada martes.
e Iré de vacaciones con mis padres.
f ¿Fuiste de paseo con el perro?

6 **Work with a partner. Take turns to tell your partner what you do during these types of holidays. (Use the texts in activity 1 to help.)**

- a beach holiday
- an activity holiday
- a holiday at home
- a sightseeing holiday
- a holiday in the country

7 **Write a 90-word account with the title *Mis vacaciones ideales*. Say how you would spend your ideal holidays.**

Pronunciación

j

The letter 'j' is pronounced like the 'ch' in the Scottish word 'loch'.

Examples: ***j****ugar*, *naran****j****a*, ***j****amón*, *me****j****or*, *hi****j****o*

Los verbos

The conditional tense

To form the conditional tense ('would' …), follow these steps.

Take the infinitive (like *viajar, comer, ir*) and add the following endings:

Person	Ending	Examples	English
yo	*-ía*	*viajaría*	I would travel
tú	*-ías*	*pagarías*	you would pay
él / ella / usted	*-ía*	*vendería*	he / she would sell
nosotros / as	*-íamos*	*comeríamos*	we would eat
vosotros / as	*-íais*	*conducirías*	you would drive
ellos / ellas / ustedes	*-ían*	*irían*	they would go

Note the irregular stem (instead of the infinitive) for these five verbs:

tener > *tendr-* (*tendr****ía****, tendr****ías***, etc.)
poder > *podr-* (*podr****ía****, podr****ías***, etc.)
hacer > *har-* (*har****ía****, har****ías***, etc.)
poner > *pondr-* (*pondr****ía****, pondr****ías***, etc.)
haber > *habría* – there would be

¡Atención!

ir de

Note the following important phrases using *ir de* …
ir de vacaciones – to go on holiday
ir de paseo – to go for a walk
ir de compras – to go shopping

7.1H Las vacaciones fueron un desastre

OBJECTIVES
- Holiday problems
- Possessive pronouns
- The conditional tense – irregular verbs

1 **You read this online forum where people have written about their holiday nightmares.**

Write **A** if only statement A is correct
B if only statement B is correct
A+B if both statements A and B are correct.

1	**A**	José was stuck in a plane for hours.
	B	The plane had a technical problem.
2	**A**	Mariana had a long, hot journey.
	B	She had a cool swim when she arrived.
3	**A**	Mateo's hotel had lovely sea views.
	B	His room overlooked a busy street.
4	**A**	Adriana broke her suitcase at the airport.
	B	She had arrived after a long flight.
5	**A**	Adriana's sister helped her.
	B	The luggage problem was eventually solved.
6	**A**	Manolo was involved in a boating accident.
	B	Manolo broke his arm.

2 **Listen to eight people (1–8) talking about their holidays. What problem did each one have? Write the answer in English.**

Los verbos

The conditional tense – irregular verbs

You saw the regular conditional tense on page 111.

The irregular verbs are the same as for the future tense. Here you can see the irregular stem of some common verbs in the 1st person singular:

add a *-d*	
venir	*ven**d**ría*
poner	*pon**d**ría*
salir	*sal**d**ría*
tener	*ten**d**ría*
valer	*val**d**ría*

lose an *-e*	
poder	*podría*
saber	*sabría*
haber	*habría*
querer	*querría*

others	
hacer	*haría*
decir	*diría*

Inicio

José

Subimos al avión para el vuelo a Nueva York, pero hacía muy mal tiempo y el avión no pudo salir. Estuvimos cinco horas esperando sentados en el avión antes de poder salir. Pensé que nunca llegaríamos.

Mariana

Estábamos haciendo un viaje por varias ciudades de México. Después de pasar varias horas en el autobús, con mucho calor, llegamos al hotel para descubrir que estaba en obras y que no había agua en la piscina.

Mateo

En las fotos, podíamos ver que el hotel tenía vistas al mar y a los jardines. Y era verdad. Desafortunadamente, nuestra habitación estaba al otro lado donde había una calle muy animada, pero muy sucia. No pudimos dormir por el ruido.

Adriana

Después del largo vuelo a Australia, nos dijeron en el aeropuerto que mis maletas estaban perdidas. Tuve que llevar la ropa de mi hermana durante cuatro días, pero finalmente encontraron **el equipaje** y lo trajeron al hotel.

Manolo

El primer día, hicimos una excursión en barco y me sentía muy enfermo. Parece que viajar por el mar me sienta mal. Luego, dimos un paseo en bicicleta y me rompí el brazo porque me caí de la bici.

el equipaje luggage

3 **Translate these sentences into Spanish.**

- a I thought that the train would leave at six.
- b He said that there would be a fridge in the room.
- c They told me that it would cost much less.
- d I decided that I would go by car.
- e She said that she would take some photos.
- f I thought that the campsite would have a shop.
- g I decided that I would buy souvenirs in the market.
- h They told me that they would reserve two rooms.

¡Atención!

You will also need these verbs in the preterite:

I thought – *pensé*; he / she said – *dijo*; they told me – *me dijeron*; I decided – *decidí*

4 **Complete the sentences with the correct possessive pronoun.**

- a Voy a poner mi ropa en el armario; puedes poner ___ (*yours, you sing.*) allí.
- b Esa maleta no es ___ (*his*); es ___ (*mine*).
- c No me gustó su hotel, prefiero ___ (*ours*).
- d Voy a poner mis billetes y ___ (*yours, you pl.*) en mi maleta.
- e Nuestro hotel es moderno; ___ (*theirs*) es un edificio histórico.
- f No tengo una bolsa de tela aquí– voy a usar ___ (*hers*).

Gramática

Possessive pronouns

Possessive pronouns tell us who something belongs to, such as 'It is **mine**' or 'She can't find **hers**.' They agree with the noun they are replacing.

	masculine sing.	feminine sing.	masculine pl.	feminine pl.
mine	*(el) mío*	*(la) mía*	*(los) míos*	*(las) mías*
yours (belonging to you, sing.)	*(el) tuyo*	*(la) tuya*	*(los) tuyos*	*(las) tuyas*
his / hers	*(el) suyo*	*(la) suya*	*(los) suyos*	*(las) suyas*
ours	*(el) nuestro*	*(la) nuestra*	*(los) nuestros*	*(las) nuestras*
yours (belonging to you, pl.)	*(el) vuestro*	*(la) vuestra*	*(los) vuestros*	*(las) vuestras*
theirs	*(el) suyo*	*(la) suya*	*(los) suyos*	*(las) suyas*

The article (*el, la, los, las*) is used before the possessive pronouns unless it comes immediately after the verb *ser*.

Examples:

*Tu habitación está allí. Esta es **mía**.* – Your room is there. This is **mine**.

*Perdí mis gafas de sol y mi amiga me prestó **las suyas**.* – I lost my sunglasses and my friend lent me **hers**.

5 **Work with a partner. Take it in turns to suggest things that went wrong during an imagined holiday. Use these ideas for help.**

Lo pasé mal porque … *Fue un desastre porque …*			
perdí … *mi billete / móvil / maleta* *mi cámara* *mi mochila / dinero* *el tren / autobús / avión*	*en el hotel, no había ….* *restaurante / piscina / gimnasio / sala de juegos / ascensor*	*la habitación no tenía ….* *nevera / vistas al mar / balcón / agua caliente*	*me puse enfermo / a* *me quemé al sol* *alguien me robó …* *había mucho ruido* *(me) rompí …*

7.2F ¿Qué tipo de vacaciones prefieres?

OBJECTIVES
- Different types of holidays
- Object pronouns
- The past continuous
- Pronunciation *ge, gi*

1 **Read what these young people say about different holidays. What type of holiday is each person describing? Write the name of each person and the letter of their holiday.**

A	beach		**E**	outdoor activity
B	cultural		**F**	theme parks
C	family reunion		**G**	volunteering
D	foreign travel		**H**	winter sports

2 **Answer the questions in English.**

a What work did Adrián do during his trip?
b Why did he feel the hard work was worthwhile?
c When did Sara go to Asturias?
d What two water-based activities did she do?
e Where is Toledo, according to Nicolás?
f Which religious buildings did he visit?
g What does Claudia say about the weather where she lives?
h What does she like to do on holiday at the end of the day?

3 **Listen to five people talking about holidays. Choose the correct options to complete the sentences.**

a Paula is going to the **countryside / mountains / coast**. Paula needs **a new suitcase / new clothes / a bigger rucksack**.
b Mateo wants **to learn English / avoid English-speaking countries / improve his English**.
c Irene loves shopping for **food / presents / clothes**. Irene **looks for bargains / doesn't worry about the price / buys gifts for family**.
d When Leo is abroad, he **doesn't like foreign food / loves trying new dishes / sticks to what he knows**.
e Carmen likes **seeing traditional costumes / dancing at parties / learning about customs**.

Adrián

El año pasado pasé dos semanas ayudando a pintar y mejorar una escuela en una zona pobre. Fue mucho trabajo, pero valió la pena; los niños estaban muy contentos y yo lo pasé muy bien.

Sara

En Semana Santa fui con mi instituto a Asturias en el norte de España. Pasamos una semana muy activa en el campo. Montamos a caballo, nadamos en el río y fuimos en un barco.

Nicolás

En verano visité Toledo, cerca de Madrid, con mis padres. Es una ciudad histórica con hermosos edificios. Visitamos la sinagoga, la mezquita, la catedral y el museo de arte.

Claudia

Yo soy del noroeste de España, donde llueve bastante. Por eso mis vacaciones ideales son ir a la playa en el sur del país. Allí, tomo el sol, nado en la piscina o en el mar y ceno al aire libre.

Pronunciación

ge, gi

The word *genial* you can hear in activity 3 is an example of the sound produced by the letter 'g' when followed by 'e' or 'i'. The 'g' sound is just like the sound made by the letter 'j' that was covered on page 111. It sounds like the 'ch' in the Scottish word 'loch'.

Other examples are: ***gi**mnasio, cole**gi**o, re**gi**ón, co**ge**r, **ge**nte, **ge**neral*

4 Complete the sentences with the correct past continuous form of the verbs in brackets. Then translate the sentences into English.

a Me caí cuando ___ (*bajar, yo*) del autobús.
b Empezó a llover cuando ___ (*conducir, nosotros*) por la ciudad.
c Compraste unas gafas de sol cuando ___ (*pasar, tú*) por el mercado.
d Se quemó cuando ___ (*tomar, ella*) el sol el primer día de las vacaciones.
e ¿Volviste al hotel porque ___ (*llover*)?
f Mis padres vieron a un actor famoso cuando ___ (*cenar, ellos*) en el restaurante.
g Llegamos a la estación y vimos que el tren ___ (*salir*).
h Perdí mi reloj cuando ___ (*nadar, yo*) en el mar.

5 Complete the sentences with the correct pronoun.

a ¿Mis gafas de sol? ___ perdí durante las vacaciones.
b ¿Mi abuela? ___ mandé un mensaje ayer.
c ¿El hotel? ___ reservamos en febrero.
d ¿Mis primos? ___ escribí el sábado pasado.
e ¿Mi mochila? Sí, ___ tengo aquí.

6 Translate these sentences into Spanish.

a He bought me a present.
b He bought us a book.
c He bought you (sing.) a drink.
d The book? She sent it to me.
e The flowers? She sent them to us.
f The photos? She sent them to him.

7 Work with a partner to take turns asking and answering these questions.

- ¿Qué te gusta hacer durante las vacaciones?
- ¿Cuál es el país que más te gustaría visitar? ¿Por qué?
- ¿Prefieres vacaciones tranquilas o activas? ¿Por qué?
- Describe un día divertido durante tus últimas vacaciones.

Example:
- ***Durante las vacaciones me gusta…***
- ***El país que más me gustaría visitar es…***
- ***Prefiero las vacaciones…***
- ***Cuando estaba de vacaciones…***

Los verbos

The past continuous

When you are talking about the past and you want to stress what you were doing at a certain time, use the past continuous tense. This is how it is formed.

Take the imperfect tense of *estar*	add the present participle	Examples
estaba *estabas* *estaba* *estábamos* *estabais* *estaban*	*-ando* for *-ar* verbs *-iendo* for *-er* and *-ir* verbs	*estaba trabajando* – I was working *estabas andando* – you were walking *estaban conduciendo* – they were driving

Gramática

Object pronouns

Object pronouns are the little words we use to stand in for a noun when we do not want to repeat ourselves. In English they come after a verb. In Spanish, they go in front of the verb.

Me *dio una entrada.* – He gave **me** the ticket.

La *compró esa tarde.* – He bought **it** that evening.

Te *escribiré.* – I will write **to you**.

Here is the full table of object pronouns.

Direct object pronouns		Indirect object pronouns	
me	*me*	to me	*me*
you (sing.)	*te*	to you (sing.)	*te*
him / it (masc.)	*lo*	to him / her / it	*le*
her / it (fem.)	*la*		
us	*nos*	to us	*nos*
you (pl.)	*os*	to you (pl.)	*os*
them (masc.)	*los*	to them (masc. / fem.)	*les*
them (fem.)	*las*		

When two object pronouns come together, put the indirect pronoun first.

Te lo *mandaré mañana.* – I will send **you it** tomorrow.

(If in doubt, the indirect pronoun is usually a person, so remember 'people before things'!)

If two 3rd person pronouns come together, then the indirect object pronoun changes from *le* to *se*.

Se lo *mandaré mañana.* – I will send **him it** tomorrow.

7.2H Una visita a la ciudad de México

OBJECTIVES
- Mexico City
- The passive with *se*
- The passive voice: *ser* + past participle

1 **Read this tourist guide to Mexico City and answer the questions.**

El sitio ideal para empezar la visita es el *Zócalo* o Plaza Mayor. Desde aquí, se puede visitar la antigua catedral cuya construcción fue iniciada en el siglo dieciséis y terminada en 1813. Allí al lado, se encuentra el Palacio Nacional que hay que visitar para disfrutar de las enormes obras del famoso artista Diego Rivera pintadas sobre las paredes.

Por la tarde, viaja al sur de la ciudad a la zona de Xochimilco, una región verde con muchos canales.

Aquí, puedes alquilar una *trajinera*, un barco de muchos colores, para hacer una excursión por el agua. Si tienes suerte, te acompañará un grupo de músicos tradicionales, los *mariachis*, que tocan la guitarra y cantan a bordo de otra *trajinera*.

Mientras estás en la ciudad, no puedes perder la oportunidad de visitar la casa de la artista Frida Kahlo, que fue famosa por sus **llamativas** pinturas y su **turbulento** matrimonio con Diego Rivera.

a What is the *Zócalo*?
b When was work on the cathedral started?
c Where did Diego Rivera paint his huge paintings? Give full details.
d Whereabouts is the Xochimilco district?
e How is this area described?
f What is a *trajinera*?
g If you are lucky, what might you come across during the boat trip? Give full details.
h What is Frida Kahlo famous for? Give **two** reasons.

llamativo	striking
turbulento	stormy

2 **Listen to four people talking about their visit to Mexico.**

Write **A** if only statement A is true
B if only statement B is true
A+B if both statements A and B are true.

Alejandro

1
A	They went to see some ancient ruins.
B	The site was to the south of Mexico City.

2
A	They saw the Temple of the Sun.
B	He was impressed by the architecture.

Fran

1
A	Rivera's works can be seen in the cathedral.
B	Rivera's paintings show the country's history.

2
A	He took lots of photos.
B	He bought a book about Rivera's work.

Arancha

1
A	They saw plants with huge yellow flowers.
B	They decided not to do the boat trip.

2
A	A guide went with them.
B	The guide explained a lot about the local nature.

Sara

1
A	They stayed in Mexico City.
B	They saw all the places of interest.

2
A	Cancún has everything for a luxury seaside holiday.
B	They avoided the touristy areas.

3 Complete the sentences with the correct form of the verbs from the box on the right.

to book	*reservar*	to produce	*producir*
to tell	*contar*	to change	*cambiar*
to receive	*recibir*	to use	*utilizar*
to build	*construir*	to serve	*servir*
to create	*crear*	to run, manage	*dirigir*

- **a** La habitación ___ (*was booked*) hace tres semanas.
- **b** La historia del país ___ (*was told*) a través de las pinturas.
- **c** Los turistas ___ (*were received*) en la recepción del hotel.
- **d** Las casas ___ (*were built*) en el siglo dieciocho.
- **e** El templo ___ (*was created*) para dar gracias al sol.
- **f** La guía ___ (*was produced*) para explicar la historia de la región.
- **g** Las reglas ___ (*were changed*) la semana pasada.
- **h** Las pinturas ___ (*were used*) en un documental sobre la historia de México.
- **i** La comida ___ (*was served*) por un camarero muy simpático.
- **j** El hotel ___ (*was run*) muy eficientemente.

Gramática

The passive voice: *ser* + past participle

To form the past participle in Spanish:

- remove *-ar* from *-ar* verbs and add *-ado* (*reservar* > *reservado*)
- remove *-er* or *-ir* from *-er* and *-ir* verbs and add *-ido* (*permitir* > *permitido*)

To form the passive, use the verb *ser* in the appropriate tense, add the past participle and make it agree with what it is describing.

*El templo fue construid**o** hace siglos.* (masculine singular ending because it refers to *templo*) – The temple was built centuries ago.

*Los recuerdos son vendid**os** en el mercado.* (masculine plural ending because it refers to *recuerdos*) – The souvenirs are sold on the market.

4 Translate these sentences into English.

- **a** No se permite hacer fotos en la iglesia.
- **b** Las playas se mantienen muy limpias.
- **c** Se utilizan productos locales en la cocina española.
- **d** Se necesitan más camareros en el restaurante.
- **e** Se sirve el desayuno entre las siete y las nueve y media.
- **f** Las comidas se preparan con cuidado y atención.
- **g** El libro sobre el arte de Rivera se publicó hace diez años.
- **h** El castillo se construyó en el siglo catorce.
- **i** Mis gafas de sol se rompieron en la maleta.
- **j** El problema con nuestra habitación se resolvió rápidamente.

Gramática

The passive with *se*

Examples:

Aquí se habla inglés.
English is spoken here.

Se venden recuerdos en el mercado.
Souvenirs are sold on the market.

Se organizaron varias actividades para niño / as.
Several children's activities were organised.

5 Work with a partner. Take turns to ask and answer questions about the text in activity 1.

¿Dónde se recomienda empezar una visita a la ciudad de México?

¿Cómo se llama la Plaza Mayor?

¿Qué edificio se terminó en el siglo diecinueve?

¿Qué se puede ver en el Palacio Nacional?

¿Qué visita se recomienda por la tarde?

¿Cómo se llaman los barcos tradicionales en los canales de México?

¿Qué son *mariachis*?

¿Dónde se puede ver a los *mariachis* cuando estás en Xochimilco?

¿Con quién estaba casado Diego Rivera?

¿Por qué razones es conocida Frida Kahlo?

6 Do some research about a place in the Hispanic world. Write a tourist guide of about 150 words about it.

Example: Si visitas..., un buen sitio para empezar es... Allí se puede ver…
También tienes que ver... Siempre vale la pena ir a... porque... Para comer, recomiendo probar…

8.1F Los cambios en la tecnología

OBJECTIVES
- How technology has changed
- The perfect tense
- Revising numbers
- Pronunciation *rr*

1 **Read the text and find the Spanish words and phrases for the following:**

a the mobile weighed **b** to recharge **c** a colour screen **d** touch screen

El primer teléfono móvil fue inventado en 1973. El 3 de abril, un ingeniero hizo la primera llamada de teléfono móvil de la historia. El móvil pesaba 1,1 kg y ¡era bastante grande! Te permitía un tiempo de conversación de solo treinta minutos y necesitaba diez horas para recargarse. En 1992 hubo un gran momento: se envió el primer mensaje de texto de la historia.

En 2002, llegó un teléfono que permitía ver las fotos en la pantalla, en lugar de tener que conectarlo a un ordenador. Este teléfono también tenía una pantalla en color y una cámara con flash. Con la llegada en 2007 del iPhone vino la primera pantalla táctil. Esta gran pantalla también permitía por primera vez navegar fácilmente por Internet.

2 **Read the text again and answer the questions.**

a What happened in 1973?
b What did an engineer do on April 3rd in that year?
c How much did the first mobile phone weigh?
d How long did it take to charge?
e What exciting event happened in 1992?
f When could you first get to see photos on a mobile?
g What other two developments came with this phone?
h What was the 2007 iPhone the first to provide?
i What advantage did the large screen give?

3 **Write these years out in words.**

a 1763
b 1891
c 1987
d 2015
e 2024

4 **Listen to this speaker talking about the first appearances of some of our most common technology. Which invention is he talking about and when did it first appear?**

	Event
A	first colour TV programmes
B	first computer
C	first laptop
D	first public TV programmes
E	first video game

	Year
1	1928
2	1946
3	1954
4	1958
5	1981

Cultura

Around 66% of young Spanish children between the ages of 10 and 15 have a mobile phone and 22% of those under 10 also have one. The use of technology increases from the age of 13 and research shows that girls use technology slightly more than boys.

Gramática

Revising numbers

When talking about specific years, you will need *mil* for one thousand and *dos mil* for two thousand. The hundreds are as follows:

*doscientos, trescientos, cuatrocientos, **quin**ientos, seiscientos, **sete**cientos, ochocientos, **nove**cientos*

Note that all but the three highlighted words are simply a combination of the basic number + *cientos*.

So, to put it all together:

1935 – mil novecientos treinta y cinco
1872 – mil ochocientos setenta y dos

2010 – dos mil diez
2025 – dos mil veinticinco

(Note that there is no 'y' where we put an 'and' in English – two thousand **and** ten)

5 **Complete the sentences with the correct perfect tense form of the verbs in brackets.**

a La tecnología ___ (*cambiar*) mucho en los últimos años.

b Mis padres ___ (*comprar*) una nueva televisión.

c Yo ___ (*jugar*) a un nuevo videojuego con mis amigos.

d Mi compañero y yo ___ (*decidir*) buscar información en Internet.

e ¿___ (*perder, tú*) tu móvil?

f ¿Por qué no ___ (*responder, tú*) a mis mensajes?

g Mi padre me ___ (*dar*) su portátil viejo.

h ¿___ (*ver, vosotros*) esa nueva serie en la tele?

i ___ (*discutir, yo*) con mi hermano por este videojuego.

j Los ingenieros ___ (*diseñar*) un nuevo móvil inteligente.

Los verbos

The perfect tense

This tense is the equivalent of the English 'has ___ -ed, have ___-ed' (I have worked, it has changed). This is how to form it:

	the present tense of *haber*	+ past participle (___-*ed*)	Examples	
I have you (sing.) have he / she / it has we have you (pl.) have they have	*he* *has* *ha* *hemos* *habéis* *han*	 *-ado* *-ido*	*he viajado* *has encontrado* *ha recibido* *hemos seguido* *habéis respondido* *han aprendido*	I have travelled you (sing.) have found he / she / it has received we have followed you (pl.) have replied they have learned

There are lots of irregular past participles in English (like eaten, fallen, understood, flown, seen) but only a few in Spanish. One common one is ***visto*** (seen): I have seen – *he visto*.

6 **Work with a partner. Use the ideas below to talk about the differences between old and new technology.**

Los móviles *Las televisiones* *Los videojuegos* *Los ordenadores* *Los portátiles*	*viejos / as* *antiguos / as* *originales*	*eran*	*grandes,* *enormes,* *pequeños / as,* *pesados / as,* *aburridos / as,* *sencillos / as,* *básicos / as,*	*pero los / las nuevos / as son más / muy*	*grandes.* *pequeños / as.* *complicados / as.* *avanzados / as.* *realistas.* *ligeros / as.**

**ligero* – light

7 **Translate these sentences into Spanish.**

a The new videogames are very realistic.

b The first laptops were very heavy.

c The mobiles of today have a touch screen.

d The first televisions were very small.

e Mobiles have changed a lot in the last ten years.

Pronunciación

rr

The double 'r' sound in Spanish is a very strong, rolled 'r'. It is just as strong when written as a single 'r' at the start of a word and after the letters 'l', 'n' and 's'. This can take a lot of practice! Here is a nonsense tongue-twister to practise:

*El pe**rr**o de San **R**oque no tiene **r**abo porque **R**amón **R**odríguez se lo ha **r**obado.*

8.1H Lo bueno y lo malo de las redes sociales

OBJECTIVES
- The advantages and disadvantages of social media
- The rules of stress and accents
- Irregular past participles

1 Read this text about social media and answer the questions.

Las redes sociales están aquí para quedarse. Hoy día es raro encontrar a una persona que no tenga un **perfil** en al menos una de las plataformas más conocidas. ¿Por qué son tan populares? Pues, para empezar, permiten conectarnos con personas de todo el mundo y mantener el contacto con antiguos amigos, aunque estén a miles de kilómetros de distancia. También pueden ayudar con aspectos tan importantes como los negocios, o incluso el amor. Las redes sociales te permiten conocer opiniones diferentes ya que **cualquier** persona puede convertirse en un *influencer* y comunicar sus opiniones al resto del mundo. Otros beneficios de las redes sociales son que puedes hacer nuevas amistades y conocer a personas con intereses comunes. Además, las plataformas ofrecen numerosas maneras de divertirse como juegos, vídeos y música.

el perfil	profile
cualquier	any

a Does the text show (A) the positive side of social media, (B) the negative side or (C) both positive and negative sides?

b Translate the first sentence of the text into English.

c According to the text, what is a rare find?

d In what ways has long-distance communication improved, according to the text?

e What two other aspects are helped along by social media?

f How do social media allow you to learn about different opinions?

g What two other benefits are mentioned?

h What types of entertainment are offered by the various platforms?

2 Listen to four people (1–4) expressing their concerns about social media. Match each speaker to the correct summary.

a	a worrying addiction	**d**	frauds and scams
b	decline of other hobbies	**e**	increasing isolation
c	distorted view of life	**f**	spreading hate

3 Listen again and answer the questions.

a How does the woman describe social media when people start using them?

b Why does the girl think social media affect your mood?

c What did the boy try to buy? What happened?

d What does the second boy hate? Why can't he forgive these actions?

Los verbos

Irregular past participles

Here are some more common irregular past participles.

cubrir	to cover	*cubierto*	covered	*he cubierto*	I have covered
decir	to say, tell	*dicho*	said, told	*has dicho*	you have said / told
escribir	to write	*escrito*	written	*ha escrito*	he / she / it has written
hacer	to do, make	*hecho*	done, made	*hemos hecho*	we have done, made
poner	to put	*puesto*	put	*habéis puesto*	you have put
ver	to see	*visto*	seen	*han visto*	they have seen
volver	to return	*vuelto*	returned	*he vuelto*	I have returned

Note that, unlike in English, the two parts of the verb are always together; no word goes between the two parts.
Examples:

***No** he visto la película.* – I have **not** seen the film.

***Solo** he visto la película una vez.* – I have **only** seen the film once.

4 Complete the sentences with the correct perfect tense form of the verbs in brackets.

a Mis compañeros y yo ___ (*escribir*) un informe sobre las redes sociales.
b Ellos ___ (*poner*) los resultados en la página web del colegio.
c Yo ___ (*hacer*) un estudio sobre el uso de YouTube entre los jóvenes.
d Mi profesora ___ (*ver*) el efecto de las redes sociales en los niños.
e ¿Le ___ (*decir, tú*) a tu madre que has perdido tu móvil?
f El personaje de Sonic ___ (*volver*) en otro videojuego de la famosa serie.
g ¿___ (*subir, vosotros*) las fotos de las vacaciones a Instagram?

5 Read the 'The rules of stress and accents' box. Underline the stressed syllable in the following words.

a palabra
b recordar
c seguridad
d español
e derechos
f animal
g programa
h imagen
i levantarse
j diferente

6 Read the rules again. Work with a partner to say these words out loud, ensuring that you stress each word in the correct place.

a política
b corazón
c educación
d artículo
e práctico
f oportunidad
g capital
h policía
i árbol
j carácter

Pronunciación

The rules of stress and accents

- Words that end in a vowel (a, e, i, o, u), an 'n' or an 's' are stressed on the last but one syllable.
  Examples:
  trabajo > tra-**ba**-jo, *practican* > prac-**ti**-can, *amigos* > a-**mi**-gos
- Words that end in any other consonant are stressed on the last syllable.
  Examples:
  compartir > com-par-**tir**, *principal* > prin-ci-**pal**, *dificultad* > di-fi-cul-**tad**

If a word has an accent on, it means that it does not follow the rule above and that you should stress it on the accented vowel.
Examples: *s**á**bado, j**ó**venes, matem**á**ticas.*

Question words have accents (*¿dónde?, ¿cómo?*) and some words have accents to differentiate them from otherwise identical words: *te* (you), *té* (tea).

8.2F ¿Cómo usas tu móvil?

OBJECTIVES
- Mobiles and their apps
- Pronunciation *h*
- Revising object pronouns

1 **What can a mobile phone do? Read the descriptions and match to the correct picture.**

a

b

c

d

e

f

auriculares	headphones

1. Los últimos móviles tienen unas cámaras excelentes y hacen fotos increíbles. También puedes cambiar el color de la foto o quitar alguna cosa de la foto que no te gusta.
2. El móvil te permite escuchar música o programas sobre las cosas que te interesan. Si te pones **auriculares**, el ruido no molesta a otras personas.
3. En los móviles puedes encontrar miles de juegos diferentes. Puedes jugar tú solo, pero la tecnología también te permite jugar con otras personas.
4. Nunca más necesitarás llevar una calculadora a todas partes porque tu móvil tiene una calculadora como una de sus funciones básicas. ¡Muy útil en tus clases de matemáticas!
5. Aunque el móvil tiene una pantalla pequeña, puedes bajar y ver programas de televisión y películas en él. Perfecto cuando tienes un viaje largo y aburrido.
6. Con tu móvil, puedes mantenerte en contacto con amigos y familia que viven cerca de tu casa o que viven lejos en otros países. Puedes llamar, mandar mensajes o enviar correos electrónicos.

2 **Read the texts again and answer the questions.**

a What do the latest phones allow you to do with a photo? Mention **two** things.
b What is the benefit of using headphones?
c What does technology allow you to do with games on your mobile?
d What basic function is installed on your mobile, according to the text?
e According to the text, when might you find it useful to watch a film on your phone?
f According to the text, in what three ways can you keep in touch with family and friends on your mobile?

3 **Listen to six people (1–6) describing different apps. What does each app do? Write the correct letter for each app.**

A	compares flight prices	E	identifies pieces of music
B	creates schedules	F	locates restaurants
C	finds lost phones	G	monitors sleep patterns
D	identifies bird song	H	provides road news

4 **Write each sentence and fill in the gaps with the correct object pronouns.**

a Esta app es muy útil; ___ uso todos los días.

b Mi móvil no funciona; ___ rompí esta mañana.

c Mi amigo vive en México; ___ mando mensajes cada semana.

d Mi prima está de vacaciones; ___ mandé esta foto ayer.

e Estas canciones son mis favoritas; ___ escucho mucho.

f No sé dónde están mis auriculares. ___ perdí la semana pasada.

g Dormía profundamente cuando el ruido de mi móvil ___ despertó.

h Si tú pagas el hotel, ___ mandaré el dinero hoy.

i Mis amigos quieren llamarme; ___ voy a mandar mi nuevo número.

j Tengo un lector electrónico; ___ uso para leer durante viajes largos.

5 **Translate these sentences into Spanish. Remember to look out for object pronouns (found after the verb in English).**

a I have a new mobile. I use it all the time.

b I like this app. It is very useful.

c My mobile has a great camera. It takes excellent photos.

d Pedro's laptop does not work; he broke it yesterday.

e I love these songs; I downloaded them on Saturday.

6 **Work with a partner. Read the passage out loud to each other. Let your partner know if there any sounds that they can improve on.**

En los Institutos españoles está prohibido usar móviles. Cuando los jóvenes están en clase, hacen actividades en el ordenador y usan diccionarios digitales. Pueden buscar información en páginas educativas en Internet, pero no está permitido jugar.

Pronunciación

h

The letter 'h' is not pronounced unless it is combined with 'c' to make 'ch' as in *mu**ch**o*.

At the beginning of the word, 'h' is silent; for example, in *horario, hotel, hijos, hablar.*

If it is in the middle of the word, as in *ahora*, pronounce the 'a' then the 'o' one after the other as if the 'h' were not there. Other examples are: *prohibir, ahorrar, enhorabuena.*

Gramática

Revising object pronouns

These are the main object pronouns. They usually go before the verb in Spanish.

me	*me*	you (pl.)	*os*
you (sing.)	*te*	them (masc.)	*los*
him / it (masc.)	*lo*	them (fem.)	*las*
her / it (fem.)	*la*	to him / her	*le*
us	*nos*	to them	*les*

Cultura

A Colombian computer engineer called Daniel Rodríguez is responsible for adapting the game Wordle for Spanish speakers. He did it over a period of two afternoons, inputting hundreds of words so that fans could play this word-guessing game in Spanish on their mobiles, tablets or computers.

8.2H La tecnología del futuro

OBJECTIVES
- Technology of the future
- The present subjunctive after certain verbs
- The present subjunctive after *para que* and *cuando*

1 **Read the text and answer the questions.**

¿Te gustaría tomar una pizza? En el futuro, cuando seas mayor, si tus hijos tienen hambre, podrías producir una pizza en una **impresora** 3D. Actualmente, los científicos están experimentando con impresoras 3D que se pueden usar en el espacio. Aquí en la Tierra, ya existen las impresoras 3D, pero son muy caras y no pueden producir una gran variedad de comidas. Sin embargo, un día se verán en todas las cocinas.
También en la cocina, la **nevera** del futuro notará cuando te hace falta algo, como leche o huevos. La nevera será capaz de pedir el producto y añadirlo a tu lista de la compra. Esta tecnología existe ya y continúa mejorando. Un día, será tan común que todas las casas la tendrán.
En el cuarto de baño, tendrás un **cepillo de dientes** inteligente. Este dispositivo te ayudará a limpiarte bien los dientes y durante el tiempo adecuado. Además, será capaz de observar tu salud dental, identificar problemas y mandar la información a tu dentista.

la impresora	printer
la nevera	fridge
el cepillo de dientes	toothbrush

a What might produce your food for you in the future?
b What are scientists currently experimenting with?
c What are the issues with the current form of this technology?
d What will the fridge of the future be able to do? Mention **two** things.
e What stage of development is this technology at?
f How will a smart toothbrush help your brushing technique?
g What will the smart toothbrush of the future do?

2 **Translate these sentences into Spanish.**

a I hope to go to the castle when I go on holiday.
b You must download this app so that you have the correct information.
c She cannot use the computer when she does her exams in summer.
d If you have a mobile, you can call your parents when it is necessary.
e We can watch the film when you come to my house on Saturday.

Los verbos

The present subjunctive after *para que* and *cuando*

After *para que* (so that) and *cuando* (when), if the action that follows has not yet happened, a tense called the present subjunctive is used. You need to know this tense in the singular for the verbs *hacer, ser, tener, ir* and *venir*. This is the present subjunctive for those verbs:

	hacer	*ser*	*tener*	*ir*	*venir*
yo	*haga*	*sea*	*tenga*	*vaya*	*venga*
tú	*hagas*	*seas*	*tengas*	*vayas*	*vengas*
él / ella	*haga*	*sea*	*tenga*	*vaya*	*venga*

When translated into English, it will sound like the ordinary present tense.

Te daré el libro ***cuando vengas*** *a mi casa.* – I will give you the book **when you come** to my house.

3 Look at the photo. Work with a partner to ask and answer the questions below.

Student A	Student B
¿Dónde está la familia? ¿Qué hace la madre? ¿Piensas que la familia está contenta? ¿Por qué? ¿Cuándo usas tú el móvil? ¿Piensas que los jóvenes usan el móvil demasiado?	¿Qué comida están tomando estas personas? ¿Qué hace el niño? ¿Cómo se siente la madre? ¿Por qué? ¿Prefieres un móvil o un portátil? ¿Por qué? ¿Piensas que la tecnología es peligrosa? ¿Por qué?

4 Translate these sentences into English.

- a Mi padre quiere que yo haga la cena.
- b Voy a pedir a Pablo que venga al baile conmigo.
- c Mi madre siempre me dice que sea más responsable.
- d Quiero que tengas un día tranquilo y relajado.
- e No tenemos pan; pediré a Dani que vaya al supermercado.

Los verbos

The present subjunctive after certain verbs

The subjunctive is also used after wishing, wanting, asking, telling, etc. when one person is trying to get someone else to do something. Note how in Spanish, the word *que* is always used.

I want you to make a sandwich. (= I want that you make a sandwich.)

Quiero que ***hagas*** *un bocadillo.*

I will ask him to come at six (= I will ask that he comes at six.)

Le pediré que ***venga*** *a las seis.*

5 Translate these sentences into Spanish, using the previous sentences and the verb box for guidance.

- a I want you to come to the cinema on Friday.
- b He will ask Ángela to do the exam next week.
- c My parents want me to be a doctor.
- d I will tell Ana to go to the market.
- e He wants me to have the party in my house.

¡Atención!

After the verb *ser*, leave out the article when talking about professions.

Soy dentista. – I'm a dentist.

¿Eres abogado? – Are you a lawyer?

6 Listen to five people (1–5) talking about inventions they would like to see in the future. Answer the questions in English.

1 a What does Martín like doing especially? Give details.
   b What invention would he like to see?
2 a What does Julia say about movement?
   b What would Julia like to invent?
3 a What sci-fi invention does Mateo want to create?
   b Why does he think it would be useful?
4 a What would Paula like to invent?
   b How would it work?
5 a Why does Leo want to help his grandfather?
   b What would the gadget do?
   c Why might the gadget help Leo's grandfather's health?

9.1F Mi pueblo y mi ciudad

OBJECTIVES
- Places in town
- Talking about the weather
- Adverbs of place
- Pronunciation *tu*

1 Look at where the places are on the town plan. Complete the sentences with the words below. You do not need to use all the words.

banco bosque campos castillo cine fábricas
hotel iglesia mercado mezquita montañas
museo parque playa puerto tiendas

- **a** Al oeste de la biblioteca hay unas ___.
- **b** En el norte del pueblo hay unos ___ con frutas y verduras.
- **c** Al este del castillo hay una zona de ___.
- **d** El mercado está al lado de las ___.
- **e** El hospital está entre la ___ y el ___.
- **f** Al este de la biblioteca hay un ___ infantil.
- **g** Al norte de las montañas hay una zona de ___.
- **h** El castillo está detrás del ___.
- **i** El banco está entre el ___ y la ___.
- **j** Al lado del mar está la ___ y el ___ para los barcos.

2 Look back at the town plan. Write out these sentences and complete them with the correct adverb.

- **a** El hospital está ___ de la iglesia.
- **b** El castillo está ___ los campos y el bosque.
- **c** El cine está ___ del parque.
- **d** El puerto está ___ de las fábricas.
- **e** La playa no está muy ___ del castillo.
- **f** Hay nieve ___ de las montañas.

Gramática

Adverbs of place

When talking about where things are in the home or in town, you will need these expressions:

lejos de – far from
cerca de – near to
detrás de – behind
entre – between
encima de – on top of
delante de – in front of
al lado de – next to

3 Listen to six people (1–6) talking about their town. Complete the table by choosing the correct letter for what facility they have in town and the letter for what they do not have.

	✓	✗
1		
2		
3		
4		
5		
6		

A	toilets
B	hotels
C	green spaces
D	bridge
E	airport
F	industry
G	offices

H	restaurants
I	theme park
J	shopping centre
K	market
L	beach
M	swimming pool
N	bullring

Pronunciación

tu

Notice the way *turistas* was pronounced in the recording. The sound 'tu' is very pure in Spanish, nothing like the 'choo' sound in 'insti**tu**te' and 'na**tu**ral'. Practise the sound in these Spanish words:

instituto, situación, cultura, actual, temperatura

4 Translate these sentences into English.

a El clima en el sur es muy agradable durante el invierno.

b En verano las temperaturas subieron hasta más de cuarenta grados.

c Iremos a las tiendas esta tarde porque ahora está lloviendo.

d Es bastante común tener lluvia durante la Semana Santa.

e Hace sol hoy, pero hace bastante viento al lado del río.

f No me gustan los inviernos de mi país; siempre tenemos cielos grises y llueve todo el tiempo.

g Cuando nieva en el norte, hay bastante nieve para hacer deportes de invierno.

5 Work with a partner and take turns. Use the town plan in activity 1. Choose a place and tell your partner where it is. You can use the adverbs of place and / or the points of the compass. Your partner must tell you which place you have chosen.

Person 1: *Este sitio está al este del castillo.*
Person 2: *Es el bosque.*

6 Write an article about where you live (approximately 90 words in Spanish).

Mention:

- what there is in your town
- what you did in town with your friends last weekend
- what else you would like to have in your town.

Example: En mi pueblo / ciudad hay... El fin de semana pasado fui al / a la... con mis amigos. En mi pueblo / ciudad, me gustaría tener...

Gramática

Talking about the weather

These are the words and phrases you will need to talk about the weather.

¿Qué tiempo hace?	What is the weather like?
hace frío	it is cold
hace fresco	it is cool
hace viento	it is windy
hace calor	it is hot
hace sol	it is sunny
hace buen tiempo	it is good weather
hace mal tiempo	it is bad weather

llueve	it rains
está lloviendo	it is raining
la lluvia	the rain
nieva	it snows
está nevando	it is snowing
la nieve	the snow
el clima	the climate
la temperatura	temperature
el grado	degree

Cultura

Almost all Spanish towns have a *Plaza Mayor*, the main square, which began to be a feature towards the end of the Middle Ages. Across the country there are a range of different styles, but most are rectangular with semi-circular arches. They are a great place to start exploring a town, to meet up with friends, eat or stop for coffee.

9.1H Lo bueno y lo malo de mi región

OBJECTIVES
- Describing your area
- *lo que; el que, la que, los que, las que*
- Using *desde hace*

1 **Read Álvaro's account of the city of Bilbao, where he lives, and write the correct letters from the grid according to what he mentions.**

A	beach
B	crime
C	entertainment facilities
D	historic area
E	industry
F	outskirts
G	port
H	shopping
I	sports facilities
J	tourism
K	transport
L	unemployment

Bilbao, la ciudad donde vivo, es grande y animada. A mí me gusta mucho vivir aquí, pero es cierto que tiene aspectos positivos y negativos. Está bien conectada con otros sitios porque hay un buen sistema de trenes y autobuses que van a las ciudades y pueblos de la región. También hay mucho que hacer; tenemos cines, un centro deportivo, un teatro, el estadio de fútbol y varios parques infantiles. El barrio antiguo tiene muchos edificios históricos como la catedral y la plaza mayor. Además, la arquitectura de las casas en las calles antiguas es fascinante. El museo moderno es el sitio de mayor interés para los turistas desde hace casi treinta años, cuando se construyó al lado del río. Antiguamente, había zonas pobres en las afueras, con mucho paro y casas en muy mal estado. Estos barrios eran feos, estaban sucios y había un alto nivel de delincuencia. Sin embargo, en los últimos años, se ha gastado mucho dinero en mejorar estas zonas y han conseguido hacerlas sitios agradables para vivir.

2 **Read the text again and answer the questions.**

- **a** What does Álvaro mean when he says the town is 'well-connected'?
- **b** What sporting facilities does he mention?
- **c** What is worth seeing in the old streets?
- **d** Where was the museum built?
- **e** How long has it been attracting tourists?
- **f** Where was the poorer area?
- **g** How does Álvaro describe that area. Mention **five** things.
- **h** What has happened to these areas recently?

3 **Listen to four people (1–4) talking about where they live and answer the questions.**

1 **a** What does Carlos think there is a shortage of?
b Why does he want to have more parks built?

2 **a** What are the tourists doing in Paula's town?
b Why is this causing a problem?

3 **a** What has happened as a result of the improvements to the roads?
b What is the positive effect of this?

4 **a** How long has Manolo lived in the town?
b What three things does he say about the underground train network?

4 Translate these sentences into English.

- a Conozco a Marcos desde hace cinco años.
- b La mezquita está en este sitio desde hace quinientos años.
- c Hay un pueblo aquí desde hace muchos siglos.
- d El señor Rodríguez dirige la empresa desde hace varios meses.
- e El ayuntamiento mantiene los parques desde hace muchos años.
- f Dani trabaja en el centro deportivo desde hace seis semanas.
- g Esta torre está aquí desde el siglo dieciséis.
- h Hay un puente sobre el río desde la Edad Media.

5 Complete the sentences with the correct phrase: *lo que, el que, la que, los que* or *las que*.

- a Fui a ver dos pisos. ___ (*The one that*) tiene dos dormitorios es demasiado pequeño.
- b ___ (*What*) necesitan hacer es construir más casas en las afueras.
- c Vimos dos películas la semana pasada. ___ (*The one that*) me gustó más fue la mexicana.
- d De todas las regiones de España, ___ (*the ones that*) reciben más lluvia están en el noroeste.
- e El ayuntamiento permitió la construcción de una fábrica, ___ (*which*) molestó a los vecinos del barrio.
- f Probamos varios platos y ___ (*the ones that*) preferíamos eran vegetarianos.

6 Work with a partner and ask and answer these questions. Remember to always expand your answers as much as you can.

- a ¿Adónde vas con tus amigos cuando sales? (centro comercial / cine / ciudad / centro de deportes, etc.)
- b ¿Qué espacios verdes hay en tu región? (parques / jardines / mucho campo, etc.)
- c ¿Qué pueden hacer los turistas en tu región? (ver los sitios históricos / ir a la costa / visitar…, etc.)
- d ¿Cómo es el clima de tu región? (llueve mucho / muchas nubes / hace viento, etc.)
- e ¿Hay un buen sistema de transporte en tu ciudad o pueblo? (trenes / autobuses)
- f ¿Piensas que es mejor vivir en el campo o en la ciudad? ¿Por qué? (El campo es mejor si… pero la ciudad es ideal si…)
- g ¿Dónde te gustaría más vivir? ¿Por qué? (Me encantaría vivir en otro país / en el campo… porque…)

Gramática

Using *desde hace*

The phrase *desde hace* appears both in the text and in the recording. Individually, *desde* means 'since' and *hace* means 'ago'. Together, they translate as 'for' in sentences like these:

Vivo en Barcelona ***desde hace*** *dos años.* – I have lived in Barcelona **for** two years.

Trabaja en el museo ***desde hace*** *tres meses.* – He has been working at the museum **for** three months.

Notice how, in Spanish, the ordinary present tense is used (*vivo, trabaja*) where in English, we say 'has / have ….-ed' or 'has / have been ….-ing'. This is because the action is still taking place in the present time.

Gramática

lo que; el que, la que, los que, las que

Lo que has two meanings. It can mean 'what', in cases where it is not a question.

Eso es ***lo que*** *voy a hacer.* – That is **what** I am going to do.

It can also mean 'which', when referring back to a whole clause and not just a noun.

La fábrica contaminó el río, ***lo que*** *enojó a los vecinos.* – The factory polluted the river, **which** annoyed the locals.

El que, la que, los que, las que mean 'the one that' or 'the ones that'. They agree with the noun that they are referring to.

Hay dos catedrales. ***La que*** *está en la plaza es la más antigua.* – There are two cathedrals. **The one that** is in the square is the oldest.

La casa tiene cuatro dormitorios. ***Los que*** *están en el primer piso tienen vistas al mar.* – The house has four bedrooms. **The ones that** are on the first floor have sea views.

9.2F El medio ambiente y yo

OBJECTIVES
- Helping the environment
- The preterite (first person singular)
- The imperative
- Pronunciation *v*

1 Read this article and match the categories from the table to each piece of advice.

el contenedor	container, bin
la calefacción	heating

Aquí tienes una lista de cosas que podrías hacer:

1 Separar la basura y ponerla en los **contenedores** correctos.
2 Bajar la **calefacción** un poco en cada habitación, reduciendo la temperatura un grado.
3 Ponerte más ropa si tienes frío, sin subir la calefacción.
4 Evitar dejar correr el agua cuando no la usas.
5 Llevar la ropa usada a una tienda de ropa de segunda mano.
6 Recoger el agua de la lluvia para regar las plantas del jardín.
7 Participar en proyectos de tu barrio, como recoger basura o plantar árboles.
8 Apagar las luces de las habitaciones donde no haya nadie.
9 Dejar comida en el jardín para los pájaros durante el invierno.
10 Ir a pie o en bicicleta al colegio en lugar de ir en coche.
11 Empezar un club en tu instituto y compartir ideas sobre proyectos que hacer en el colegio.

Un grupo de jóvenes voluntarios plantando un árbol.

Categories	
a	caring for wildlife
b	keeping warm
c	recycling
d	saving energy
e	saving water
f	working with others

Cultura

All areas of Spain suffer periods of drought from time to time, but climate change has made the situation worse. Research shows that Spain is suffering the driest climate for 1,200 years. The millions of tourists that go to Spain every year use water without realising what a precious resource it is.

2 Read the text again. What suggestions are given about the following?

a tap water
b rain water
c birds
d old clothes
e transport
f local volunteering
g feeling cold

3 Listen to four students (1–4) reporting on the environmental projects that the student committee organised this year.

1 a In autumn, where did they plant trees?
  b What two reasons does she give for the planting?
2 a In winter, what did the students collect?
  b What does the supermarket plan to do?
3 a In spring, what did the committee organise?
  b Why was this possible?
4 a In summer, what competition did they organise?
  b What will happen to the winning design?

Pronunciación

v

The sound made by the letter 'v' at the beginning of a word is very strong, like a 'b'. You heard *verano* in the recording. Practise saying these words in Spanish:

verano, voy, vamos, viernes, viaje, vender, vale, visitar

4 Translate these sentences into English.

- **a** Pon las flores en la mesa.
- **b** Protege las plantas jóvenes del sol.
- **c** Recicla las botellas de plástico.
- **d** Respeta a los animales y a los pájaros.
- **e** Ahorra energía en cada habitación.
- **f** Usa menos agua cuando te limpias los dientes.
- **g** Haz un anuncio para el concurso.
- **h** Ven aquí y ayúdame a plantar este árbol.

5 Look back to activity 1 where all the advice was given in the infinitive. Turn the verbs into commands.

1 Separar la basura y ponerla en los contenedores correctos.
*Example: **Separa** la basura y **ponla** en los contenedores correctos.*

6 Look back at the list of advice in activity 1. Use the ideas there to answer these questions about last week.

- **a** ¿Qué hiciste para proteger el medio ambiente? (separated rubbish)
- **b** ¿Cómo ahorraste energía? (turned down heating in each room)
- **c** ¿Cómo ahorraste agua? (did not let water run)
- **d** ¿Qué hiciste con la ropa usada? (took old clothes to second-hand shop)
- **e** ¿Cómo ahorraste agua? (saved rainwater for plants in garden)
- **f** ¿Cómo ahorraste energía (turned off lights at home)
- **g** ¿Cómo ayudaste a la naturaleza? (left food in the garden for the birds)
- **h** ¿Qué más hiciste? (started a club at school to share ideas)

7 Work with a partner to talk about what you are going to do in the future to help the environment. Use *Voy a* + infinitive or *No voy a* + infinitive and see if you can use these verbs.

Example: En el futuro voy a respetar la naturaleza.
No voy a tirar basura en el campo.

Los verbos

The imperative

When giving advice or instructions, the imperative is often used. In Spanish the regular verbs follow this pattern when you are speaking to one person.

Infinitive	Ending	Example	English
-ar	*-a*	*Apag**a** la luz.*	Turn off the light.
-er	*-e*	*Recog**e** la basura.*	Pick up the rubbish.
-ir	*-e*	*Conduc**e** con cuidado.*	Drive with care.

If a verb is radical changing, the change will also occur in this form of the imperative.

*V**ue**lve a casa pronto.* – Come home soon.

Object pronouns go on the end of these commands.

*Pon**te** las gafas de sol.* – Put on your sunglasses.

Common irregular verbs in the imperative include:

haz – make, do | *di* – tell, say | *ten* – have, take
pon – put | *ven* – come | *ve* – go
sal – go out, leave | *sé* – be

Los verbos

The preterite (first person singular)

To talk about something you did in the past, the preterite is the most used tense.

To put *-ar* verbs into the first person singular preterite, remove the *-ar* and add *-é*.

Be careful with:

- infinitives that end in *-gar*: in the first person singular these will become *-gué*. *(cargar > car**gué*** – to carry)
- infinitives that end in *-zar*: in the first person singular these will become *-cé*. *(caza > ca**cé*** – to hunt)
- infinitives that end in *-car*: in the first person singular these will become *-qué*. *(aparcar > apar**qué*** – to park)

recoger	to pick up, collect	*reciclar*	to recycle	*encender*	to turn on
apagar	to turn off, turn out	*proteger*	to protect	*limpiar*	to clean
respetar	to respect	*usar*	to use	*ahorrar*	to save
tirar	to throw, throw away	*plantar*	to plant	*separar*	to separate

9.2H Protegiendo el planeta

OBJECTIVES
- Global environmental issues
- *acabar de* + infinitive
- The imperative (2nd person plural)

1 Read about the work of these different environmental campaigns. Write one short sentence to summarise the aim of each campaign.

RespiraVida fue creada como consecuencia de las cifras de un informe sobre el impacto de la contaminación del aire en la vida de las personas. El efecto era especialmente grave en las ciudades más **pobladas** del mundo. La campaña pide a los gobiernos que tomen medidas para bajar la contaminación del aire. También pide a los ciudadanos que usen el transporte público en vez del coche propio, o la bicicleta, si las distancias no son muy largas.

Menoscarne recomienda reducir el consumo de carne. Según esta organización, ninguna acción destinada a resolver los problemas del medio ambiente será efectiva si no comenzamos a cambiar el consumo de carne por el de otros alimentos. La **ganadería** es responsable de una gran parte de los gases que contribuyen al **efecto invernadero**, además de la contaminación de las aguas y la destrucción de los bosques.

Vivan las abejas busca concienciar del peligro que corren las abejas. Las abejas son una de las especies más importantes para el planeta porque gran parte de los cultivos de la Tierra dependen de ellas. Todos los años hay un concurso de dibujo infantil y la imagen que gana se usa en los anuncios de la campaña del año

2 Read the text again and answer the questions.

a Where did the figures that inspired the setting up of *RespiraVida* come from?
b Where is the impact especially serious?
c What does the campaign aim to do?
d According to *Menoscarne*, why is its work so essential for the planet?
e What is the main reason we should reduce the amount of cattle farming?
f Why are bees so important for the planet?
g What type of competition does the campaign organise?

3 Listen to these news reports and decide which of the following statements are correct.

Write **A** if only statement A is correct
B if only statement B is correct
A+B if both statements A and B are correct.

1

A	There has been heavy rain in the north.
B	The rain is likely to continue all day.

2

A	Building works have destroyed natural habitat.
B	The green areas are home to threatened species.

3

A	A chemical plant is being inspected.
B	Locals have just noticed the smell of the fumes.

4

A	More electric car charging points are announced.
B	A shortage of charging points is causing lack of sales.

5

A	The initiative focuses on light pollution.
B	It will encourage us to appreciate the wonders of the night sky.

poblado	populated
la ganadería	cattle farming
el efecto invernadero	greenhouse effect
la abeja	bee

4 **Translate these sentences into Spanish, using the 2nd person plural form of the imperative.**

a Pick up the litter.
b Turn out the lights.
c Buy an electric car.
d Reduce the fumes from the factory.
e Clean the rivers.
f Respect the green spaces.
g Protect the trees.
h Recycle paper.
i Eat less meat.

5 **Translate these sentences into Spanish.**

a He has just started the project.
b I have just lit a fire.
c You (sing.) have just turned out the lights.
d I have just cleaned my bedroom.
e They have just seen the litter.
f She has just gone out to the park.
g We have just arrived.
h They have just closed the factory.

6 **Work with a partner and take it in turns to describe what you see in the picture below.**

7 **You are writing an article (approximately 150 words in Spanish) for a Spanish website on the environment.**

Mention:

- A local environmental problem that needs to be solved
- What other environmental changes you would like to see in the future.

Los verbos

The imperative (2nd person plural)

Here is how to give commands when talking to two or more people.

With -*ar* verbs, remove the -*ar* and add -*ad*.
*Esper**ad**.* – Wait.

With -*er* verbs, remove the -*er* and add -*ed*.
*Com**ed** las verduras.* – Eat the vegetables.

With -*ir* verbs, remove the -*ir* and add -*id*.
*Ven**id** aquí.* – Come here.

Los verbos

acabar de + infinitive

To say 'has / have just' done something, you need the verb *acabar de* + infinitive.

acabar		Examples	
acabo	+ de + infinitive	*acabo de llegar*	I have just arrived
acabas		*acabas de mandar*	you (sing.) have just sent
acaba		*acaba de ver*	he / she has just seen
acabamos		*acabamos de comer*	we have just eaten
acabáis		*acabáis de recibir*	you (pl.) have just received
acaban		*acaban de salir*	they have just gone out

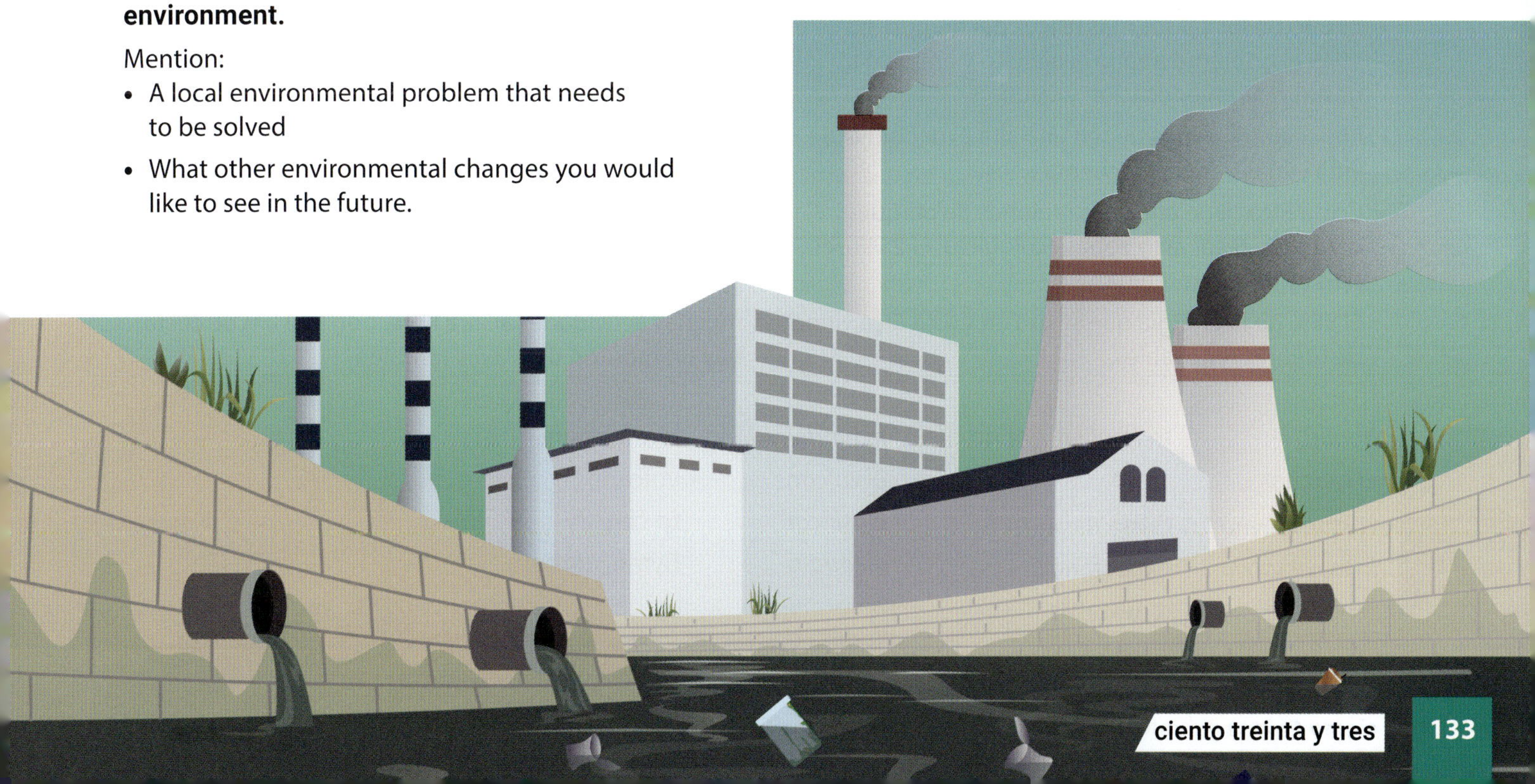

Cultura
Aspectos del mundo hispánico

1 **Look at the map. Read the descriptions and work out the names of countries A–L.**

- **Brasil** es el país más grande de Sudamérica. Se habla portugués.
- **Chile** es el país muy, muy largo y delgado al oeste del continente.
- **México** es el país más al norte. Tiene frontera con Guatemala y Belice.
- **Argentina** es el segundo país más grande; está en el sur del continente.
- El país más pequeño entre Argentina y Brasil es **Uruguay**.
- El país bastante grande al noroeste, con frontera con Ecuador, es **Colombia**.
- Al este de Colombia se encuentra **Venezuela**.
- El país en el centro del continente, de color amarillo en el mapa, es **Bolivia**.
- El país en el oeste, con fronteras con Brasil y Bolivia, es **Perú**.
- El pequeño país ahí, entre Perú y Colombia, es **Ecuador**.
- El pequeño país en el centro, de color rosa, es **Paraguay**.
- La isla más grande del mar Caribe es **Cuba**.

2 **Work with a partner. Each one reads the 4 facts in one of the columns and then tells the other what they have learned about Costa Rica.**

Student A	Student B
• Es uno de los países más felices del mundo. En 1949 el gobierno abolió el ejército y empezó a gastar más en educación y salud. • Los costarriqueños tienen una alta expectativa de vida – más o menos ochenta años. • Costa Rica tiene enormes regiones de parques naturales, reservas y zonas ecológicas. El 25% del país es tierra protegida. • El 98% de la energía que se usa en Costa Rica viene de fuentes renovables.	• Es el país con más biodiversidad del mundo. Tiene más de 500.000 especies de animales, plantas, insectos y pájaros. • Costa Rica tiene unos cien volcanes; pero no te preocupes, solo cinco se clasifican como volcanes activos. • Los costarriqueños se despiertan cada mañana al son del himno nacional. Se oye cada día en la radio a las siete. • El turismo es muy importante para el país y ofrece muchas actividades al aire libre. Con 800 km de costa, hay un montón de playas también.

abolir	to abolish, get rid of	*la biodiversidad*	biodiversity
el ejército	army	*el volcán*	volcano
costarriqueño	Costa Rican	*clasificar*	to classify
la expectativa	expectancy	*el himno*	hymn, anthem
renovable	renewable		

3 ✏ **Find out about these three directors and answer these questions.**

Three famous Mexican directors

a Which director won Oscars for *Gravity* (2014) and *Roma* (2018)?

b Which director won Oscars for *Birdman* (2014) and *The Revenant* (2016)?

c Which director won an Oscar for *The Shape of Water* (2018)?

d Which film from 2006 did Guillermo del Toro write, produce and direct?

e Which director was in charge of a Harry Potter film?

f Which director was chosen to lead the panel of judges for the Cannes Film Festival 2019?

4 📖 **Put the topics in the grid (A–F) in the same order that they appear in the text.**

A	geographical location
B	permission to settle
C	setting sail
D	survival of the language
E	taming the landscape
F	the aim of the settlers

The Welsh community in Patagonia

En 1865 un grupo de más de 150 galeses salió en barco del puerto de Liverpool para empezar una nueva vida en la región de Patagonia, en el extremo sur de Argentina. El gobierno de Argentina les ofreció tierras para desarrollar una nueva comunidad donde podrían conservar su lengua y su estilo de vida. Trabajaron mucho y al final lograron transformar la zona, creando campos para la agricultura. Hoy día, unos 5.000 habitantes todavía hablan galés y varios pueblos tienen nombres galeses como Trelew, Trevelin o Dolavon.

5 🎧 **Listen to the descriptions and match each one to the correct soap opera.**

South American soap operas		
A	*Betty la fea* Colombian	Plain but bright, the star of the show is unloved and underappreciated by her colleagues.
B	*Cristal* Venezuelan	1980's classic of love and scandal set in the glamorous world of a successful fashion house.
C	*Diseñando tu amor* Mexican	Girl loses boyfriend in tragedy and moves town, where she meets the love of her life.
D	*Mi marido tiene familia* Mexican	A ground-breaking series which moved away from the traditional portrayal of straight couples.
E	*Rebelde Way* Argentinian	The series explores the lives of a group of teenagers, with a passion for music, at a private school in Buenos Aires.

Grammar practice

The conditional tense

1 Complete the sentences with the correct conditional form of the verbs in brackets.

- a Para llegar antes de las doce, yo ___ (*salir*) ahora.
- b De todos los países, el que más me ___ (*gustar*) visitar es México.
- c Creo que ___ (*ser*) mejor hacer el viaje en tren.
- d Los niños no ___ (*poder*) ir en autobús; es un viaje demasiado largo.
- e Decidí que ___ (*poner, yo*) mis maletas en la habitación primero.
- f ¿No dijiste que ___ (*hacer, tú*) la reserva hoy?
- g Creo que ___ (*costar*) mucho pasar la noche en ese hotel.
- h Pensé que ___ (*haber*) un café en la playa.
- i No ___ (*valer*) la pena reservar dos habitaciones; podemos compartir una.
- j Dijeron que ___ (*venir, ellos*) con nosotros para mostrarnos el camino.
- k Creímos que la habitación ___ (*tener*) vistas al mar.
- l Normalmente ___ (*ir, nosotros*) en coche, pero está roto en este momento.
- m Yo no ___ (*saber*) cómo encontrar el camping; no me acuerdo de la dirección.
- n Mis padres te ___ (*decir*) que me paso todo el día mirando el móvil.

Possessive pronouns

2 Complete the sentences with the correct possessive pronouns.

Este es mi billete. ¿Dónde está ___? (*yours, sing.*)

Example: Este es mi billete. ¿Dónde está el tuyo?

- a Tengo mis gafas de sol aquí. ___ están en la mesa. (*hers*)
- b Sus excursiones son muy caras. ___ son más baratas. (*ours*)
- c Si tú pones la ropa en la bolsa, yo pondré ___ en la maleta. (*mine*)
- d Ese plano de la ciudad no es muy útil. ___ es mucho mejor. (*yours, sing.*)
- e Nuestra habitación es un poco pequeña. ___ es más grande. (*yours, pl.*)
- f No me gusta nuestro hotel. ___ es más bonito. (*theirs*)
- g Tus billetes están encima de la mesa, pero ¿dónde están ___? (*mine*)
- h Mi cámara no es muy buena; ___ es mejor para hacer fotos así. (*his*)

Past continuous tense (translation)

3 Translate these sentences into Spanish. Use the past continuous.

- a They were selling souvenirs.
- b He was driving a car.
- c I was looking for the swimming pool.
- d We were eating in the hotel.
- e You (sing.) were visiting the mosque.
- f The train was arriving.
- g Were you (pl.) looking at the plan?
- h The children were swimming in the sea.
- i I was sunbathing on the beach.
- j We were buying the tickets.

Object pronouns

4 Complete the sentences with the correct object pronoun: *lo*, *la*, *los* or *las*.

- a Tengo una tableta nueva. ___ uso para ver películas.
- b Mi portátil está roto. ___ rompí ayer.
- c ¿Viste mis fotos? ___ subí a Instagram esta mañana.
- d ¿Sabes dónde están mis zapatos? ___ quiero poner en la maleta.
- e Es un libro muy bueno. ___ leí el año pasado.
- f Mamá, ¿dónde está la mochila? ___ necesito para el camping.
- g Las maletas pesan mucho. ___ podemos dejar en la recepción.
- h Aquí están tus gafas de sol; ___ encontré en la mesa.
- i Pero, ¿dónde están los billetes? ¿___ tienes tú?
- j Voy a comprar un plano de la ciudad. ___ necesitaremos más tarde.

5 **Choose the correct translation for each sentence.**

1 He gave her the tickets.
 a Te dio los billetes.
 b Les dio los billetes.
 c Le dio los billetes.

2 I sent them the money.
 a Les mandé el dinero.
 b Os mandé el dinero.
 c Nos mandé el dinero.

3 She showed us the room.
 a Os mostró la habitación.
 b Nos mostró la habitación.
 c Les mostró la habitación.

Passive voice (translation)

6 **Translate these sentences (in the passive voice) into Spanish. Use *ser* and the past participle. Remember to make the past participle agree.**

a The paper was recycled.
b The trees were protected.
c The fumes were reduced.
d The rivers will be cleaned.
e The litter will be picked up.

Reflexive verbs and passive voice (translation)

7 **Translate these sentences (in the passive voice) into Spanish. Use the reflexive.**

Many species were lost.

Example: Se perdieron muchas especies.

a The rivers were cleaned.
b The litter was picked up.
c The forest was destroyed.
d The factory was closed.
e Many birds were saved.
f The trees were cut down.
g The fire was put out.
h Green spaces were created.
i The chemical products were removed.
j Nature is respected in this country.

Present perfect tense

8 **Complete the sentences with the correct present perfect form.**

a Este mes ___ (*llover*) más de lo normal.
b El ayuntamiento ___ (*construir*) una nueva carretera.
c ___ (*comprar, nosotros*) billetes para una excursión muy interesante.
d ___ (*reservar, yo*) el vuelo para Mallorca.
e ¿___ (*ir, tú*) al nuevo supermercado?
f El pueblo ___ (*cambiar*) mucho en los últimos años.
g ¿___ (*viajar, vosotros*) mucho por España?
h ___ (*encontrar, yo*) una cámara al lado de la piscina.
i Barcelona es estupenda. ___ (*ser*) una semana excelente.
j ¿___ (*comer, tú*) alguna vez en ese restaurante?

Irregular present perfect

9 **Complete the sentences with the correct present perfect form. (These sentences have irregular past participles.)**

a El chico ___ (*poner*) nuestras maletas en la habitación.
b Me ___ (*cubrir, yo*) la cabeza porque entramos en una mezquita.
c ¿___ (*escribir, tú*) al hotel para hacer la reserva?
d Los guías nos ___ (*decir*) que la historia del castillo es muy interesante.
e Te ___ (*hacer, nosotros*) un plano de la ciudad para que no te pierdas.
f ¿___ (*ver, vosotros*) el tráfico en la ciudad? No sé qué pasa.
g Mi hijo ___ (*volver*) de sus vacaciones en la montaña con una pierna rota.

Grammar practice

Numbers

10 Write out these numbers in figures.

a Dos mil diecinueve
b Mil setecientos cincuenta y uno
c Novecientos sesenta y ocho
d Quinientos veintidós
e Mil trescientos diez

11 Write these numbers out in words.

a 1936
b 2024
c 1579
d 713
e 95

Prepositions

12 Complete the sentences with the Spanish translation of the words in brackets. Remember that *de* combines with *el* to become *del*. Then translate the sentences into English.

a El río no está ___ (*very far from*) la ciudad.
b El hotel está ___ (*close to*) el barrio chino.
c El jardín está ___ (*behind*) la casa.
d El museo está ___ (*between*) la plaza y el mercado.
e Hay un pájaro ___ (*on top of*) la iglesia.
f Hay espacio para tu coche ___ (*in front of*) el restaurante.
g Hay una estación de metro ___ (*next to*) el aeropuerto.
h Verás la sinagoga ___ (*at the end of*) la calle.
i Los principales monumentos históricos están ___ (*in the centre of*) la ciudad.
j El barco pasó ___ (*underneath*) el puente.

The imperative

14 Translate these sentences into English.

a Ten cuidado de no molestar a los pájaros en el parque.
b Proteged las especies que están en peligro.
c Haz algo cada día para proteger el medio ambiente.
d Para llegar al río, sal de aquí y sigue ese camino.
e Dime a qué hora vas a llegar.
f Pon las maletas en la habitación.
g Venid a visitarme durante las vacaciones de verano.
h Cierra la ventana por favor.
i Probad estas tapas; están deliciosas.
j Dame tu móvil y te haré una foto.

Irregular forms of the preterite

15 Complete the sentences with the preterite form (first person singular) of the verbs in brackets.

a Cuando salí de la habitación, ___ (*apagar*) la luz.
b Después de comer, ___ (*empezar*) con los deberes.
c Al llegar a Córdoba, ___ (*buscar*) mi hotel.
d Les ___ (*explicar*) a los turistas cómo llegar a la estación.
e Llamé a mis padres cuando ___ (*llegar*) al pueblo.
f En verano, ___ (*organizar*) actividades para los niños en el camping.
g Ayer ___ (*tocar*) la guitarra en un concierto de mi instituto.

Using *acabar de*

16 Translate these sentences into Spanish.

a He has just arrived.
b They have just gone out.
c She has just written.
d I have just remembered.
e You (sing.) have just started.

Stressed vowels

17 Underline the stressed vowel in these words.

a desayuno
b practico
c práctico
d Navidad
e bicicletas
f organizar
g contaminación
h juguete
i autobús
j alquilan
k simpático
l afortunadamente

The subjunctive

18 Complete the sentences with the present subjunctive form of the verbs in brackets.

a Te daré el dinero para que ___ (*hacer, tú*) la reserva.
b Necesitaré una mochila cuando ___ (*ir, yo*) de vacaciones.
c Cuando ___ (*venir, tú*) a verme, te recogeremos en la estación.
d Espero viajar por el mundo cuando ___ (*ser, yo*) mayor.
e Haz una foto del grupo para que ___ (*tener, tú*) un recuerdo del día.
f Cuando ___ (*ir, tú*) a Málaga, tienes que visitar el castillo.
g Llama a tu hermano para que ___ (*venir*) a ayudar.
h Esta casa no será cómoda cuando ___ (*hacer*) frío este invierno.

The subjunctive (translation)

19 Translate these sentences into Spanish.

a I want you to come to the party.
b She will tell me to make the dinner.
c They will ask him to be more careful.
d I am surprised that you are going by plane.
e He wants me to do the exam today.
f He will tell you to go shopping tomorrow.
g I will ask her to come to the station.
h I am glad that your job is so interesting.

Using *desde hace*

20 Translate these sentences into English.

a Mi marido trabaja en Madrid desde hace tres meses.
b Vivimos en esta casa desde hace un año.
c El castillo está aquí desde hace cuatro siglos.
d Nuestro hijo estudia medicina desde hace dos años.
e Esperamos el tren desde hace casi una hora.
f Mi hermano está de viaje por Europa desde hace varias semanas.

Relative clauses

21 Complete the sentences with *lo que, el que, la que, los que* or *las que*.

a Hay varias iglesias; ___ prefiero es la más grande.
b Tenemos dos planos de la ciudad; ___ será más útil es este.
c El café hace diferentes tipos de tapas; ___ más me gustan son las de pescado.
d Si quieres una de las maletas, ___ te recomiendo es la marrón.
e ___ que tienes que hacer es visitar el barrio antiguo de la ciudad.

Gramática

lo que; el que, la que, los que, las que

Lo que has two meanings. It can mean 'what', in cases where it is not a question.

*Eso es **lo que** voy a hacer.* – That is **what** I am going to do.

It can also mean 'which', when referring back to a whole clause and not just a noun.

*La fábrica contaminó el río, **lo que** enojó a los vecinos.* – The factory polluted the river, **which** annoyed the locals.

El que, la que, los que, las que mean 'the one that' or 'the ones that'. They agree with the noun that they are referring to.

*Hay dos catedrales. **La que** está en la plaza es la más antigua.* – There are two cathedrals.
The one that is in the square is the oldest.

Higher Vocabulary

Words that are highlighted in grey in this list are words that may be useful, but you won't need to know them for the exam.

7.1F ¿Qué haces durante las vacaciones?

al aire libre in the open air, outdoors
alojarse to stay
aprender to learn
el baloncesto basketball
el bosque wood, forest
buscar to look for
la carretera road
la ciudad town, city
cocinar to cook
conducir to drive
conocer to know (a person or place)
la costa coast
decidir to decide
descansar to rest
el edificio building
emocionante exciting
el/la empleado/a employee
el equipo equipment
la estrella star
excelente excellent
la excursión trip
la foto photo
fresco/a cool, fresh
el fuego fire
la habitación room
hacer camping to go camping
el hotel hotel
el interés interest
el invierno winter
ir de compras to go shopping
la isla island
el jardín garden
el lado side
lleno/a full
el lugar place
la maleta suitcase
el mercado market
mirar to look at
la mochila rucksack
montar to set up, to ride
la naturaleza nature
nuestro/a our
el país country
el paisaje country, countryside
pasado/a (adj.) past
perderse to get lost
la piscina swimming pool
el plano map, street plan
la playa beach
principal main
probar to try, try out
la recepción reception
el recuerdo souvenir
el regalo present, gift
reservar to book
el restaurante restaurant
el sitio place
sobre on
tener calor to be hot
la tienda tent, shop
tomar el sol to sunbathe
el/la turista tourist
vender to sell
el verano summer
el viento wind
visitar to visit

7.1H Las vacaciones fueron un desastre

el aeropuerto airport
animado/a lively
el apartamento apartment
el armario cupboard, wardrobe
el ascensor lift, elevator
el autobús bus, coach
el balcón balcony
el barco boat
el billete ticket
la bolsa bag
el brazo arm
caer(se) to fall (off, down)
el camping campsite
la cuenta bill
dar un paseo to go for a walk, stroll, ride
descubrir to discover
después de after
enfermo/a ill
el equipaje luggage
esperar to wait, to hope
fenomenal amazing
hacer fotos to take potos
la maleta suitcase
mío/a mine
la nevera fridge
las obras roadworks, building works
la policía police (force)
qué tal …? how is, was, are, were …?
quemar, quemarse to burn, get sunburnt
la reserva reservation
robar to steal
romper to break
el ruido noise
la sala de juegos games room
sentar/sentarse to sit, seat/to sit down
subir a to get onto (transport)
sucio/a dirty
la tela cloth, fabric
el tren train
varios/as several
la verdad truth
el viaje journey
la vista view
el vuelo flight

7.2F ¿Qué tipo de vacaciones prefieres?

bajar de to get off (transport)
caer(se) to fall, to fall over/down
caliente warm, hot
la catedral cathedral
celebrar(se) to celebrate, to hold (event)
cenar to dine, have the evening meal
conducir to drive
la cosa thing
la costumbre custom
el edificio building
el extranjero abroad
las gafas de sol sunglasses
hermoso beautiful
ir al extranjero to go abroad
llover to rain
mandar to send
mejorar to improve

el ***mensaje*** message
mezquita mosque
montar a caballo to ride a horse, go horse riding
el ***mundo*** world
el ***museo*** museum
la ***nacionalidad*** nationality
los/as ***niños/as*** children
el ***noroeste*** north-west
el ***norte*** north
la ***oportunidad*** opportunity
el ***país*** country
la ***parte*** part
pasarlo bien to have a good time
pintar to paint
pobre poor
practicar to practise
qué tal how is
quedar(se) to stay, remain
quemar, quemarse to burn, get sunburnt
el ***reloj*** watch, clock
la ***Semana Santa*** Easter Week, Holy Week
la ***sinagoga*** synagogue
los ***tíos*** uncle(s) and aunt(s)
la ***tradición*** tradition
valer la pena to be worth it
la ***zona*** area

7.2H Una visita a la ciudad de México

a bordo de on board
acompañar to accompany
al final at the end
alquilar to hire, rent
amarillo/a yellow
antiguo/a old
la ***arquitectura*** architecture
el ***artista*** artist
la ***atención*** attention
el/la ***camarero/a*** waiter/waitress
el ***canal*** canal
cantar to sing
el ***color*** colour
el ***comienzo*** the start, beginning
cultural cultural
cuyo whose
desde since, from
dieciséis sixteen
dirigir to run, manage
disfrutar to enjoy
encontrar, encontrarse to find, to be found
enorme enormous
entre between, among
el/la ***guía*** guide
la ***guitarra*** guitar
hace + time ago
la ***iglesia*** church
increíble incredible
iniciar to begin
llamar to call
llamativo/a striking
el ***lujo*** luxury
mantener to maintain, keep
maravilloso/a marvellous
el ***matrimonio*** marriage
el/la ***músico/a*** musician
nacional national
la ***obra*** work (of art, literature)
el ***palacio*** palace
la ***pared*** wall
la ***pintura*** painting
la ***planta*** plant
la ***plaza mayor*** main square
producir to produce
publicar to publish
recomendar to recommend
la ***ruina*** ruin
el ***siglo*** century
el ***templo*** temple
tener suerte to be lucky
tocar to play (instrument, music)
turbulento/a turbulent, stormy
utilizar to use

8.1F Los cambios en la tecnología

avanzado/a advanced
básico/a basic
el/la ***compañero/a*** classmate, partner
la ***conversación*** conversation
digital digital
discutir to discuss, argue
diseñar to design
enviar to send
la ***información*** information
el/la ***ingeniero/a*** engineer
inteligente intelligent, smart
inventar to invent
el ***juego*** game
el ***kilo*** kilo
ligero/a light (in weight)
la ***llamada*** call
la ***llegada*** arrival
el ***minuto*** minute
el ***momento*** moment
navegar to surf, navigate (i.e. the Internet)
original original
permitir to allow, permit
pesado/a heavy
pesar to weigh
el ***portátil*** laptop
público/a public
realista realistic
recargar to charge, recharge
responder to reply
sencillo/a simple
la ***serie*** series
táctil touch (ie. touch screen)
el ***teléfono*** telephone
la ***televisión*** television
el ***tenis*** tennis
la ***transmisión*** broadcast
treinta thirty
último/a last, latest
el ***videojuego*** video game

8.1H Lo bueno y lo malo de las redes sociales

afectar to affect
al menos at least
la ***amistad*** friendship
anunciar to announce
aquel/aquella that (one)
causar to cause
el ***colegio*** school
común common
comunicar to communicate
el ***concierto*** concert
continuamente continuously
convertirse en to become
criticar to criticise
cualquier any
el ***daño*** damage, harm
desaparecer to disappear
detestar to detest
la ***distancia*** distance

el ***efecto*** effect
encontrar to find
el ***estudio*** study, studio
horrible horrible
hoy día these days
el ***humor*** mood
incluso even, including
el ***informe*** report
insultar to insult
la ***manera*** manner, way
molestar to annoy
la ***música*** music
el ***negocio*** business
numeroso numerous
la ***oferta*** offer
ofrecer to offer
otra vez again
peligroso/a dangerous
perdonar to forgive
el ***perfil*** profile
el ***personaje*** character
la ***plataforma*** platform
el/la ***profesor(a)*** teacher
el ***resto*** rest
el ***resultado*** result
tan so
el ***uso*** use
el ***vídeo*** video
ya que since, as

8.2F ¿Cómo usas tu móvil?

alguno/a some
la ***app*** app
los ***auriculares*** headphones
la ***calculadora*** calculator
el/la ***cantante*** singer
como as, like
las ***compras*** shopping
la ***cosa*** thing
despertar to wake up
el ***diccionario*** dictionary
educativo/a educational
el ***ejemplo*** example
electrónico/a electronic
el ***familiar*** family member
la ***función*** function
gratis free
el ***lector electrónico*** e-book
lejos far
la ***lista*** list
mantenerse to keep (oneself)
medio/a average
molestar to bother, annoy
el ***nombre*** name
el ***número*** number
oír to hear
el/la ***primo/a*** cousin
profundamente deeply
prohibido/a forbidden, banned
quién who
quitar to remove
el ***ruido*** noise
saber to know
la ***tecnología*** technology
todas partes everywhere
el ***tráfico*** traffic

8.2H La tecnología del futuro

absorber to absorb
actualmente currently, at present
el ***agua*** water
añadir to add
apagar to turn off, out out
capaz de capable of
cargar to charge
el ***castillo*** castle
el ***cepillo*** brush
la ***ciencia*** science
el/la ***científico/a*** scientist
el ***cine*** cinema
continuar to continue
la ***cuestión*** issue, matter
dental dental
el/la ***dentista*** dentist
detectar to detect
el ***dispositivo*** gadget
el ***examen*** exam
existir to exist
experimentar to experiment, experience
la ***ficción*** fiction
hacer falta to be lacking, missing
los ***hijos*** children, sons and daughters
identificar to identify
la ***impresora*** printer
la ***invención*** invention
ir de vacaciones to go on holiday
limpiar to clean
la ***medicina*** medicine
la ***mentira*** lie
mover to move
necesario/a necessary
notar to notice
observar to observe
los ***padres*** parents
la ***pizza*** pizza
el/la ***segundo/a*** second
el ***sistema*** system
tener hambre to be hungry
la ***Tierra*** Earth
ya now, already

9.1F Mi pueblo y mi ciudad

agosto August
al lado de next to, at the side of
el ***árbol*** tree
así like this, like that
el ***baño*** bathroom
el ***bosque*** wood, forest
el ***campo*** field, country(side)
el ***castillo*** castle
el ***centro comercial*** shopping centre
el ***cielo*** sky
el ***clima*** climate
delante de in front of
detrás de behind
encima de on top of
la ***estación*** station
el ***este*** east
la ***fábrica*** factory
faltar to be lacking, to be short of
el ***grado*** degree (ie. temperature)
el ***hospital*** hospital
imposible impossible
lejos de far from
llegar a to arrive, get to
mal bad, badly
la ***mezquita*** mosque
la ***nieve*** snow
el ***parque de atracciones/temático*** theme park
la ***plaza de toros*** bullring
la ***plaza mayor*** main square
el ***puente*** bridge
el ***puerto*** port, harbour
los ***servicios*** toilets
la ***tarde*** afternoon, evening
único/a only
las ***verduras*** (green) vegetables

9.1H Lo bueno y lo malo de mi región

la ***abuela*** grandmother
las ***afueras*** outskirts
animado/a lively
atraer to attract
el ***ayuntamiento*** town hall, council
el ***barrio*** neighbourhood, district, area
el ***centro deportivo*** sports centre
cierto/a true
conseguir to manage
la ***construcción*** building, construction
cruzar to cross
la ***delincuencia*** crime
el ***delito*** crime, offence
desde hace for
la ***edad*** age
la ***empresa*** company, firm
la ***escalera*** stairs
el ***estado*** state
gastar to spend
gracias thanks
la ***industria*** industry
infantil children's, of children
mal bad, badly
el ***mes*** month
el ***metro*** underground
el ***nivel*** level
el ***noroeste*** north-west
el ***paro*** unemployment
el ***piso*** flat, apartment
roto/a broken
la ***semana pasada*** last week
el ***sistema*** system
la ***torre*** tower
el ***transporte*** transport

9.2F ¿Qué puedo hacer para proteger el medio ambiente?

el ***anuncio*** advert
la ***basura*** rubbish, litter
la ***botella*** bottle
la ***calefacción*** heating
el ***colegio*** school
el ***contenedor*** container, bin
el ***cuidado*** care
dejar to leave, let, allow
el ***entorno*** surroundings
evitar to avoid
ir a pie to go on foot, walk
la ***lluvia*** rain
el ***medio ambiente*** environment
nadie no one
organizar to organise
el ***otoño*** autumn
el ***plan*** plan
plantar to plant
el ***plástico*** plastic
preocuparse por to worry about
la ***primavera*** spring
reciclar to recycle
recoger to collect, pick up
regar to water, irrigate
separar to separate
la ***Tierra*** Earth
tirar to throw

9.2H Protegiendo el planeta

la ***abeja*** bee
la ***acción*** action, act
advertir to warn
el ***alimento*** food, foodstuff
alrededor de around
amenazar to threaten
artificial artificial
aumentar to increase
buscar to look for, to seek
la ***campaña*** campaign
la ***cifra*** figure
el/la ***ciudadano/a*** citizen
como consecuencia de as a result of
concienciar to make aware, raise awareness
consciente aware
el ***consumo*** consumption
la ***contaminación*** pollution
contaminar to pollute
contribuir to contribute
crear to create
el ***cultivo*** crop
dejar de + infinitive to stop … ing
destinado a aimed at
destruir to destroy
efectivo/a effective
eléctrico/a electric
emitir to emit, give off
en vez de instead of
la ***especie*** species
fundar to set up
la ***ganadería*** cattle farming
el ***gas*** gas
el ***gobierno*** government
el ***hogar*** home
el ***humo*** smoke, fume
la ***imagen*** image
el ***impacto*** impact
el ***informe*** report
la ***iniciativa*** initiative
el ***invernadero*** greenhouse
la ***investigación*** research, investigation
la ***luz*** light
la ***medida*** measure
el ***millón*** million
la ***necesidad*** need
el ***olor*** smell
la ***organización*** organisation
el ***planeta*** planet
poblado/a populated
prohibir to prohibit, ban
químico/a (adj.) chemical
reciente recent
reportar to report
según according to
tantos/as so many, as many
el ***transporte*** transport

Test and revise: Higher Listening

1 These residents are attending an online meeting. What aspect of the town are they concerned about? Complete the sentences in English.

a Rodrigo wants to improve… **1 mark**

b Laura wants the council to change its mind about… **1 mark**

c Felipe wants the council to build… **1 mark**

d Emma wants to know why the council has not… **1 mark**

Consejo

When you have to complete sentences, like in activity 1, the beginnings of the sentences will cue you in the key part of the recording. Listen carefully for the cue and then focus on the section that follows – this will be the required answer.

2 These people are talking about different aspects of technology.

Write **A** if only statement A is correct
B if only statement B is correct
A+B if both statements A and B are correct.

a A Mateo is concerned about his mother's computer.
B Mateo's mother has bought a new computer. **1 mark**

b A Isabel forgot to save her work on the computer.
B She hopes her Dad can help get the work back. **1 mark**

c A Leo's brother is always playing computer games.
B Leo's brother's school work is suffering. **1 mark**

d A Elena uses social media quite a lot.
B She thinks there is a lot of rubbish on social media. **1 mark**

3 Pablo and his family have moved house. He is talking to his grandmother on the phone. When do these things take place?

Write **P** if it is something that happened **in the past**
N if it is something that is happening **now**
F if it is something that will happen **in the future**.

Answer **all** parts of the question.

a doing homework **1 mark**

b sharing a bedroom **1 mark**

c mother's shopping trip **1 mark**

d working on the garden **1 mark**

4 These people are talking about problems that happened on holiday. What went wrong for each of them? Write down the correct letter.

a Miguel had a problem when …
A their coach broke down.
B he got food poisoning.
C he ended up sleeping on the floor. **1 mark**

b Sandra had a problem …
A when they found people sleeping in their hotel room.
B because the noise from the hotel disco kept them awake.
C and had to confront the people in the room next door. **1 mark**

c Carlos had a problem when …
A the bus left him behind after a day out.
B his coach broke down on the way to a festival.
C his hotel turned out to be miles from town. **1 mark**

d Ana had a problem when …
A she rented out her apartment to an elderly lady.
B she couldn't find anywhere to stay.
C the hotel she had booked had lost her reservation. **1 mark**

5 A guide on a country walk is talking to the group. What advice is he giving? Complete the sentences in English.

a While you are in the country… **1 mark**

b To avoid disturbing the birds… **1 mark**

c If you stay for a picnic, remember that… **1 mark**

d At the end of the day… **1 mark**

Consejo

It is very important to take account of the context of the question. Activity 5 is about advice during a walk in the country. Knowing this will help you see what is likely or possible and what is simply not appropriate. For example, the answer to 5d is not going to be 'turn the lights off'.

6 This couple is discussing a flat they have just been to visit. Which aspect of the flat did each person like and dislike? Write down the correct letter for each aspect.

A	cost
B	kitchen
C	location
D	lounge
E	parking
F	views

a Blanca: Liked Disliked **2 marks**

b Arturo: Liked Disliked **2 marks**

Dictation A

You will now hear 5 short sentences.

- Listen carefully and using your knowledge of Spanish sounds, write down in **Spanish** exactly what you hear for each sentence.
- You will hear each sentence **three** times: the first time as a full sentence, the second time in short sections and the third time again as a full sentence.
- Use your knowledge of Spanish sounds and grammar to make sure that what you have written makes sense. Check carefully that your spelling is accurate.

10 marks

Consejo

Learn the word CAROL as a way to remember the only double consonants you will meet in the exam. Double 'c' exists in words like *acción*; double 'r' is in words like *perro*, and double 'll' can be found in words like *llamar*.

Dictation B

You will now hear 5 short sentences.

- Listen carefully and using your knowledge of Spanish sounds, write down in **Spanish** exactly what you hear for each sentence.
- You will hear each sentence **three** times: the first time as a full sentence, the second time in short sections and the third time again as a full sentence.
- Use your knowledge of Spanish sounds and grammar to make sure that what you have written makes sense. Check carefully that your spelling is accurate.

10 marks

Test and revise: Higher Speaking

Role Play

You are talking to your Cuban friend.

Your teacher (or partner) will play the part of your friend and will speak first.

You should address your friend as *tú*.

When you see this – ? – you will have to ask a question.

In order to score full marks, you must include a verb in your response to each task.

1 Say what you used your mobile for last weekend. (Give **two** details.)

2 Say why you think social networks are popular. (Give **two** details.)

3 Say what is a disadvantage of using social networks. (Give **one** disadvantage.)

4 Say how you will use technology for your studies next week. (Give **one** detail.)

5 **?** Ask your friend a question about their favourite apps.

Consejo

As you are required to ask a question in the role play, it is essential to learn question words. It is a good idea to keep a list of these and make sure that learning them is part of your exam preparation.

Reading aloud task

When your teacher (or partner) asks you, read aloud the following text in **Spanish**.

La región donde vive mi amigo está bastante sucia. No quiere quedarse a vivir allí. Cuando sea mayor, dice que va a trabajar en el extranjero.

En esta zona hay demasiados coches y el ruido es horrible. Además, todos los humos hacen daño al medio ambiente. Preferiría vivir en el campo.

You will then be asked four questions in **Spanish** that relate to the topic of **The environment and where people live**. Make sure you answer **all four questions as fully as you can**.

Consejo

Bear in mind that the questions you will be asked in relation to the reading aloud task will be on the same topic as the text. Use some of your preparation time to anticipate what those questions might be and start to consider your responses.

Photo card

- During your preparation time, look at the two photos. You may make as many notes as you wish on an Additional Answer Sheet and use these notes during the test.
- Your teacher (or partner) will ask you to talk about the content of these photos. The recommended time is approximately **one and a half minutes. You must say at least one thing about each photo.**
- After you have spoken about the content of the photos, your teacher (or partner) will then ask you questions related to **any** of the topics within the theme of **Communication and the world around us.**

Consejo

Don't panic if you see a photo and realise you can't remember a certain word. For example, in Photo 1, it doesn't matter if you don't know 'motorway' or 'traffic jam', you can still talk about lots of cars, too much traffic, contamination and noise.

Photo 1

Photo 2

Test and revise: Higher Reading

1 Read this email from Lorena to Óscar. Answer the questions in English.

Vas a llegar el jueves y el día después tengo clases, así que tendrás que ir al instituto conmigo. Ese día tengo dibujo, religión, química y francés. Será interesante para ti y mis amigos tienen muchas ganas de conocerte. Normalmente tengo una clase de baile los viernes, pero esta semana no, porque es el final del trimestre*.
El sábado te voy a llevar a la plaza de toros. No hay corrida, pero el edificio es histórico y muy hermoso. Sé que no te interesa el fútbol y por eso no he organizado una visita al famoso estadio. El domingo vendrás a la iglesia con mi familia. No vamos mucho, pero es Semana Santa y es bonito ir.
Creo que el centro comercial es exactamente como los de tu país, aburrido. Sin embargo, tengo dos entradas para el parque temático la semana de después, ¡será estupendo!

**trimestre* – term

a What day will Óscar be going into school with Lorena? **1 mark**

b What does Lorena say about her friends? **1 mark**

c What change has happened because it is the end of term? **1 mark**

d Why is Lorena taking Óscar to the bullring? **1 mark**

e Will they visit the stadium? Why / Why not? **1 mark**

f Why are the family going to church this Sunday? **1 mark**

g Why doesn't Lorena plan to take Óscar to the shopping centre? **1 mark**

h What does she tell him about next week? **1 mark**

i Read the first paragraph again. What do you think *química* is?

A A hobby

B A school subject

C An item of equipment **1 mark**

Consejo

Be careful not to make rapid assumptions when you see a word you recognise. Question 1 asks you to name a day, but read the text carefully and don't jump at the first day of the week that you see.

2 You read this tourist guide about Menorca.

Menorca es quizás la isla con más riqueza histórica de todas las islas españolas. Durante su historia, culturas diferentes han dejado su impacto en varios sitios en la isla.

La capital, Mahón, es uno de los puertos naturales más grandes del mundo. En otras partes de la isla, hay tumbas* y monumentos de piedra que vienen de un período de la historia antigua.

Calas* bonitas y playas de arena se encuentran por toda la isla además de zonas de interés como Es Grau en el norte. Muchos turistas suben el *Monte Toro* porque desde encima las vistas son preciosas.

Las fiestas principales son las de San Juan en junio y las de Gracia en septiembre. El caballo y los trajes hacen un papel importante en los desfiles por las calles. Por la noche las hogueras y los fuegos artificiales crean un espectáculo precioso contra el cielo oscuro.

**tumba* – tomb

**cala* – cove

Which statements are correct? Write **A**, **B** or **A+B**.

a A Menorca is rich in history.
B Other cultures have left their mark on the island. **1 mark**

b A Mahón is inland.
B There are ancient stone monuments. **1 mark**

c A The island's beaches are rocky.
B Monte Toro is a hill. **1 mark**

d A The main festivals are in winter.
B The costumes and parades are an important feature. **1 mark**

e Read the last paragraph again. What do you think *hogueras* are?
A bonfires B dances C flowers **1 mark**

3 An environmental group has produced this report.

INFORME	
Febrero	El ayuntamiento promete aumentar los gastos de conservación para proteger los bosques naturales y prohibir cortar los árboles para obras de construcción.
Mayo	Los supermercados se quejan de la falta de productos como frutas y verduras después de una fría primavera que ha destruido muchos cultivos.
Agosto	Doscientas personas abandonaron sus hogares cuando los incendios amenazaban con destruir sus casas. Afortunadamente, nadie sufrió daños.
Noviembre	Los dueños de los hoteles de la ciudad acordaron cobrar a los turistas un euro por noche en impuestos. Se usará el dinero para resolver el problema de la falta de agua.

Which headline corresponds to which month of the news report?

	Headlines
A	Ancient trees cut down
B	Forest fires leave several injured
C	Homeowners evacuated
D	Hotels rationing water
E	More funding to save woodland
F	Supermarkets raise prices
G	Tourist tax imposed
H	Wintry weather ruins crops

a February **1 mark**

b May **1 mark**

c August **1 mark**

d November **1 mark**

Consejo

You will often find that two of the options (or 'headlines' in this case) are closely linked to the answer you are looking for. You need to read the relevant part of the text with great care to eliminate the wrong option and select the one that matches in all its details.

4 Translate these sentences into English.

a El gobierno debe tomar medidas para reducir el cambio climático.

b Este es el dispositivo que estábamos usando para grabar la conversación.

c Sé que estaba de mal humor porque utilizó un emoticón con una cara enojada.

d Ella antes llevaba gafas de sol, pero ahora las ha perdido.

e Mándame un mensaje cuando tengas un momento libre. **10 marks**

Consejo

You will come across verbs in various tenses in the translation sentences. As you translate each sentence, take your time to look at the verb endings and the stems to help you identify what tense each verb is in.

5 Translate these sentences into English.

a Los humos de la fábrica estaban contaminando el aire de los pueblos vecinos.

b Han alquilado un coche, pero no se acuerdan de dónde lo han dejado.

c En los últimos años, muchos jóvenes han cerrado sus cuentas en las redes sociales.

d Creo que lo mejor sería ir en barco cuando vayas de vacaciones.

e Estos días, se sirven platos vegetarianos en casi todos los restaurantes. **10 marks**

Test and revise: Higher Writing

1 Translate the following sentences into Spanish.

a That is my bedroom. Yours is here.

b The church was built centuries ago.

c He said that he would like to buy a new mobile phone.

d I have taken lots of photos; I will show them to you on Saturday.

e I have just turned off the heating; I do not want you to be too hot.

10 marks

Consejo

On occasions, there may be more than one way of translating a word. For example, if you don't know 'centuries' you could say 'hundreds of years'. There are also a couple of words that could be used for 'bedroom'.

Either Question 2.1 *or* Question 2.2

2.1 You are writing to your Peruvian friend about your town and neighbourhood.
Write approximately 90 words in Spanish.
You must write something about each bullet point.

Mention:

- what you think of your town
- what you did in town last weekend
- what you would like to change about your area in the future.

15 marks

2.2 You are writing an article about technology.
Write approximately 90 words in Spanish.
You must write something about each bullet point.

Mention:

- what you think about social media
- what aspects of technology you used last week
- how you will use technology in the future to help your studies.

15 marks

Consejo

Remember that you will not get extra marks for writing a lot. You can impress with the 90 words stated in the instructions; better to aim for quality than quantity.

Either Question 3.1 *or* Question 3.2

3.1 You are writing a post for a Spanish website on the environment.
Write approximately 150 words in Spanish.
You must write something about both bullet points.

Describe:

- what you and your family do at home in order to be environmentally friendly
- what projects are going to happen in your area to improve the environment.

25 marks

3.2 You are writing an article for a Spanish magazine called *Mi Verano*.
Write approximately 150 words in Spanish.
You must write something about both bullet points.

Describe:

- how you like to spend you summer holidays
- problems you had during your last summer holidays.

25 marks

Consejo

These question types, requiring you write approximately 150 words, give you the opportunity to narrate a series of events or to give all the details about one complex event. Take a moment to read both questions, have a quick think about what you could write about (you can jot down a few ideas and notes to remind you) and then decide which question to go for.

Test and revise: Higher Listening

1 Jordi and Emma are talking about how they plan to improve their lifestyle. What does each one plan to do? Write the correct letter.

a Jordi plans to…

A reduce the amount he eats.

B eat less fatty food.

C cut out snacks between meals. **1 mark**

b Jordi also plans to…

A use his car less.

B go cycling with his dad.

C walk to school. **1 mark**

c Emma hopes to…

A be on the basketball team.

B get new sports equipment.

C lose some weight. **1 mark**

d Emma also plans to…

A do weights at the gym.

B go running.

C go swimming four times a week. **1 mark**

Consejo

Look carefully at the layout of the questions. How many questions do you need to answer for each recording? In activity 1, you need to answer two questions from each speech. It's important to know this, because you need to read the options before the recording starts and to know how much you are listening out for.

2 Cristina and Marco are walking home from school, talking about their day.

Write **A** if only statement A is correct

B if only statement B is correct

A+B if both statements A and B are correct.

a When considering the exchange visit, Cristina…

A is concerned about the standard of her English.

B worries about staying with a family. **1 mark**

b Cristina says that…

A they might be changing the school uniform.

B students have to vote for what colour they would prefer. **1 mark**

c Marco…

A thinks his history teacher is being unfairly negative.

B has never liked history lessons. **1 mark**

d Marco…

A has suffered bullying at school recently.

B wants David to walk home with them. **1 mark**

3 Hugo and Julia are talking about hopes and plans for the future. For each one, write what they want to do and what they do not want to do.

a Hugo's dream is to…

He does **not** want to… **2 marks**

b Julia's ambition is to…

She does **not** want to… **2 marks**

4 Sofía and her mother have different ideas about their visit to Andalusia, in the south of Spain. Answer the questions in English. Give full details.

a Exactly when does Sofía suggest they go, and why? **1 mark**

b What is there to see at the Jerez festival? Mention **one** thing. **1 mark**

c What happens during the *Fiesta de los Patios*? **1 mark**

d What is Sofía's mother's solution to their different ideas. **1 mark**

Consejo

If you see instructions like 'Give full details' or the question has the word 'exactly' in it, this is to remind you that all the relevant information in the recording is required in the answer. Do not leave out any details.

5 Adrián and Mia are talking about their free time.

a What does Adrián do in his free time?

yesterday	today	tomorrow
finished reading a novel		

2 marks

b What does Mia do in her free time?

yesterday	today	tomorrow
		prepare a meal for her boyfriend

2 marks

Consejo

There will often be a question on verb tenses in the reading or listening exams. A good way to prepare for it, apart from learning time phrases, is to make a grid of three columns: past, present and future. Write examples of the different tenses for each time frame in the different columns. For example, in the 'past' column, you would write examples of the perfect, the preterite and the imperfect tenses.

6 Mateo and Diego are discussing a TV programme. Write the correct letter. Answer all the questions.

a What type of programme is Diego asking about?

A a talent show

B a reality TV show

C a general knowledge quiz **1 mark**

b Who benefits from the programme?

A young people with talent

B charity associations

C overseas aid **1 mark**

c Who surprised Diego?

A a newsreader

B a TV presenter

C a weather forecaster **1 mark**

d The winner was…

A an actress.

B a journalist.

C a writer. **1 mark**

Dictation A

You will now hear 5 short sentences.

- Listen carefully and using your knowledge of Spanish sounds, write down in **Spanish** exactly what you hear for each sentence.
- You will hear each sentence **three** times: the first time as a full sentence, the second time in short sections and the third time again as a full sentence.
- Use your knowledge of Spanish sounds and grammar to make sure that what you have written makes sense. Check carefully that your spelling is accurate.

10 marks

Dictation B

You will now hear 5 short sentences.

- Listen carefully and using your knowledge of Spanish sounds, write down in **Spanish** exactly what you hear for each sentence.
- You will hear each sentence **three** times: the first time as a full sentence, the second time in short sections and the third time again as a full sentence.
- Use your knowledge of Spanish sounds and grammar to make sure that what you have written makes sense. Check carefully that your spelling is accurate.

10 marks

Test and revise: Higher Speaking

Role Play

You are talking to your Peruvian friend.

Your teacher (or partner) will play the part of your friend and will speak first.

You should address your friend as *tú*.

When you see this – **?** – you will have to ask a question.

In order to score full marks, you must include a verb in your response to each task.

1 Say what items you recycle at home. (Give **two** details.)

2 Tell your friend about the green spaces in your area. (Give **two** details.)

3 Talk about the environmental problems in your area. (Give **two** details.)

4 Tell your friend about something you did at school to help the environment.

5 **?** Ask your friend a question about the environment where they live.

Consejo

Use the preparation time wisely. Look at the amount of detail you are required to give for each bullet point in the role play, and only plan for the information necessary. You will be wasting precious time if you spend minutes thinking about what else you could say.

Reading aloud task

When your teacher (or partner) asks you, read aloud the following text in **Spanish**.

Mi hija mayor asiste a un club de baile los viernes. Participa en un concierto una vez al año y ha ganado varios premios.

Es una actividad un poco cara porque necesita zapatos y trajes especiales. Tenemos que llevarla a las clases en coche también.

Me imagino que seguirá bailando en el futuro.

You will then be asked four questions in **Spanish** that relate to the topic of **Free-time activities**. Make sure you answer **all four questions as fully as you can**.

Consejo

Remember that the letter 'j', and the letter 'g' when followed by 'e' and 'i', are both pronounced like the 'ch' in the Scottish word 'loch'. There are three examples of this sound in the reading aloud task.

Photo card

- During your preparation time, look at the two photos. You may make as many notes as you wish on an Additional Answer Sheet and use these notes during the test.
- Your teacher (or partner) will ask you to talk about the content of these photos. The recommended time is approximately **one and a half minutes. You must say at least one thing about each photo.**
- After you have spoken about the content of the photos, your teacher (or partner) will then ask you questions related to **any** of the topics within the theme of **Communication and the world around us.**

Consejo

Remember to think ahead about typical questions that might come up in relation to the photos on a card. These photos show a city flat and a country house so you could imagine being asked about the advantages and disadvantages of living in the city or the country, for example.

Photo 1

Photo 2

Test and revise: Higher Reading

1 You see this report in a magazine. Have the numbers of young people doing these activities gone up, gone down or stayed the same?

Hace poco hicieron una encuesta a dos mil personas sobre las tendencias en el uso del tiempo libre y han descubierto unas respuestas interesantes. Parece que hoy día no va tanta gente al cine porque prefiere ver películas en casa. Se quejan del costo de las entradas y de las bebidas. La lectura de periódicos, revistas y novelas es mucho menos popular entre los jóvenes de hoy. En cuanto a* la televisión, el número de jóvenes que ve la tele como pasatiempo principal no ha cambiado. Con respecto a los ordenadores, cada vez más jóvenes pasan su tiempo libre navegando en Internet y jugando con los videojuegos. Respecto al deporte, las cifras destacan que el número de chicos y chicas que participan es el mismo ahora que en el pasado.

**en cuanto a* – as regards

Write **U** if the numbers have gone **up**
D if the numbers have gone **down**
S if the numbers have stayed the **same**.

a Going to the cinema **1 mark**

b Reading **1 mark**

c Watching TV **1 mark**

d Use of technology **1 mark**

e Sport **1 mark**

f Look at the first sentence again. What do you think *una encuesta* is?
A An interview B A leaflet
C A survey **1 mark**

Consejo !

With this type of exercise, the answers can be found in the text in the same order that they appear in the question. So, if you have found the answer to 1b and the answer to 1d, this helps you to know where in the text you will find the information you need to answer 1c.

2 You read this in a magazine problem page. Complete each sentence by selecting the correct letter.

Me siento muy enojada porque mis padres me tratan de manera distinta a mi hermano. A mi hermano le dan mucha libertad; entra y sale cuando quiere y respetan sus decisiones. Pero conmigo siempre quieren saber dónde estoy, con quién salgo, con quién estoy hablando en el móvil y todo. Quiero hacerles entender que esto no es justo. ¿Qué puedo hacer?

Mónica

a Mónica is feeling…
A angry. B ill. C tired. **1 mark**

b Mónica thinks that her parents are…
A putting too much pressure on her.
B being unfair.
C getting impatient. **1 mark**

c Mónica says that her brother…
A works really hard.
B gets a lot of pocket money.
C is given a lot of independence. **1 mark**

d Mónica feels that her parents ask too many questions about…
A her future plans. B her school work.
C her friends. **1 mark**

3 You see this report on a health and fitness website. Answer the questions in English.

Hay una tendencia en este momento de beber agua constantemente: eso está bien hasta cierto punto, pero es mejor no hacerlo antes de acostarte porque pasarás la noche sin dormir.

Lo que sí se recomienda es terminar los deberes antes de las nueve para que tengas tiempo para relajarte antes de irte a la cama. Además de tu cuerpo, tu cerebro necesita tiempo para desconectar también.

Luego, al levantarte, debes tomar un desayuno sano para que te dé la energía que necesitas para el resto del día.

Claro que el ejercicio es esencial, pero evita hacerlo a primera hora de la mañana porque tu cuerpo todavía no está despierto.

a Why **shouldn't** you drink water in the evening? **1 mark**

b What must you do to give you time to relax before bedtime? **1 mark**

c How can you be sure to have enough energy during the day? **1 mark**

d Why should you not exercise first thing in the morning? **1 mark**

e Read the second paragraph again. What do you think *desconectar* means?

A to refresh

B to wake up

C to wind down **1 mark**

4 Your Spanish friend Javi has filled in this questionnaire about work. Look at the answers he has circled and answer the questions in English.

1 ¿Sabes qué tipo de trabajo te gustaría hacer en el futuro?
(A) No tengo la menor idea.
B Hay varias posibilidades que estoy investigando.
C Ya sé exactamente lo que voy a hacer.

2 ¿Cómo reaccionarías a la idea de trabajar en el extranjero?
A Me encantaría.
B Pues depende; lo consideraría.
(C) La rechazaría en seguida.

3 ¿En qué aspecto tienes más talento?
A Resolver problemas
(B) Diseño y creatividad
C Tratar con la gente

4 ¿Cómo describirías tus conocimientos de informática?
(A) Excelentes
B Bastante buenos
C Básicos

What do we learn about Javi from…

a the first question and answer? **1 mark**

b the second question and answer? **1 mark**

c the third question and answer? **1 mark**

d the fourth question and answer? **1 mark**

Consejo

This type of question is common on the higher reading paper. In order to answer successfully, you are required to put together information from both the question from the questionnaire and the answer. The questions cannot be answered from just one of these elements alone.

5 Translate these sentences into English.

a Intenté comprar huevos, pero no había en las tiendas.

b Tomar el sol durante las horas más calientes del día es muy peligroso.

c Miles de estudiantes participaron en la manifestación anoche.

d He perdido mis llaves; creo que podrían estar detrás del armario.

e Escribió un informe sobre el impacto del calentamiento global. **10 marks**

6 Translate these sentences into English.

a Mis hermanos se peleaban mucho cuando eran jóvenes.

b El teclado está roto. Tendré que pedir un nuevo portátil.

c Acaban de quejarse al dueño de los problemas en el piso.

d El pueblo todavía huele a humo, después del incendio.

e La película tuvo mucho éxito y ganó varios premios. **10 marks**

Consejo

When translating sentences, do not offer alternatives (i.e. leave two possible translations for the examiner to choose from). You must decide which version to go with and cross out the other.

Test and revise: Higher Writing

1 Translate the following sentences into Spanish.

a My city is in the south of the country.

b You will get on very well with my family.

c They used to play basketball in the park on Sundays.

d I am very hungry. At what time are we going to eat?

e My sister is very clever; she would like to study law.

10 marks

Consejo

It is a good idea to learn a group of phrases that use *tener* in Spanish, where in English we use 'to be'. Some of these are: *tener hambre* (to be hungry), *tener sed* (to be thirsty), *tener calor / frío* (to be hot / cold), *tener razón* (to be right) and *tener suerte* (to be lucky).

Either Question 2.1 *or* Question 2.2

2.1 You post your ideas on healthy living on a Spanish blog.
Write approximately 90 words in Spanish.
You must write something about each bullet point.

Mention:

- what you think of school meals
- the sport or exercise you did last week
- what meals you are going to have this weekend.

15 marks

2.2 Your Spanish friend Oliver is coming to stay and will spend a day with you in school. Write to tell him about it.
Write approximately 90 words in Spanish.
You must write something about each bullet point.

Mention:

- what you think about the school and its facilities
- a trip you went on with school
- what Oliver will do in school when he visits.

15 marks

Consejo

Each time you make a point in the writing task, try to extend your answer by adding extra information such as an opinion and / or a reason. For instance, when you say what you think about your school, say why. You could even add what you would like to have in your school.

Either Question 3.1 *or* Question 3.2

3.1 You enter a Spanish writing competition about fame and famous people.
Write approximately 150 words in Spanish.
You must write something about both bullet points.

Mention:

- the advantages and disadvantages of being famous
- a celebrity that you admired when you were younger.

25 marks

3.2 You are writing an article for a Spanish magazine called *Estudiar y trabajar*.
Write approximately 150 words in Spanish.
You must write something about both bullet points.

Describe:

- how your studies are going
- your ambitions for study and work in the future.

25 marks

Consejo

Keep an eye on your word count. It is no advantage at all to write pages and pages – you are given a word guide of approximately 150 words. If you write lots more, you will rush and allow more errors to creep in.

Grammar

Contents

Glossary of terms

Adjectives ***los adjetivos***

Words that describe somebody or something:

pequeño	small
tranquilo	quiet, peaceful

Adverbs ***los adverbios***

Words that complement (add meaning to) verbs, adjectives or other adverbs:

mal	badly
lentamente	slowly

Articles ***los artículos***

Short words used to introduce nouns:

un/una	a, an
unos/unas	some, any
el/la/los/las	the

The infinitive ***el infinitivo***

The verb form given in the dictionary:

ir	to go
tener	to have

Nouns ***los nombres***

Words that identify a person, a place or a thing:

madre	mother
casa	house

Prepositions ***las preposiciones***

Words used in front of nouns to give information about when, how, where, etc.:

con	with	*en*	in
de	of, from		

Pronouns ***los pronombres***

Words used to replace nouns. For example, subject pronouns:

yo	I	*él*	he
tú	you	*ella*	she

Verbs ***los verbos***

Words used to express an action or a state:

trabajo	I work
vive	he lives

1 Nouns

Masculine and feminine nouns

All Spanish nouns are either masculine or feminine.

- In the singular, masculine nouns are introduced with *el* or *un*:

***el** padre*	**the** father
***un** libro*	**a** book

- Feminine singular nouns are introduced with *la* or *una*:

***la** madre*	**the** mother
***una** mesa*	**a** table

- Some nouns have two different forms, masculine and feminine:

un amigo	a male friend
una amiga	a female friend
un profesor	a male teacher
una profesora	a female teacher

- Some nouns stay the same for masculine and feminine.

el artista	the male artist
la artista	the female artist

- Some nouns which relate to jobs such as ***el jefe*** (the boss) usually stay the same in the feminine form, i.e. ***la jefe***. However, the use of feminised forms of the noun, in this instance ***la jefa***, have become increasingly widespread.
- Infinitives can be used as nouns:
  Leer es mi pasatiempo favorito.
  Reading is my favourite hobby.
- The process of turning a verb or adjective into a noun is called nominalisation. Masculine adjectives are used for languages:
  francés → (el) francés (French)
- Adjectives of nationality follow the same pattern. The adjective must match the gender of the noun.

la inglesa	the English person (female)
los españoles	Spanish people

- Adding -ito or -ita to a noun changes the meaning of the noun to be 'little'.

librito	a little book

Singular and plural forms

As in English, Spanish nouns can either be singular (one) or plural (more than one).

- Nouns ending in a vowel add *–s* for the plural.
  un año → ***dos años***
  one year → two years
- Nouns ending in a consonant add *–es* for the plural.
  un país → *dos país**es***
  one country → two countries
- For nouns ending in *–z*, change the *z* to *c* and add *–es*:
  *una lu**z*** → *dos luces*
  one light → two lights
- If a noun ends in *–ión*, drop the accent and add *–es*:
  *una situac**ión*** → *dos situaciones*
  one situation → two situations

2 Articles

Definite articles: *el, la los, las* (the)

- The word for 'the' depends on whether the noun it goes with is masculine, feminine, singular or plural.

masculine singular	feminine singular	masculine plural	feminine plural
el	la	los	las

***el** abuelo*	the grandfather
***la** fruta*	the fruit
***los** billetes*	the tickets
***las** palabras*	the words

- When the masculine singular definite article *el* follows the prepositions *de* (from, of) and *a* (at, to), the *e* is omitted to form ***del*** and ***al***.

*¿Cómo vas **al** instituto?*	How do you get to school?
*cerca **del** mar*	near the sea

Indefinite articles: *un, una, unos, unas* (a, an, some)

- The word for 'a / an' and 'some' also depends on whether the noun it goes with is masculine or feminine, singular or plural.

masculine singular	feminine singular	masculine plural	feminine plural
un	una	unos	unas

***un** avión*	a plane
una** biciclet**a	a bicycle
unos** coche**s	some cars

- When talking about jobs, *un* and *una* are not used in Spanish where 'a' or 'an' is used in English.
  Mi padre es electricista. My father's an electrician.
- Spanish uses the definite article more than English, particularly for general statements, or where the noun relates to a concept:
  La educación es importante. Education is important.

The neuter article: *lo*

- Use *lo* with an adjective to mean 'the … thing'. The adjective after *lo* is always masculine and singular.
  lo importante the important thing
- Use it with an adjective + *es que*:
  ***Lo bueno** es que hay fruta fresca.*
  The good thing is that there is fresh fruit.
- Use it with an adjective + *es* + an infinitive:
  ***Lo importante es** comer comida sana.*
  The important thing is to eat healthy food.

3 Adjectives

Feminine and masculine, singular and plural adjectives

In Spanish, adjectives have different endings depending on whether they describe masculine, feminine, singular or plural nouns:

- The masculine singular form usually ends in *–o*:
  *El barco es blanc**o**.* The boat is white.
- If the noun is feminine singular, the adjective will usually end in *–a*:
  *Mi hermana es tranquil**a**.* My sister is quiet.
- Add *–s* to the masculine adjective if the noun is masculine plural:
  *Los barcos son blanc**os**.* The boats are white.
- Add *–s* to the feminine adjective if the noun is feminine plural:
  *Mis hermanas son tranquil**as**.* My sisters are quiet.
- When an adjective describes a group of both masculine and feminine nouns, it has to be in the masculine plural form:
  *Mis padres son alt**os**.* My parents are tall.

- There are exceptions: adjectives that end in *–e* don't change in the feminine:

*un chico inteligen**te***	an intelligent boy
*una chica inteligen**te***	an intelligent girl

- to form the plural, simply add an *–s*:

*unos chicos inteligente**s***	some intelligent boys
*unas chicas inteligente**s***	some intelligent girls

- Adjectives that end in *-ista* don't change in the masculine:

*el chico optimist**a***	the optimistic boy
*la chica optimist**a***	the optimistic girl

- to form the plural, simply add an *–s*:

*unos chicos optimista**s***	some optimistic boys
*unas chicas optimista**s***	some optimistic girls

- Adjectives that end in a consonant (except ***r***) do not change in the feminine:

*un avión **azul***	a blue plane
*una camisa **azul***	a blue shirt

- to form the plural, add *-**es***:

*los aviones azul**es***	the blue planes
*las camisas azul**es***	the blue shirts

- If an adjective ends in *-**z***, change to ***z*** to ***c*** before adding *-**es*** to form the plural:

*unos niños feli**ces***	some happy (little) boys
*unas niñas feli**ces***	some happy (little) girls

- Adjectives of nationality often end in *–o* and follow the same rules as other adjectives ending in *–o*:

*un chico mexican**o***	a Mexican boy
*una chica mexican**a***	a Mexican girl
*unos chicos mexican**os***	some Mexican boys
*unas chicas mexican**as***	some Mexican girls

- For adjectives of nationality that end in a consonant, add *–a* for the feminine singular form, *–es* for the masculine plural form and *–as* for the feminine plural form:

un chico español	a Spanish boy
*una chica español**a***	a Spanish girl
*unos chicos español**es***	some Spanish boys
*unas chicas español**as***	some Spanish girls

- Attention! Some adjectives of nationality, such as *francés*, (French) behave like this:

masculine singular	feminine singular	masculine plural	feminine plural
*franc**és***	*franc**esa***	*franc**eses***	*franc**esas***

- Also note that adjectives of nationality do not begin with a capital letter.
- Spanish verbs 'to be', *ser* and *estar*, are used in different contexts. The usual rule is *ser* describes character, and *estar* an emotion.

Soy artístico.	I am artistic.
¿Estás nervioso?	Are you nervous?

Sometimes the meaning of the adjective changes depending on the use of *ser* or *estar*.

Es listo.	He's clever.
Está listo.	He's ready.

- Adding *-ísimo* or *-ísima* to an adjective means 'very' or 'extremely'. Sometimes to form the adjective you have to remove the *-o* / *-a* ending first.

peligrosísimo	very dangerous
facilísimo	very easy

The position of adjectives

- Most adjectives follow the noun they describe:

*una dieta **sana***	a ***healthy*** diet

- However, a few adjectives, such as *alguno, ninguno, primero, segundo, tercero, bueno* and *malo* come in front of the noun and lose their final *–o* when the following noun is masculine singular. Notice that an accent is sometimes needed to keep the stress on the correct syllable:

ningún *deporte*	no sport
ninguna *idea*	no idea

- The meaning of an adjective can change depending on whether it comes before or after a noun, for example, *único* which can mean 'only' or 'unique'.

Llevo una falda única.	I'm wearing a unique skirt.
Esa es mi única falda.	That's my only skirt.

Comparatives and superlatives

- To make comparisons, use:

  más … que more … than, …er than

  *Mi casa es **más pequeña** que la tuya.*

  My house is **smaller than** yours.

  *La fruta es **más cara** en Inglaterra **que** en España.*

  Fruit is **more expensive** in England **than** in Spain.

  menos … que less … than

  *Mi hermano es **menos alto que** mi padre.*

  My brother is **less tall than** my father.

  tan + … + como as … as

  *Los tomates son **tan sanos como** las naranjas.*

  Tomatoes are **as healthy as** oranges.

- For 'better than', use *mejor que*:

  ***Es mejor** estudiar **que** trabajar.*

  Studying **is better than** working.

- For 'worse than', use *peor que*:

  *Te pagan **peor que** en la ciudad.*

  They pay **worse than** in the city.

- For superlatives, use:

  el / la / los / las + más the most, the …est

  *Esta casa es **la más vieja** de la región.*

  This house is **the oldest** in the area.

  el / la / los / las + menos the least

  *Este hotel es **el menos caro** de la región.*

  This hotel is the least expensive in the area.

Demonstrative adjectives: *este, esta, estos, estas; ese, esa, esos, esas; aquel, aquella, aquellos, aquellas* (this, that, these, those)

- Spanish has three groups of demonstrative adjectives: one group for 'this' and 'these' (*este, esta, estos, estas*), one for 'that' and 'those' (*ese, esa, esos, esas*), and one to indicate more distant things ('that / those over there' – *aquel, aquella, aquellos, aquellas*).

this		**these**	
este	*esta*	*estos*	*estas*
that (not very distant)		**those (not very distant)**	
ese	*esa*	*esos*	*esas*
that (more distant)		**those (more distant)**	
aquel	*aquella*	*aquellos*	*aquellas*

***este** cine* — **this** cinema

***esa** estrella* — **that** star

***aquellas** películas* — **those** films

Indefinite adjectives: *cada, otro, todo, mismo, alguno, ninguno, algún, ningún*

- Although *cada* is an adjective, it never changes:

  ***cada** sección* — **each** section

  ***cada** resultado* — **each** result

- *otro, todo* and *mismo* must agree with the noun they describe:

  ***otra** ciudad* — **another** city

  *la **misma** idea* — the **same** idea

  ***todo** el mundo* — **all** the world (= everyone)

  ***todas** las chicas* — **all** the girls

  *los **mismos** libros* — the **same** books

- *alguno* means 'some' and *ninguno* means 'no, none'. They must agree with the noun they describe.

  ***algunas** chicas* — **some** girls

  ***ningunos** estudiantes* — **no** students

They drop the *–o* ending and gain an accent when they are placed before a masculine singular noun:

***algún** pan* — **some** bread

***ningún** juego* — **no** game

Possessive adjectives

Possessive adjectives are used to demonstrate relations and that something belongs to someone:

mi / mis — my

tu / tus — your

su / sus — his / her / its

- A possessive adjective must agree with the noun that follows it:

  ***mi** padre* — **my** father

  ***mi** madre* — **my** mother

  ***mis** padres* — **my** parents

  ***tu** padre* — **your** father

  ***tu** madre* — **your** mother

  ***tus** padres* — **your** parents

  ***su** pie* — **his / her / its** foot

  ***su** puerta* — **his / her / its** door

  ***sus** ventanas* — **his / her / its** windows

- When the relation or possession is plural the adjectives are:

  nuestro — our

  vuestro — your

  su / sus — their*

They also must agree with the noun that follows them:

nuestro *padre*	**our** father
nuestra *madre*	**our** mother
nuestros *padres*	**our** parents
vuestro *padre*	**your** father
vuestra *madre*	**your** mother
vuestros *amigos*	**your** friends
su *hermano*	**their** brother
su *hermana*	**their** sister
sus *profesores*	**their** teachers

- Spanish doesn't have three different words for 'his', 'her' and 'its'. With a Spanish possessive adjective, what counts is whether the noun it describes is masculine, feminine, singular or plural. Like other adjectives, they agree with their noun.

4 Adverbs

Adverbs are used with a verb, an adjective or another adverb to express how, when, where, or to what extent something happens.

Adverbs of manner

These adverbs describe how something happens. They are used placed directly after the verb.

- Many Spanish adverbs are formed by adding *–mente* (the equivalent of '–ly' in English) to the feminine form of the adjective:

masculine adjective	feminine adjective	adverb
rápido	*rápida*	*rápidamente* - quickly
tranquilo	*tranquila*	*tranquilamente* - slowly

- Some common adverbs are completely irregular:

bien	well
Habla ***bien****.*	He / She speaks **well**.
mal	badly
Come ***mal****.*	He / She eats **badly**.

Adverbs of time

hoy	today
mañana	tomorrow
ayer	yesterday
pasado mañana	the day after tomorrow
ahora	now
ya	already

- Adverbs of time are usually placed at the beginning or end of a sentence:
  Ayer *yo fui al cine.* **Yesterday** I went to the cinema.
  ¿Quieres ir conmigo ***mañana****?*
  Do you want to go with me **tomorrow**?

Adverbs of frequency

a veces	sometimes
frecuentemente / a menudo	often
siempre	always
raramente	rarely, not very often

Adverbs of sequence

antes	before
después	then, afterwards
luego	next
por último	finally

Adverbs of place

Adverbs of place are positioned before the verb they are describing.

dentro de	inside
fuera de	outside
aquí	here
allí	(over) there
lejos	far

Quantifiers and intensifiers

- This group of adverbs (qualifying words) enables you to indicate intensity and quantity when you use an adjective or adverb:

bastante	enough / quite
demasiado	too (much)
mucho	a lot
un poco	a little
muy	very

La gramática es un poco complicada, pero es ***bastante*** *interesante.*

Grammar is a bit complicated, but it's **quite** interesting.

Interrogative adverbs

- Note that these words all have an accent when they are used as an interrogative.
  ¿cómo? how?
  ¿cuándo? when?
  ¿dónde? where?
  ¿por qué? why?

5 Pronouns

Subject pronouns: *yo, tú, él, ella, usted, nosotros, nosotras, vosotros, vosotras, ellos, ellas, ustedes* (I, you, he, she, it, we, they)

In Spanish, subject pronouns are usually only used with the verb to emphasise who or what performs the action.

yo – I
tú – you
él – he / it
ella – she / it
usted – you (formal)
nosotros – we (m) *nosotras* – we (f)
vosotros – you (m) *vosotras* – you (f)
ellos – they (m)
ellas – they (f)
ustedes – you (formal plural)
***Ella** es estudiante, pero **él** ha acabado de estudiar.*
She is a student, but **he** has finished studying.

- In Spanish there are two ways to translate 'you': *tú* (plural: *vosotros*) and *usted* (plural: *ustedes*).

Use *tú* when talking to someone (one person) of your own age or to someone in your family.

Use *vosotros* when talking to more than one person of your own age or to your relatives.

Use *usted* when talking to an adult not in your family (e.g. your teacher).

Use *ustedes* when talking to more than one adult not in your family.

Direct object pronouns: *me, te, lo / la, nos, os, los / las*

Direct object pronouns replace a noun that is not the subject of the verb.

singular	plural
me – me	*nos* – us
te – you	*os* – you
lo – him / it (masculine)	*los* – them (masculine)
la – her / it (feminine)	*las* – them (feminine)

- These pronouns come in front of the verb, unlike in English:
  ***Los** compré en Barcelona.* I bought **them** in Barcelona.

- If there are two verbs in a construction, the direct object pronoun can go before the first verb or it can attach to the second verb.
  ***Lo** puedes comprar en Barcelona.*
  You can buy **it** in Barcelona.
  *Puedes comprar**lo** en Barcelona*
  You can buy **it** in Barcelona.

- A positive imperative form of the verb attaches the direct object pronoun to the end of it, usually with an accent placed on the first vowel:
  *¡Cómpra**los**!* Buy **them**!

Indirect object pronouns: *me, te, le, nos, os, les*

Indirect object pronouns are used to replace a noun which is not the direct object of the verb.

singular	plural
me – (to) me *te* – (to) you *le* – (to) him / her / it	*nos* – (to) us *os* – (to) you *les* – (to) them

***Les** dio mil euros. **Le** escribieron para dar**le** las gracias.*
He gave **them** a thousand euros. They wrote **to him** to thank **him**.

- If there are two verbs in a construction, the indirect object pronoun can go before the first verb, or it can attach to the second verb.
  *Quiero dar**les** mil euros.*
  I want to give **them** a thousand euros.
  ***Le** puedo ayudar.* I can help **him**.

- A positive imperative form of the verb attaches the direct object pronoun to the end of it, usually with an accent placed on the first vowel:
  *Si no puedes hacerlo, **dámelo**.*
  If you can't do it, **give it** to me.

- Note that when two pronouns are used together in the same sentence, the indirect object pronoun always comes before the direct object pronoun.
  *Tengo un móvil. Mis padres **me lo** regalaron por mi cumpleaños.*
  I have a mobile. My parents gave **it to me** for my birthday.
  me – indirect object pronoun, *lo* – direct object pronoun

Reflexive pronouns: *me, te, se, nos, os, se*

Reflexive pronouns are used in Spanish when the subject and object of the verb are the same. They come before the verb.

singular	plural
me – myself *te* – yourself (informal) *se* – himself, herself, itself, yourself (formal)	*nos* – ourselves *os* – yourselves (informal) *se* – themselves, yourselves (formal)

***Me** lavo.* I am washing **myself**.

- If there are two verbs in a construction, the reflexive pronoun can go before the first verb or it can attach to the second verb.
  ***Se** debe lavar* → *Debe lavar**se**.*
  One should wash (themselves).
- A positive imperative form of the verb attaches the reflexive pronoun to the end of it, usually with an accent placed on the first vowel:
  *¡Láva**te**!* Wash **yourself**!

Interrogative pronouns: *cuánto, cuál, quién*

- As in English, interrogative pronouns usually come at the beginning of a sentence:
  ***¿Cuántas** personas viven en la casa?*
  How many people live in the house?
  ***¿Cuál** de estas preguntas es más difícil?*
  Which one of these questions is harder?
  ***¿Cuáles** prefieres?* **Which ones** do you prefer?
  ***¿Qué** quieres?* **What** do you want?
  ***¿Quién** habla?* **Who** is speaking?
  ***¿Quiénes** son?* **Who** are they?
- However, if a preposition is used with the interrogative, it is the preposition which comes first:
  *¿Con **quién** vas a la fiesta?*
  Who are you going to the party with?

Indefinite pronouns: *algo, alguien, alguno, ninguno*

- The Spanish for 'something' is *algo*:
  *¿Quieres **algo** de comer?*
  Do you want **something** to eat?
- The Spanish for 'someone' is *alguien*:
  *Busco a **alguien**.* I'm looking for **someone**.
- The Spanish for 'some' or 'any' is *alguno*:
  *Muchas de mis asignaturas son fáciles pero **algunas** son difíciles.*
  Many of my subjects are easy but **some** are difficult.
- The Spanish for 'none' is *ninguno*:
  ***Ninguno** de ellos me preguntaron.*
  None of them asked me.

Relative pronouns: *que, lo que, el cual, la cual, los cuales, las cuales*

Relative pronouns are used to link phrases together.

- *que* is used as the subject of the relative clause. It can refer to people and things, and means 'who', 'that' or 'which':
  *el amigo **que** vive en Barcelona*
  the friend **who** lives in Barcelona
- Remember that *que* is not optional. Although it is often not translated in English, you cannot leave it out in Spanish.
  *La película **que** estaba viendo era muy divertida.*
  The film (**that**) I was watching was very funny.
- Use *lo que* to refer to a general idea:

***Lo que** me gusta de mi barrio es que hay un centro comercial.*

What I like about my neighbourhood is that there is a shopping centre.

- The pronouns *el que, la que, los que, las que* (note the necessary agreement with singular, plural, masculine and feminine nouns) are used after prepositions, to refer to both people and things:
  *Mi hermana, **la que** es peluquera, vive en Madrid.*
  My sister, **the one who** is a hairdresser, lives in Madrid.
- *el cual, la cual, los cuales, las cuales* are relative pronouns that can be used in place of *el que, la que, los que* and *las que*. They are not used in everyday conversation and tend to be used more in formal written Spanish:
  *Me queda un poco de dinero, **el cual** no quiero gastar.*
  I have a little money left, **which** I don't want to spend.

Disjunctive pronouns: *mí, ti, él, ella, usted, nosotros, nosotras, vosotros, vosotras, ellos, ellas, ustedes*

These are also called emphatic pronouns.

- Use them for emphasis:
  ***Para mí**, las vacaciones de invierno son las más divertidas.*
  For me, winter holidays are the most fun.

- Use them after a preposition:
  ***A mí** no me gusta el pescado.* **Me**, I don't like fish.
- To say 'with me', 'with you (*tú*)' there is a special form:
  conmigo with me
  contigo with you
  *Mi hermano viene **conmigo**.*
  My brother is coming **with me**.

Possessive pronouns

A possessive pronoun is used to replace a possessive adjective and its noun.

¿Ése es su perro? *No, no es el **suyo**.*
Is that their dog? No, it isn't **theirs**.

masculine singular	feminine singular	masculine plural	feminine plural	
mío	*mía*	*míos*	*mías*	mine
tuyo	*tuya*	*tuyos*	*tuyas*	yours
suyo	*suya*	*suyos*	*suyas*	his / hers / its
nuestro	*nuestra*	*nuestros*	*nuestras*	ours
vuestro	*vuestra*	*vuestros*	*vuestras*	yours
suyo	*suya*	*suyos*	*suyas*	theirs

Use possessive pronouns with the definite article *el / la / los / las* and remember that they must agree with the noun they replace.

*Me gusta más la casa de Julia que **la mía**.*
I like Julia's house more than **mine**.

Relative clauses using wh- pronouns: *cuando, donde*

You can link phrases together with the question words *cuando* and *donde*.

*Me compré un vestido **cuando** fui de compras.*
I bought a dress **when** I went shopping.
*Fui a un café **donde** tomé un bocadillo.*
I went to a restaurant **where** I had a sandwich.

Demonstrative pronouns: *esto, eso, aquello*

There are also three neutral demonstrative pronouns: *esto*, *eso* and *aquello*. These do not agree in number or gender with a noun because they represent an idea rather than a person or a thing:

***Eso** es cierto.* **That**'s true.
*Martina es demasiado habladora. No me gusta **eso**.*
Martina is too talkative. I don't like **that**.

6 Verbs

- Spanish verbs have different endings depending on who is doing the action and whether the action takes place in the past, the present or the future. The verb tables at the end of the grammar section set out the patterns of endings for some useful verbs.
- When using a name or a singular noun instead of a pronoun, use the same form of the verb as for *él / ella*:
  *Jamie **habla** español.* Jamie **speaks** Spanish.
- When using two names or a plural noun, use the same form of the verb as for *ellos / ellas*:
  *Laura y Javier **viven** en Sevilla.*
  Laura and Javier **live** in Seville.
- When referring to yourself and someone else, use the same form of the verb as for *nosotros*:
  *Laura y yo **vamos** a Madrid.*
  Laura and I **are going** to Madrid.

The infinitive

The infinitive is the form of the verb you find in a dictionary, e.g. *hablar*, *comer*, *vivir*. It never changes.

- When two verbs follow each other, the second one is always in the infinitive.
  ***Me gusta dormir** bien.* **I like to sleep** well.
  ***Prefiero salir** con mis amigos.*
  I prefer to go out with my friends.
- *ir a* + infinitive is a useful expression meaning 'to be going to do something' in the immediate future. The verb *ir* is conjugated, but the second verb will remain in the infinitive. The preposition *a* is always used:
  ***Voy a visitar** España.* **I am going to visit** Spain.
- *llegar a* + infinitive means 'to manage to' or 'to succeed in'.
  ***Llegaré a ver** el efecto.* **I will get to see** the effect.
- *acabar de* + infinitive means 'to have just done something very recently'. Note that the preposition *de* is needed in this expression.
  ***Acabas de invitar** a muchos amigos.*
  You have just invited many friends.

7 Verb tenses

The present indicative

- Use the present tense to describe:
  something that is taking place now:
  ***Como** una manzana.* **I am eating** an apple.
  something that happens regularly:
  ***Voy** al cine muy a menudo.* **I often go** to the cinema.
- Verb endings change depending on who is doing the action:
  *Mi amigo **habla** español.* My friend **speaks** Spanish.
  ***Hablamos** inglés.* We **speak** English.
- Most verbs follow a regular pattern, as in the table below. See the verb tables on pages 194–197 for irregular verb forms.

	–*ar* verbs	**–*er* verbs**	**–*ir* verbs**
	hablar – to speak	*comer* – to eat	*vivir* – to live
(yo)	*habl**o***	*com**o***	*viv**o***
(tú)	*habl**as***	*com**es***	*viv**es***
(él / ella)	*habl**a***	*com**e***	*viv**e***
(nosotros)	*habl**amos***	*com**emos***	*viv**imos***
(vosotros)	*habl**áis***	*com**éis***	*viv**ís***
(ellos / ellas)	*habl**an***	*com**en***	*viv**en***

Other **–*ar*** verbs:

ayudar to help
ganar to win
invitar to invite
tocar to play

Other **–*er*** verbs:

deber to owe
proteger to protect

Other **–*ir*** verbs:

producir to produce
salir to go out

A few common verbs have an irregular first person in the present tense:

dar → *doy*
decir → *digo*
estar → *estoy*
hacer → *hago*
poner → *pongo*
saber → *sé*
salir → *salgo*
ser → *soy*
tener → *tengo*
venir → *vengo*
conocer → *conozco*
parecer → *parezco*
coger → *cojo*

Radical-changing verbs

- The biggest group of Spanish irregular verbs is called radical-changing, or stem-changing verbs.
  The first part of the verb changes when stressed:
  In one type, *u* changes to *ue*
  jugar – to play
  ***jue**go* *jugamos*
  ***jue**gas* *jugáis*
  ***jue**ga* ***jue**gan*
  In another type, *o* changes to *ue*
  poder – to be able to
  ***pue**do* *podemos*
  ***pue**des* *podéis*
  ***pue**de* ***pue**den*
  In another type, *e* changes to *ie*
  preferir – to prefer
  *pref**ie**ro* *preferimos*
  *pref**ie**res* *preferís*
  *pref**ie**re* *pref**ie**ren*

The changes do not happen in the *nosotros* and *vosotros* parts of the verb, because the stress is not on the stem.

The gerund

- The gerund (or present participle) is formed by replacing the infinitive verb ending *–ar* with *–ando*, and the *–er* and *–ir* verb endings with *–iendo*:

  hablar → *hablando*

  *Estoy **hablando**.* I am **talking**.

  comer → *comiendo*

  *¿Qué estás **comiendo**?* What are you **eating**?

  salir → *saliendo*

  *Ana está **saliendo**.* *Ana is **going out**.*

Some irregular gerunds are:

dormir → *durmiendo*
leer → *leyendo*
oír → *oyendo*
preferir → *prefiriendo*
sentir → *sintiendo*
vestir → *vistiendo*

Note that where in English we often use the gerund of a verb in sentences like:

I love **swimming**. My brother prefers **going** on bike rides.

Spanish uses the infinitive.

*Me gusta **nadar**. Mi hermano prefiere **dar** paseos en bici.*

The gerund is also used to convey ongoing actions in the present.

- *seguir* + gerund means 'to continue' or 'to still be' doing something. The verb 'seguir' is conjugated, and the second verb is in the present participle.

  ***Sigo estudiando** español.*

  I am still studying Spanish.

- *llevar* + time period + gerund means 'to have been doing something' for a certain amount of time. The verb *llevar* is conjugated, and the time period is specified, followed by the present participle.

  ***Llevo dos años estudiando** medicina.*

  I have been studying medicine **for two years.**

The present continuous

The present continuous tense is the Spanish equivalent of the English form 'I am ...ing, you are ...ing' etc. It indicates something that is happening at the time of speaking. It is formed by adding the gerund to the present tense of *estar*:

*¿Qué **estás leyendo**?* What **are you reading**?

***Estoy leyendo** un libro estupendo.*

I'm reading a fantastic book.

The preterite

- Use the preterite tense to talk about a single, completed event in the past.

  *Por la tarde **recibí** un mensaje de mi amiga.*

  In the afternoon **I got** a message from my friend.

  Regular verbs:

To form the preterite tense, remove the infinitive endings, *–ar*, *–er* or *–ir* to leave the stem, then add the following endings:

	***–ar* verbs**	***–er* verbs**	***–ir* verbs**
	hablar – to speak	*comer* – to eat	*vivir* – to live
(yo)	*habl**é***	*com**í***	*viv**í***
(tú)	*habl**aste***	*com**iste***	*viv**iste***
(él / ella)	*habl**ó***	*com**ió***	*viv**ió***
(nosotros)	*habl**amos***	*com**imos***	*viv**imos***
(vosotros)	*habl**asteis***	*com**isteis***	*viv**isteis***
(ellos / ellas)	*habl**aron***	*com**ieron***	*viv**ieron***

Note that the endings for *–er* and *–ir* verbs are the same.

- Some regular verbs have spelling changes in the first person in the preterite tense. These changes are there in order to keep the consonant sounds the same:

  empezar → *empe**cé*** to begin → I began
  jugar → *ju**gué*** to play → I played
  sacar → *sa**qué*** to take → I took out
  tocar → *to**qué*** to play (instrument) → I played

- Irregular verbs:

Some common Spanish verbs are irregular in the preterite tense: *ser* and *estar*, *hacer*, *ir*, *poner*, *tener* and *ver*. The verb tables on pages 178–181 set out the patterns for these. The verbs *ser* (to be) and *ir* (to go) are the same in the preterite and you have to use the context to work out which verb is being used:

fui I was / went
fuiste you were / went
fue he / she / it, you was / were / went
fuimos we were / went
fuisteis you were / went
fueron they, you were / went

*Por la mañana **fuimos** al partido.*

We went to the match in the morning.

*El ambiente en el estadio **fue** fantástico.*

The atmosphere in the stadium **was** fantastic.

The present perfect

- Use the present perfect tense to say what you have done recently:
  He comprado *un móvil.* **I've bought** a mobile phone.
- The perfect tense is formed with the present tense of *haber* (to have) plus the past participle:
  haber – to have

he	*hemos*
has	*habéis*
ha	*han*

To form the past participle add *–ado* to the stem of *–ar* verbs and *–ido* to the stem of *–er* and *–ir* verbs.

hablar → *habl**ado***	to live → lived
comer → *com**ido***	to speak → spoken
vivir → *viv**ido***	to eat → eaten

Este marzo ***he ido*** *a Valencia a ver la fiesta.*

This March **I went** to Valencia to see the fiesta.

Some Spanish verbs have irregular past participles. Here are some common ones:

decir → *dicho*	to say → said
hacer → *hecho*	to make → made
volver → *vuelto*	to come back → came back
poner → *puesto*	to put → put
ver → *visto*	to see → saw / seen

Ya ***hemos visto*** *esta película.*

We have already **seen** this film.

The imperfect

- Use the imperfect tense to say what was happening at a certain time in the past:
  Trabajaba *entonces en Madrid.*
  At that time **I was working** in Madrid.
- To describe something that used to happen regularly in the past:
  Iba *al cine todos los sábados.*
  I used to go to the cinema every Saturday.
- To form the imperfect tense of regular verbs, add the following endings to the stem of the verb:

	–ar **verbs**	***–er*** **verbs**	***–ir*** **verbs**
	hablar – to speak	*comer* – to eat	*vivir* – to live
(yo)	*habl**aba***	*com**ía***	*viv**ía***
(tú)	*habl**abas***	*com**ías***	*viv**ías***
(él / ella)	*habl**aba***	*com**ía***	*viv**ía***
(nosotros)	*habl**ábamos***	*com**íamos***	*viv**íamos***
(vosotros)	*habl**abais***	*com**íais***	*viv**íais***
(ellos / ellas)	*habl**aban***	*com**ían***	*viv**ían***

En los cumpleaños siempre ***preparábamos*** *una cena especial.*

- **We always used to prepare** a special meal for birthdays.
- Three common Spanish verbs are irregular in the imperfect tense: *ser*, *ir* and *ver*:

	ser **– to be**	***ir*** **– to go**	***ver*** **– to see**
(yo)	*era*	*iba*	*veía*
(tú)	*eras*	*ibas*	*veías*
(él / ella)	*era*	*iba*	*veía*
(nosotros)	*éramos*	*íbamos*	*veíamos*
(vosotros)	*erais*	*ibais*	*veíais*
(ellos / ellas)	*eran*	*iban*	*veían*

Después de la cena ***íbamos*** *a la iglesia a celebrar la Misa de Gallo a medianoche.*

After the meal **we used to go** to church to celebrate Midnight Mass.

The imperfect continuous

The imperfect continuous tense is used to describe an ongoing action more vividly. It is formed using the imperfect of *estar* and the gerund:

Estaba comiendo *cuando llegó mi hermano.*

I was eating when my brother arrived.

Preterite or imperfect?

To help you decide between the preterite and the imperfect:

Remember that the following time expressions describe a single, completed action and should be used with the preterite:

ayer	yesterday
el otro día	the other day
la semana pasada	last week
hace tres años	three years ago

These time expressions indicate a repeated action and are used with the imperfect:

siempre	always
frecuentemente	frequently
a veces	sometimes
todos los días	every day

The immediate future

- Use the present tense of *ir* + *a* followed by an infinitive to say what you are going to do or what is going to happen:
  Voy a continuar *trabajando hasta los 65 años.*
  I'm going to carry on working until the age of 65.
- To talk about possibility in the immediate future, use *si*.
  Si sigues estos consejos, ***vas a salvar*** *a uno o más árboles.*
  If you follow this advice, **you are going to save** one or more trees.

The future

- The future tense expresses what will happen or will be happening in the future:
  En el futuro, las especies en peligro de extinción ***desaparecerán*** *por completo.*
  In the future, endangered species **will disappear** completely.
- You can also use *si* to talk about possibility in the future.
  Si sigues estos consejos, ***podrás ahorrar*** *57.000 litros de agua.*
  If you follow this advice, **you will save** 57,000 litres of water.
- To form the future tense, add the correct ending to the infinitive of the verb:

	–*ar* verbs	**–*er* verbs**	**–*ir* verbs**
	hablar – to speak	*comer* – to eat	*vivir* – to live
(yo)	*hablar**é***	*comer**é***	*vivir**é***
(tú)	*hablar**ás***	*comer**ás***	*vivir**ás***
(él / ella)	*hablar**á***	*comer**á***	*vivir**á***
(nosotros)	*hablar**emos***	*comer**emos***	*vivir**emos***
(vosotros)	*hablar**éis***	*comer**éis***	*vivir**éis***
(ellos / ellas)	*hablar**án***	*comer**án***	*vivir**án***

- A few verbs have an irregular stem in the future (see the verb tables on pages 178–181), but all have the same future endings:

hacer – to do	*haré, harás, hará, haremos, haréis, harán*
poder – to be able	*podré*, etc.
poner – to put	*pondré*, etc.
tener – to have	*tendré, tendrás, tendrá, tendremos, tendréis, tendrán*
haber (*hay*) – there is / are	*habrá*

The conditional

- You use the conditional in Spanish when 'would' is used in English:
  Me gustaría ir *a Perú.* **I would like to go** to Peru.
  Sería *una oportunidad fantástica.*
  It would be a fantastic opportunity.
- The conditional has the same stem as the future tense and the same endings as the imperfect tense of *–er* and *–ir* verbs:

	–*ar* verbs	**–*er* verbs**	**–*ir* verbs**
	hablar – to speak	*comer* – to eat	*vivir* – to live
(yo)	*hablar**ía***	*comer**ía***	*vivir**ía***
(tú)	*hablar**ías***	*comer**ías***	*vivir**ías***
(él / ella)	*hablar**ía***	*comer**ía***	*vivir**ía***
(nosotros)	*hablar**íamos***	*comer**íamos***	*vivir**íamos***
(vosotros)	*hablar**íais***	*comer**íais***	*vivir**íais***
(ellos / ellas)	*hablar**ían***	*comer**ían***	*vivir**ían***

As the conditional tense uses the same stem as the future tense, the irregular stems are exactly the same as the future tense irregulars.

The imperative

- Use the imperative to give advice or instructions. They are either informal (*tú / vosotros*) or formal (*usted / ustedes*).
- To form positive commands with regular verbs: For *tú*, simply use the *tú* form of the verb, but without the final *–s*:

Come *mucha fruta.*	**Eat** a lot of fruit.
Compra *aquel vestido.*	**Buy** that dress.

For the *vosotros* form, remove the *–r* from the end of the infinitive and replace it with *–d*:

Escuchad *con atención.*	**Listen** carefully.
Escribid *la carta.*	**Write** the letter.

Usted and *ustedes* use the third person of the present subjunctive:

Hable *inglés.*	**Speak** English.
Coman *las patatas fritas.*	**Eat** the chips.

Here are some common irregular imperative forms:

	tú	**vosotros**	**usted**	**ustedes**
decir	*di*	*decid*	*diga*	*digan*
hacer	*haz*	*haced*	*haga*	*hagan*
ir	*ve*	*id*	*vaya*	*vayan*
ser	*sé*	*sed*	*sea*	*sean*
tener	*ten*	*tened*	*tenga*	*tengan*
venir	*ven*	*venid*	*venga*	*vengan*
poner	*pon*	*poned*	*ponga*	*pongan*
salir	*sal*	*salid*	*salga*	*salgan*

The subjunctive

- The subjunctive is a form of the verb that is used when there is an element of wishing or doubt.
- It is also used in certain set expressions of surprise or exclamation:

¡Viva la Reina!	Long live the Queen!
¡Que aproveche!	Enjoy your meal!

- Some verbal expressions are followed by the subjunctive: Wishes, advice and requests such as *querer que, pedir que, decir que.*

Mi madre no quiere que salga *con ese chico.*

My mother doesn't want me to go out with that boy.

Emotional reactions: joy, hope, sorrow, anger, fear such as *me gusta que, siento que:*

Tengo miedo de que me esté *buscando.*

I'm afraid that she is looking for me.

Doubt, uncertainty, possibility such as es *posible que, es probable que, no es cierto que:*

No es posible que yo venga *ahora.*

It's not possible that I will come now.

Expressions of purpose: *para que, a menos que:*

Te prestaré dinero ***para que puedas*** *ir de vacaciones.*

I'll lend you some money **so you can go** on holiday.

Conjunctions of time – *cuando, hasta que* – when they refer to the future:

Cuando vengas *vamos a hacer la fiesta.*

When you come we'll have a party.

- To form the present subjunctive, take the *yo* form of the present tense of the verb and replace the –o ending with the following endings:

	–*ar* verbs	**–*er* verbs**	**–*ir* verbs**
	hablar – to speak	*comer* – to eat	*vivir* – to live
(yo)	*habl**e***	*com**a***	*viv**a***
(tú)	*habl**es***	*com**as***	*viv**as***
(él / ella)	*habl**e***	*com**a***	*viv**a***

8 Reflexive verbs

Reflexive verbs have a reflexive pronoun in front of the verb:

(yo)	*me quejo*	I complain
(tú)	*te quejas*	you complain
(él / ella)	*se queja*	he / she complains
(usted)	*se queja*	you complain (formal singular)
(nosotros)	*nos quejamos*	we complain
(vosotros)	*os quejáis*	you complain
(ellos / ellas)	*se quejan*	they complain
(ustedes)	*se quejan*	you complain (formal plural)

- Plural reflexive pronouns (*nos*, *os*, *se*) with certain verbs describe the action as being to done to 'each other'

  ***Nos vemos** todas las semanas.*

  We see each other every week.

  Os entendéis. You understand each other.

  Se besan. They kiss (each other).

9 Modal verbs and expressions

- Modal verbs express things like ability, desire, permission, possibility, obligation, knowledge. For example, they say how you **can**, **might**, **should**, **must** etc. do something. In Spanish, verbs that express these meanings are always followed by the infinitive.

  poder can (to be able to)

  deber must (to have to)

  tener que to have to

  ***Puedo** descargar la película de Internet.*

  I can download the film from the Internet.

  *Para participar en el concurso, **debes** mandar un correo electrónico a…*

  To enter the competition, **you must** send an email to…

  *Después de cenar, **tenéis** que hacer los deberes.*

  After dinner, **you have to** do your homework.

  querer (to want to)

  ***Quiero** jugar a videojuego.*

  I want to play the videogame.

  saber (to know how to)

  *¿**Sabes** tocar la giutarra?*

  Do you know how to play guitar?

  Fixed phrases that are modal verb + infinitive:

  quisiera – I / he / she / it would like to

  ***Quisiera** dar las gracias a mis profesores.*

  I would like to thank my teachers.

  me / te / le gustaría – I / he / she / it would like to

  ***Le gustaría** ir a España.* He would like to go to Spain.

10 Negatives

- To make a sentence negative, you normally put *no* before the verb:

  ***No** tengo dinero.* I haven't any money.

- Other common negative expressions: *nunca, nadie, nada, ni … ni ninguno, ya no, tampoco*; never, no one, nothing, neither … nor no / not any, no longer / no more, neither / either. There are two ways of using *nunca, nadie, nada*. They can go at the start of the sentence or *no* can go before the verb with *nunca, nadie, nada* after the verb.

  nunca / jamás never

  ***No** voy **nunca** a Madrid. / **Nunca** voy a Madrid.*

  I **never** go to Madrid.

  nadie no one

  ***No** habla **nadie**. / **Nadie** habla.* **No one** talks.

  nada nothing

  ***No** me preocupa **nada**. / **Nada** me preocupa.*

  I am not worried about **anything**.

  ni … ni neither … nor

  *No soy **ni** guapo **ni** feo.*

  I'm **neither** good-looking **nor** ugly.

  no … ningún (o / a) no / not any

  ***No tengo ningún** problema.* I **don't have a** problem.

  ya no no longer / no more

  ***Ya no** vivo en esa ciudad.*

  I **no longer** live in that city.

  tampoco neither / either

  *No me gusta el fútbol **tampoco**. / **Tampoco** me gusta el fútbol.*

  I don't like football **either**.

11 Questions (Interrogatives)

- Forming questions in Spanish is easy. You can turn statements into questions by adding an inverted question mark at the beginning and a question mark at the end:

  Nati habla español. Nati speaks Spanish.

  ¿Nati habla español? Does Nati speak Spanish?

- These are common question words – note that they all have an accent:

  ¿Dónde? Where?

  ¿Cómo? How?

  ¿Cuál(es)? What? (Which?)

  ¿Cuándo? When?

  ¿Cuánto? How much?

  ¿Qué? What?

  ¿Quién(es)? Who?

  ¿Por qué? Why?

- When a question word is used, it is followed by the verb and then the subject:

  *¿**Qué** hace la chica?* **What** is the girl doing?

  *¿**Dónde** está Ana?* **Where** is Ana?

- In Spanish, you can form a question and omit the subject entirely:

  ¿Dónde está (Daniel)? Where is **he** (Daniel)?

12 Impersonal verbs

- The most common impersonal verbs in Spanish are *gustar* (to like) and *encantar* (to love).
  Me gusta esta isla.
- This sentence means 'I like this island.' Its literal translation, however, is 'This island pleases me.'
- Note that you need to include the indirect object pronoun to show who is doing the liking:
  *¿**Te** gusta esta isla? Sí, **me** encanta.*
  Do you like this island? Yes, I love it.
  ***Me** preocupan las emisiones de CO2.*
  I worry about CO2 emissions.
- Here are other impersonal verb expressions:

hay	there is / are
había	there was / were

  ***Hay** muchas cosas que hacer.*
  There are many things to do.
- The expression *hay que* means 'one must'

***Hay que** ser honesto.*	**You have to** be honest.

- The pronoun 'se' and the correctly conjugated verb express a general 'you / one' statement:

***No se puede** fumar aquí.*	**You can't** smoke here.

  ***Se necesita** pasaporte para viajar.*
  You need a passport to travel.
- The verb *hacer* and a noun is used to describe weather:

Hace sol	It's sunny.
Hace frío	It's cold.

- Other impersonal phrases:

vale la pena + infinitive	it's worth + present participle
***Vale la pena hacer** ejercicio.*	**It's worth doing** exercise.
hace falta + infinitive	it's necessary
***Hace falta** comer bien.*	**One must** eat well.

13 The passive

- The passive is used to say what is done to someone or something. It is formed from *ser* and a past participle:

active form:

Los habitantes construyeron el castillo.

The inhabitants built the castle.

passive form:

El castillo fue construido por los habitantes.

The castle was built by the inhabitants.

- The passive is quite rare in Spanish – it is very formal. To avoid using the passive, Spanish speakers often use the reflexive pronoun *se* and the third person singular or plural of the verb:

***Se comió** la torta.*	The cake was eaten.
***Se venden** caramelos aquí.*	Sweets are sold here.

14 Uses of *ser* and *estar*

- *ser* and *estar* both mean 'to be'.
  ser describes who someone is, or what something is.

***Es** mi hermana.*	**She is** my sister.
***Es** una revista.*	**It is** a magazine.

  It describes something that is unlikely to change.

*Madrid **es grande**.*	Madrid **is big.**
*Mi madre **es habladora**.*	My mother **is chatty.**

  estar describes the location of someone or something.
  *Mis padres **están en Barcelona**.*
  My parents **are in Barcelona**.
  It is used with the past participle to describe a condition that might change. In such expressions the past participle works like an adjective, agreeing with its noun.

***Estamos preocupados**.*	We are worried.

15 Expressions with *tener*

- *tener* is a useful verb in Spanish. As well as its basic meaning 'to have', it is used in a range of expressions:
  tener que — to have to
  tener sed / hambre / sueño / miedo / frío / calor / suerte
  to be thirsty / hungry / tired / afraid / cold / hot / lucky
  tener prisa — to be in a hurry
  tener éxito — to be successful

16 Prepositions

Prepositions of place with *estar*

- Because *estar* is the verb for 'to be' when you want to state where something is, the following prepositions are often seen after *estar*.

arriba	upstairs, above
debajo de	under
delante de	in front of
detrás de	behind
encima de	on top of
enfrente de	opposite
a la derecha de	to the right of
a la izquierda de	to the left of
al lado de	next to

- Prepositions with the points of the compass:

en el norte	in the north
al sur de	in / to the south of
en el centro de	in the centre of

Verbs with prepositions

Many Spanish verbs are followed by a particular preposition, which you need to learn. Here is a list of common combinations. If you are still unsure which preposition to use with a verb, you can check in a dictionary.

Verbs followed by *a*	*aprender a, atreverse a, ayudar a, decidirse a, empezar a, ir a, llegar a, volver a*	to learn to, to dare to, to help to, to decide to, to begin to, to go to, to arrive at, to return to / to do something again
Verbs followed by *de*	*acabar de, acordarse de, dejar de, olvidarse de, terminar de, tratar de, ir de*	to have just (done s / th), to remember to, to stop (doing s / th), to forget to, to finish, to try to, to go for / on / to go …ing
Verbs followed by *en*	*consistir en, insistir en, pensar en*	to consist of, to insist on, to think about
Verbs followed by *con*	*contar con, soñar con*	to count on, to dream about

The personal *a*

- When the object of a verb is a person, you need to include the personal *a* before that person:
  *Vi **a** María en el cine.* I saw Maria in the cinema.

de

- When you want to say that something belongs to someone or someplace, use *de* before the person or place:
  La casa de Miguel. Miguel's house.
  Las tiendas de la ciudad. The city's shops.

para, sin + infinitive

- *para* means 'in order to', 'for the purpose of', 'intended for':
  ***para** reducir la contaminación* **to** reduce pollution
  *Esta carta es **para** ti.* This letter is **for** you.
- *sin* means 'without':
  ***sin** decir nada* without a word
  *Salí **sin** desayunar.* I left without having breakfast.

17 Expressions of time

antes de and *después de*

- To indicate sequences of events, you can use *antes de / después de* + infinitive:
  ***Antes de salir** de casa, tomé un café con leche.*
  Before leaving home, I drank a white coffee.
  ***Después de llegar** al instituto, compré fruta para desayunar.*
  After arriving at school, I bought some fruit for breakfast.

desde hace

- To say how long you have been doing something which you are still doing, use the present tense with *desde hace*:
  *Vivo en Madrid **desde hace** diez años.*
  I have been living in Madrid **for** ten years.

18 Conjunctions

The following words are used to link parts of sentences together:

pero but
*Hace frío **pero** no me importa.*
It's cold **but** I don't mind.
porque because
*Estoy viendo la tele **porque** está nevando.*
I'm watching television **because** it is snowing.

19 Numbers, days, dates and time

1 *uno*	17 *diecisiete*
2 *dos*	18 *dieciocho*
3 *tres*	19 *diecinueve*
4 *cuatro*	20 *veinte*
5 *cinco*	21 *veintiuno*
6 *seis*	22 *veintidós*
7 *siete*	23 *veintitrés*
8 *ocho*	24 *veinticuatro*
9 *nueve*	25 *veinticinco*
10 *diez*	26 *veintiséis*
11 *once*	27 *veintisiete*
12 *doce*	28 *veintiocho*
13 *trece*	29 *veintinueve*
14 *catorce*	30 *treinta*
15 *quince*	31 *treinta y uno*
16 *dieciséis*	32 *treinta y dos*

40 *cuarenta*	100 *cien*
41 *cuarenta y uno*	101 *ciento uno*
50 *cincuenta*	102 *ciento dos*
51 *cincuenta y uno*	200 *doscientos*
60 *sesenta*	201 *doscientos uno*
61 *sesenta y uno*	300 *trescientos*
70 *setenta*	301 *trescientos uno*
71 *setenta y uno*	1000 *mil*
80 *ochenta*	1001 *mil uno*
81 *ochenta y uno*	1002 *mil dos*
90 *noventa*	2000 *dos mil*
91 *noventa y uno*	

Ordinal numbers: *primero, segundo*, etc.

- The Spanish for 'first' is *primero* in the masculine and *primera* in the feminine:
  use *primer* before a masculine singular noun:
  *mi **primer** hijo* my **first** child
- To say 'second', 'third', etc:

segundo	second
tercero	third
cuarto	fourth
quinto	fifth
sexto	sixth
séptimo	seventh
octavo	eighth
noveno	ninth
décimo	tenth

Days and dates

lunes	Monday
martes	Tuesday
miércoles	Wednesday
jueves	Thursday
viernes	Friday
sábado	Saturday
domingo	Sunday

enero	January	*julio*	July
febrero	February	*agosto*	August
marzo	March	*septiembre*	September
abril	April	*octubre*	October
mayo	May	*noviembre*	November
junio	June	*diciembre*	December

- Use normal numbers for dates:
  *Mi cumpleaños es **el 27** de diciembre.*
  My birthday is **on the 27th** of December.
  But *el primero* can be used, as well as *el uno* for 'the 1st':
  ***El primero de mayo** tenemos una fiesta.*
  On the 1st of May we have a party.
  Days of the week and months do not start with a capital letter in Spanish:
  *El cumpleaños de mi madre es el 13 de **abril**.*
  My mother's birthday is on the 13th of April.
- Use *el* + *lunes / martes*, etc. to say 'on Monday / Tuesday', etc.:
  ***El domingo** un amigo me regaló un nuevo libro.*
  On Sunday a friend gave me a new book.
- Use *los* + *lunes / martes*, etc. to say 'on Mondays / Tuesdays', etc.:
  *Normalmente **los sábados** voy a una clase de música.*
  On Saturdays I normally go to a music lesson.

Time

- The 12-hour clock goes as follows:

Es la una.	It's one o'clock.
Son las dos.	It's two o'clock.
Es la una y cinco.	It's five past one.
Son las dos y diez.	It's ten past two.
Son las dos y cuarto.	It's a quarter past two.
Son las dos y media.	It's half past two.
Son las tres menos veinte.	It's twenty to three.
Son las tres menos cuarto.	It's a quarter to three.
A mediodía.	At midday.
A medianoche.	At midnight.

- As in English, when using the 24-hour clock, use numbers such as *trece, dieciocho*, etc.:
  a las veinte diez at 20.10
- To ask the time:
  ¿Qué hora es? What time is it? / What's the time?

20 Verb tables

Verb tables help you to use verbs, particularly irregular verbs, correctly.

The first column in the table shows the infinitive in Spanish and English, and then the participles for the verb. The **present participle** (or **gerund**) ends in *–ando* or *–iendo* and is used to translate the –ing form of the English verb (e.g. to speak ⟶ speaking). The **past participle** is used to form the perfect tense (e.g. to speak ⟶ I have spoken).

Regular *–ar* verbs

infinitive + participles	present	preterite	imperfect	future	conditional
hablar **to speak** *hablando* *hablado*	*hablo* *hablas* *habla* *hablamos* *habláis* *hablan*	*hablé* *hablaste* *habló* *hablamos* *hablasteis* *hablaron*	*hablaba* *hablabas* *hablaba* *hablábamos* *hablabais* *hablaban*	*hablaré* *hablarás* *hablará* *hablaremos* *hablaréis* *hablarán*	*hablaría* *hablarías* *hablaría* *hablaríamos* *hablaríais* *hablarían*

Regular *–er* verbs

comer **to eat** *comiendo* *comido*	*como* *comes* *come* *comemos* *coméis* *comen*	*comí* *comiste* *comió* *comimos* *comisteis* *comieron*	*comía* *comías* *comía* *comíamos* *comíais* *comían*	*comeré* *comerás* *comerá* *comeremos* *comeréis* *comerán*	*comería* *comerías* *comería* *comeríamos* *comeríais* *comerían*

Regular *–ir* verbs

vivir **to live** *viviendo* *vivido*	*vivo* *vives* *vive* *vivimos* *vivís* *viven*	*viví* *viviste* *vivió* *vivimos* *vivisteis* *vivieron*	*vivía* *vivías* *vivía* *vivíamos* *vivíais* *vivían*	*viviré* *vivirás* *vivirá* *viviremos* *viviréis* *vivirán*	*viviría* *vivirías* *viviría* *viviríamos* *viviríais* *vivirían*

Irregular verbs

infinitive + participles	present	preterite	imperfect	future	conditional
dar **to give** *dando* *dado*	*doy* *das* *da* *damos* *dais* *dan*	*di* *diste* *dio* *dimos* *disteis* *dieron*	*daba* *dabas* *daba* *dábamos* *dabais* *daban*	*daré** *darás** *dará** *daremos** *daréis** *darán**	*daría** *darías** *daría** *daríamos** *daríais** *darían**
decir **to say** *diciendo* *dicho*	*digo* *dices* *dice* *decimos* *decís* *dicen*	*dije* *dijiste* *dijo* *dijimos* *dijisteis* *dijeron*	*decía* *decías* *decía* *decíamos* *decíais* *decían*	*diré* *dirás* *dirá* *diremos* *diréis* *dirán*	*diría* *dirías* *diría* *diríamos* *diríais* *dirían*
estar **to be** *estando* *estado*	*estoy* *estás* *está* *estamos* *estáis* *están*	*estuve* *estuviste* *estuvo* *estuvimos* *estuvisteis* *estuvieron*	*estaba* *estabas* *estaba* *estábamos* *estabais* *estaban*	*estaré** *estarás** *estará** *estaremos** *estaréis** *estarán**	*estaría** *estarías** *estaría** *estaríamos** *estaríais** *estarían**
haber **to have** *habiendo* *habido*	*he* *has* *ha* *hemos* *habéis* *han*	*hube* *hubiste* *hubo* *hubimos* *hubisteis* *hubieron*	*había* *habías* *había* *habíamos* *habíais* *habían*	*habré** *habrás** *habrá* *habremos** *habréis** *habrán**	*habría** *habrías** *habría* *habríamos** *habríais** *habrían**
hacer **to do, to make** *haciendo* *hecho*	*hago* *haces* *hace* *hacemos* *hacéis* *hacen*	*hice* *hiciste* *hizo* *hicimos* *hicisteis* *hicieron*	*hacía* *hacías* *hacía* *hacíamos* *hacíais* *hacían*	*haré* *harás* *hará* *haremos** *haréis** *harán**	*haría* *harías* *haría* *haríamos** *haríais** *harían**

*These verb forms are included for reference only. You won't be tested on them in your exams.

infinitive + participles	present	preterite	imperfect	future	conditional
ir **to go** *yendo* *ido*	*voy* *vas* *va* *vamos* *vais* *van*	*fui* *fuiste* *fue* *fuimos* *fuisteis* *fueron*	*iba* *ibas* *iba* *íbamos* *ibais* *iban*	*iré** *irás** *irá** *iremos** *iréis** *irán**	*iría** *irías** *iría** *iríamos** *iríais** *irían**
poder **to be able to** *pudiendo* *podido*	*puedo* *puedes* *puede* *podemos* *podéis* *pueden*	*pude* *pudiste* *pudo* *pudimos* *pudisteis* *pudieron*	*podía* *podías* *podía* *podíamos* *podíais* *podían*	*podré* *podrás* *podrá* *podremos** *podréis** *podrán**	*podría* *podrías* *podría* *podríamos** *podríais** *podrían**
poner **to put** *poniendo* *puesto*	*pongo* *pones* *pone* *ponemos* *ponéis* *ponen*	*puse* *pusiste* *puso* *pusimos* *pusisteis* *pusieron*	*ponía* *ponías* *ponía* *poníamos* *poníais* *ponían*	*pondré* *pondrás* *pondrá* *pondremos** *pondréis** *pondrán**	*pondría* *pondrías* *pondría* *pondríamos** *pondríais** *pondrían**
querer **to want** *queriendo* *querido*	*quiero* *quieres* *quiere* *queremos* *queréis* *quieren*	*quise* *quisiste* *quiso* *quisimos* *quisisteis* *quisieron*	*quería* *querías* *quería* *queríamos* *queríais* *querían*	*querré* *querrás* *querrá* *querremos* *querréis* *querrán*	*querría* *querrías* *querría* *querríamos* *querríais* *querrían*
saber **to know** *sabiendo* *sabido*	*sé* *sabes* *sabe* *sabemos* *sabéis* *saben*	*supe* *supiste* *supo* *supimos* *supisteis* *supieron*	*sabía* *sabías* *sabía* *sabíamos* *sabíais* *sabían*	*sabré* *sabrás* *sabrá* *sabremos* *sabréis* *sabrán*	*sabría* *sabrías* *sabría* *sabríamos* *sabríais* *sabrían*

infinitive + participles	present	preterite	imperfect	future	conditional
salir	*salgo*	*salí*	*salía*	*saldré*	*saldría*
to go out, to	*sales*	*saliste*	*salías*	*saldrás*	*saldrías*
leave	*sale*	*salió*	*salía*	*saldrá*	*saldría*
	salimos	*salimos*	*salíamos*	*saldremos*	*saldríamos*
saliendo	*salís*	*salisteis*	*salíais*	*saldréis*	*saldríais*
salido	*salen*	*salieron*	*salían*	*saldrán*	*saldrían*
ser	*soy*	*fui*	*era*	*seré**	*sería**
to be	*eres*	*fuiste*	*eras*	*serás**	*serías**
	es	*fue*	*era*	*será**	*sería**
siendo	*somos*	*fuimos*	*éramos*	*seremos**	*seríamos**
sido	*sois*	*fuisteis*	*erais*	*seréis**	*seríais**
	son	*fueron*	*eran*	*serán**	*serían**
tener	*tengo*	*tuve*	*tenía*	*tendré*	*tendría*
to have	*tienes*	*tuviste*	*tenías*	*tendrás*	*tendrías*
	tiene	*tuvo*	*tenía*	*tendrá*	*tendría*
teniendo	*tenemos*	*tuvimos*	*teníamos*	*tendremos**	*tendríamos**
tenido	*tenéis*	*tuvisteis*	*teníais*	*tendréis**	*tendríais**
	tienen	*tuvieron*	*tenían*	*tendrán**	*tendrían**
traer	*traigo*	*traje*	*traía*	*traeré**	*traería**
to bring	*traes*	*trajiste*	*traías*	*traerás**	*traerías**
	trae	*trajo*	*traía*	*traerá**	*traería**
trayendo	*traemos*	*trajimos*	*traíamos*	*traeremos**	*traeríamos**
traído	*traéis*	*trajisteis*	*traíais*	*traeréis**	*traeríais**
	traen	*trajeron*	*traían*	*traerán**	*traerían**
venir	*vengo*	*vine*	*venía*	*vendré*	*vendría*
to come	*vienes*	*viniste*	*venías*	*vendrás*	*vendrías*
	viene	*vino*	*venía*	*vendrá*	*vendría*
viniendo	*venimos*	*vinimos*	*veníamos*	*vendremos*	*vendríamos*
venido	*venís*	*vinisteis*	*veníais*	*vendréis*	*vendríais*
	vienen	*vinieron*	*venían*	*vendrán*	*vendrían*
ver	*veo*	*vi*	*veía*	*veré**	*vería**
to see	*ves*	*viste*	*veías*	*verás**	*verías**
	ve	*vio*	*veía*	*verá**	*vería**
viendo	*vemos*	*vimos*	*veíamos*	*veremos**	*veríamos**
visto	*veis*	*visteis*	*veíais*	*veréis**	*veríais**
	ven	*vieron*	*veían*	*verán**	*verían**

*These verb forms are included for reference only. You won't be tested on them in your exams.

Glossary

a bordo de on board
a causa de because of
¿adónde? where to?
a mi modo de ver as I see it
a pesar de despite
a pie on foot
¿a quién / quiénes? whom, to whom?
a veces sometimes
abandonar to leave
la **abeja** bee
el / la **abogado / a** lawyer
abril April
abrir to open
absorber to absorb
abstracto / a abstract
el / la **abuelo / a** grandfather / grandmother
los **abuelos (m. pl.)** grandparents
aburrido / a boring
el **accidente** accident
la **acción** action, act
el **aceite** oil
aceptar to accept
acompañar to accompany
acosar to harass
el **acoso** bullying, harassment
acostarse to go to bed
la **actitud** attitude
la **actividad** activity
activo / a active
el / la **actor / actriz** actor / actress
actual current
la **actualidad** at present, now
actualmente now, currently, at present
adaptarse to adapt
además furthermore, moreover
además de as well as
la **administración** administration
adoptado / a adopted
el / la **adulto / a** adult
advertir to warn
el **aeropuerto** airport
afectar to affect
aficionado / a fan, enthusiast
afroamericano / a African American
las **afueras** outskirts
agosto August
agradable pleasant
agresivo / a aggressive
el (fem.) **agua** water
ahora now
ahorrar to save
el **aire** air
al aire libre in the open air, outdoors
al final at the end
al lado de next to, at the side of
al menos at least
alegre cheerful
la **alegría** joy
alemán / alemana (adj.) German
algo something
alguien someone
alguno / a some
el **alimento** food, foodstuff
allí there
alojarse to stay
el **alpinismo** mountain climbing
alquilar to hire, rent
alrededor de around
alto / a tall
el / la **alumno / a** pupil
amarillo / a yellow
ambicioso / a ambitious
el **ambiente** atmosphere
amenazar to threaten
el / la **amigo / a** friend
la **amistad** friendship
el **amor** love
añadir to add
andaluz(a) Andalusian
andar to walk
animado / a lively
animal (adj.) animal
el **año** year
anoche last night
anterior previous
antes before
antes (de) before
el / la **anticuario / a** antique dealer
la **antigüedad** antique
antiguo / a old
antipático / a unpleasant
anunciar to announce
el **anuncio** advert
apagar to turn off, out out
aparecer to appear
el **apartamento** apartment
apoyar to support
el **apoyo** support
la **app** app
apreciar to appreciate
aprender to learn
aprobar to pass (eg. exam)
apropiado / a appropriate
aquel / aquella that (one)
aquí here
el **árbol** tree
argentino / a Argentinian
el **armario** cupboard, wardrobe
la **arquitectura** architecture
arruinar to ruin
el **arte** art
el **artículo** article
artificial artificial
el / la **artista** artist
artístico / a artistic
la **ascendencia** heritage
el **ascensor** lift, elevator
así like this, like that
la **asignatura** subject
asistir (a) to attend
el **aspecto** aspect
el / la **astronauta** astronaut
la **astronomía** astronomy
la **atención** attention
atraer to attract
aumentar to increase
aunque although
los **auriculares** headphones
el **autobús** bus, coach
el **automovilismo** car racing
avanzado / a advanced
la **aventura** adventure
el **avión** plane
ayer yesterday
ayudar to help
el **ayuno** fasting
el **ayuntamiento** town hall, council
el **azúcar** sugar
azul blue
bailar to dance
el **baile** dance
bajar to descend, to go down
bajar de to get off (transport)
bajo / a short
el **balcón** balcony
el **ballet** ballet
el **baloncesto** basketball
el **banco** bank
la **banda** (music) band
el **baño** bathroom
barato / a cheap
el **barco** boat
el **barrio** neighbourhood, district, area
básico / a basic
bastante quite
la **basura** rubbish, litter
beber to drink
la **bebida** drink
el **beneficio** benefit
la **biblioteca** library
la **bicicleta** bicycle
bien well
el **billete** ticket
biológico / a biological
el **bocadillo** sandwich
la **bolsa** bag
bonito / a pretty, lovely
el **bosque** wood, forest
la **botella** bottle
el **brazo** arm
bueno / a good
buscar to look for, search for, seek
el **caballo** horse
la **cabeza** head
cada each, every

caer to fall
caerse to fall off / over / down
el *café* coffee
la *caja* box, till
la *calculadora* calculator
la *calefacción* heating
caliente warm, hot
la *calle* street
el *calor* heat
la *cama* bed
la *cámara* camera
el / la *camarero / a* waiter / waitress
cambiar to change
el *cambio* change
caminar to walk
la *camiseta* t-shirt, football shirt
la *campaña* campaign
el *camping* campsite
el *campo* field, country(side)
el *canal* canal
la *canción* song
el / la *candidato / a* candidate
el / la *cantante* singer
cantar to sing
capaz (de) capable
la *cara* face
el *carácter* carácter
el *caramelo* sweet
cargar to charge
caribeño / a Caribbean
el *cariño* affection
el *carnaval* carnival
la *carne* meat
caro / a expensive, dear
la *carrera* career, degree course, race
la *carretera* road
la *carta* letter
la *casa* house
casarse to get married
casi almost, nearly
el *castillo* castle
la *catedral* cathedral
católico / a Catholic
causar to cause
la *celebración* celebration
celebrar to celebrate
celebrarse to hold (event)
la *cena* dinner, tea, evening meal
cenar to have dinner
el *centro* centre
el *centro comercial* shopping centre
el *centro deportivo* sports centre
el *cepillo* brush
cerca (de) near, close (to)
los *cereales* cereals
la *ceremonia* ceremony
cerrado / a closed, shut
cerrar to close, shut
la *chaqueta* jacket
el / la *chico / a* boy / girl
chileno / a Chilean
chino / a (adj.) Chinese
el *chocolate* chocolate
el *cielo* sky
la *ciencia* science
el / la *científico / a* scientist
cierto / a certain, true
la *cifra* figure
cinco five
el *cine* cinema
el *circuito* circuit
la *ciudad* town, city
el / la *ciudadano / a* citizen
claro clear, of course
la *clase* class
clásico / a classical
el / la *cliente* customer
el *clima* climate
el *club* club
el *coche* car
la *cocina* cooking, kitchen
cocinar to cook
el / la *cocinero / a* cook, chef
coger to catch
coleccionar to collect
el *colegio* school
el *color* colour
la *combinación* combination
Comecocos Pac-Man
comenzar to begin, start
comer to eat
la *comida* food, meal
el *comienzo* the start, beginning
como as, like
cómo how
¿cómo? how?
como consecuencia de as a result of
cómodo / a comfortable
el / la *compañero / a* classmate, partner, colleague
la *compañía* company
compartir to share
completo / a complete
complicado / a complicated
el *comportamiento* behaviour
comprar to buy
las *compras* shopping
comprensivo / a understanding
común common
comunicar to communicate
la *comunidad* community
con with
concienciar to make aware, raise awareness
el *concierto* concert
el *concurso* contest, game show, competition
conducir to drive
la *confianza* confidence, trust
conmigo with me
conocer to know, to get to know
conocido / a known, familiar
el *conocimiento* knowledge
consciente aware
la *consecuencia* consequence
conseguir to manage
considerar to consider
consistir (en) to consist (of)
la *consola* games console
la *construcción* building, construction
construir to build
el *consumo* consumption
el *contacto* contact
la *contaminación* pollution
contaminar to pollute
contar to tell, count
el *contenedor* container, bin
contento / a happy, pleased, glad
continuamente continuously
continuar to continue
contribuir to contribute
la *conversación* conversation
convertirse en to become
la *copa* cup, wine glass, trophy
copiar to copy
el *corazón* heart
correcto / a correct
correr to run
corto / a short
la *cosa* thing
la *costa* coast
costar to cost
la *costumbre* custom, tradition
crear to create
creer to think, believe
la *crema* cream
criticar to criticise
cruzar to cross
¿cuál / cuáles? which (ones)?
cualquier any
cuando when
¿cuándo? when?
¿cuánto / a / os / as? how much?, how many?
cuatro four
cubano / a Cuban
cubrir to cover
la *cuenta* bill
el *cuerpo* body
la *cuestión* issue, matter
el *cuidado* care
el / la *cuidador(a)* carer
cuidar to care for, look after
el *cultivo* crop
la *cultura* culture
cultural cultural
el *currículum* CV
cuyo whose
el *daño* damage, harm
la *danza* dance
dar to give
dar un paseo to go for a walk, stroll, ride

de moda fashionable
de momento at the moment
de niño/a as a child
¿de quién/quiénes? whose?
de segunda mano second hand
de vez en cuando from time to time
deber to owe (must)
los ***deberes*** homework
decidir to decide
decir to say, tell
declarar to declare
la ***decoración*** decoration
dedicar to dedicate, devote
la ***definición*** definition
dejar to leave, let, allow
dejar de + infinitive to stop … ing
delante de in front of
delgado/a slim, thin
la ***delincuencia*** crime
el ***delito*** crime, offence
demasiado too, too much
demostrar to show, demonstrate
dental dental
el/la ***dentista*** dentist
depender to depend
el ***deporte*** sport
el/la ***deportista*** sportsman/sportswoman, athlete
deportivo/a (of) sports
la ***derecha*** right
desafortunadamente unfortunately
desaparecer to disappear
el ***desayuno*** breakfast
descansar to rest
describir to describe
descubrir to discover
desde since, from
desde hace for
desfavorecido/a disadvantaged
el ***desfile*** parade
deshonesto dishonest
despertar(se) to wake up
después (de) after, afterwards
destacar to highlight, emphasise
destinado a aimed at
destruir to destroy
la ***desventaja*** disadvantage
el ***detalle*** detail
detectar to detect
detestar to detest
detrás de behind
el ***día*** day
diario daily
dibujar to draw
el ***dibujo*** art, drawing
los ***dibujos animados*** cartoons
el ***diccionario*** dictionary
dieciséis sixteen
el ***diente*** tooth
la ***dieta*** diet
la ***diferencia*** difference
diferente different
difícil difficult
digital digital
el ***dinero*** money
dirigir to run, manage
discutir to discuss, argue
el/la ***diseñador(a)*** designer
diseñar to design
disfrutar to enjoy
el ***dispositivo*** gadget
la ***distancia*** distance
distinto/a different
diverso/a various
divertido/a fun, enjoyable
divertirse to enjoy oneself, to have fun
divorciado/a divorced
divorciarse to get divorced
doce twelve
el/la ***doctor(a)*** doctor
el ***documental*** documentary
doler to hurt
el ***domingo*** Sunday
donar to donate
donde where
dónde where
¿dónde? where?
dormir to sleep
dormirse to fall asleep
el ***dormitorio*** bedroom
dos two
la ***duda*** doubt
el/la ***dueño/a*** owner
dulce sweet
durante for, during
duro/a hard
económico/a inexpensive
la ***edad*** age
el ***edificio*** building
la ***educación*** education
educado/a polite
educativo/a educational
efectivo/a effective
el ***efecto*** effect
los ***efectos especiales*** special effects
egoísta selfish
el ***ejemplo*** example
el ***ejercicio*** exercise
eléctrico/a electric
electrónico/a electronic
emitir to emit, give off
emocionante exciting
empezar to start, begin
el/la ***empleado/a*** employee
el ***empleo*** work, employment
la ***empresa*** firm, company
empujar to push
en cambio on the other hand
en sí mismo/a in itself
en vez de instead of
en vivo live
encantar to love (lit. to delight)
encima de on top of
encontrar to find
encontrarse to be found
la ***energía*** energy
la ***enfermedad*** illness, disease
el/la ***enfermero/a*** nurse
enfermo/a ill, sick
enojado/a angry
enorme enormous
la ***ensalada*** salad
enseñar to teach, show
los ***enseres*** goods
entender to understand
el ***entorno*** surroundings
la ***entrada*** ticket
entre between, among
entrenar(se) to train
la ***entrevista*** interview
enviar to send
la ***época*** era, period
equilibrado/a balanced
el ***equipaje*** luggage
el ***equipo*** team, equipment
la ***escalada*** rock climbing
la ***escalera*** stairs
escoger to choose
esconder to hide
escribir to write
escuchar to listen (to)
la ***escuela*** (primary) school
el ***esfuerzo*** effort
el ***espacio*** space
España Spain
español(a) (adj.) Spanish
especialmente especially
la ***especie*** species
el ***espectáculo*** show, spectacle
esperar to wait, hope, expect
el ***establecimiento*** establishment, shop
la ***estación*** station
el ***estadio*** stadium
el ***estado*** state
Estados Unidos United States
estar to be
estar de acuerdo (con) to agree (with)
estar en forma to be fit
estar seguro/a to be sure
el ***este*** east
este/esta this
el ***estilo*** style
la ***estrella*** star
el ***estreno*** premiere
el ***estrés*** stress
estricto/a strict
el/la ***estudiante*** student
estudiar to study
el ***estudio*** study, studio
estupendo/a great, brilliant
el ***euro*** euro

Europa Europe
europeo/a European
evitar to avoid
exagerar to exaggerate
el *examen* exam
excelente excellent
la *excursión* trip
existir to exist
el *éxito* success
exótico/a exotic
la *experiencia* experience
la *experiencia laboral* work experience
experimentar to experiment, experience
explicar to explain
expresivo/a expressive
extendido/a extended
extra extra
el *extranjero* abroad
extranjero/a (adj.) foreign
la *fábrica* factory
fácil easy
la *falda* skirt
falso/a false
la *falta* lack, shortage
faltar to be lacking, missing, to be short of
la *fama* fame
la *familia* family
la *familia reconstituida* step family
familiar (adj.) (of the) family
el *familiar* family member
el/la *famoso* celebrity
fascinar to fascinate
fatal terrible
favorito/a favourite
feliz happy
fenomenal amazing
feo/a ugly
la *feria* fair
la *ficción* fiction
la *fiesta* party, festival
el *fin de semana* weekend
finalmente finally
la *física* physics
físico/a (adj.) physical
la *flor* flower
el *fondo* the end, bottom
la *forma* shape, form, way
la *formación* training
el *fósil* fossil
la *foto* photo
el *fotógrafo/a* photographer
el *francés (n.)* French (language)
francés/francesa (adj.) French
la *frecuencia* frequency
fresco/a cool, fresh
frío/a cold
frito/a fried
la *fruta* fruit
el *fuego* fire
fuerte strong
fumar to smoke
la *función* function
funcionar to work, function
fundar to set up
el *futuro* future
las *gafas* glasses
las *gafas de sol* sunglasses
la *ganadería* cattle farming
ganar to earn, win
el *gas* gas
gastar to spend
general general
generoso/a generous
genial great
la *gente* people
la *geografía* geography
el *gimnasio* gym
el/la *gimnasta* gymnast
el *gobierno* government
gracias thanks
gracioso/a funny
el *grado* degree (ie. temperature)
grande big
la *grasa* grease, fat
gratis free
grave serious
gris grey
gritar to shout
el *grupo* group
guapo/a good-looking
guardar to keep
guay cool
el/la *guía* guide
la *guitarra* guitar
gustar to like (lit. to please)
la *habitación* room
hablar to speak, talk
hace falta it is necessary, you must
hace… ...ago
hacer to do, make
hacer camping to go camping
hacer falta to be lacking, missing
hacer fotos to take potos
hacer preguntas to ask questions
el (fem.) *hambre* hunger
la *hamburguesa* burger
hasta until, up to
hay there is, there are
hay que you/one must, it is necessary to
el/la *hermanastro/a* stepbrother/stepsister
el/la *hermano/a* brother/sister
hermoso/a beautiful
el/la *hijo/a* son/daughter
los *hijos (m. pl.)* children, sons and daughters
la *historia* story, history
histórico/a historic
el *hogar* home
el *hombre* man
la *hora* hour, time
el *horario* timetable, schedule
horrible horrible
el *hospital* hospital
el *hotel* hotel
hoy today
hoy día these days
el *huevo* egg
humano/a human
humilde humble
el *humo* smoke, fume
el *humor* mood
el *icono* icon
la *idea* idea
ideal ideal
identificar to identify
el *idioma* language
la *iglesia* church
igual equal, same
la *imagen* image
el *impacto* impact
la *importancia* importance
importante important
importar to matter
imposible impossible
la *impresora* printer
incluso even, including
increíble incredible
independiente independent
indígena native, indigenous
individual individual
la *industria* industry
infantil children's, of children
el/la *influencer* influencer
la *influencia* influence
la *información* information
la *informática* ICT
el *informe* report
el/la *ingeniero/a* engineer
el *inglés (n.)* English (language)
inglés/inglesa (adj.) English
iniciar to begin
la *iniciativa* initiative
inspirar to inspire
la *instalación* facility
el *instituto (insti)* secondary school
insultar to insult
inteligente intelligent, smart
intentar to try
el *interés* interest
interesante interesting
interesar to interest
el/la *Internet*
la *invención* invention
inventar to invent
el *invernadero* greenhouse
la *investigación* research, investigation
investigar to research
el *invierno* winter
ir to go
ir a pie to go on foot, walk
ir al extranjero to go abroad

ir de compras to go shopping
ir de vacaciones to go on holiday
la isla island
la izquierda left
jamás never
el jamón ham
la Janucá Hanukkah
el jardín garden
el/la jefe/jefa boss
joven (adj.) young
el/la joven (n.) young person
el juego game
el jugador(a) player
jugar to play
el juguete toy
juntos/as together
el kayak kayak
el kilo kilo
el kilómetro kilometre
el lado side
largo/a long
la lástima pity, shame
latino/a Latin
latinoamericano/a Latin American
la leche milk
el lector electrónico e-book
leer to read
lejos far
lejos (de) far (from)
la lengua language
lento/a slow
la letra lyric
levantar to raise
levantarse to get up
libre free, unoccupied
el libro book
ligero/a light (in weight)
el límite limit
limpiar to clean
limpio/a clean
la lista (n.) list
listo/a (adj.) clever
la llamada call
llamar to call
llamar la atención to stand out, be noteworthy
llamarse to be called
llamativo/a striking

la llegada arrival
llegar (a) to arrive, get to
llegar a ser to become
llenar to fill
lleno/a full
llevar to take, carry, wear, lead
llevarse bien/mal (con) to get on well/badly (with)
llover to rain
la lluvia rain
lo que what
loco/a crazy
lograr to manage
los abuelos (m. pl.) grandparents
los/las demás the others, the rest
luego then
el lugar place
el lujo luxury
la luna moon
el lunes Monday
la luz light
la madrastra stepmother
la madre mother
mal bad, badly
maleducado/a impolite
la maleta suitcase
malo/a bad
la mañana morning
mandar to send
la manera manner, way
la mano hand
mantener to maintain, keep
mantenerse to keep (oneself)
la manzana apple
maravilloso/a wonderful, marvellous
la marca brand
el marido husband
marrón brown
el martes Tuesday
más more, most
más tarde later
la mascota pet
matemáticas Maths
el matrimonio marriage
mayor older, bigger, main

la medicina medicine
el/la médico/a doctor
la medida measure
medio/a half, average
el medio ambiente environment
mediterráneo Mediterranean
mejor better, best
mejorar to improve
menor younger, smaller
menos less, least
el mensaje message
mental mental
mentir to lie, tell a lie
la mentira lie
el mercado market
la merienda afternoon snack
el mes month
la mesa table, desk
el metro underground
mexicano/a Mexican
la mezcla mixture
mezquita mosque
el miedo fear
el miembro member
mientras while
mil thousand
el millón million
el minuto minute
mío/a mine
mirar to look at
mismo/a same
la mitad half
la mochila rucksack
la moda fashion
el/la modelo a seguir role model
moderno/a modern
molestar to bother, annoy
el momento moment
monoparental single parent
la montaña mountain
montar to ride, set up
montar a caballo to ride a horse, go horse riding
el montón load, lot
la mordida bite
moreno/a brown, dark

morir to die
mostrar to show
mover to move
el móvil mobile (phone)
el mueble furniture
muerto/a dead
la mujer woman/wife
mundialmente worldwide
el mundo world
el museo museum
la música music
el/la músico/a musician
musulmán/musulmana Muslim
muy very
nacer to be born
nacional national
la nacionalidad nationality
nada nothing
nadar to swim
nadie no one, nobody
la natación swimming
natural natural
la naturaleza nature
navegar to surf, navigate (i.e. the Internet)
la Navidad Christmas
necesario/a necessary
la necesidad need
necesitar to need
negativo/a negative
el negocio business
negro/a black
nervioso/a nervous
la nevera fridge
ni neither, nor
la nieve snow
el/la niñero/a nanny/au pair
ninguno/a no, none, not any
el/la niño/a child, (little) boy/girl
el nivel level
la noche night
la Nochebuena Christmas Eve
la Nochevieja New Year's Eve
el nombre name
la nominación nomination
normal normal

normalmente normally
el ***noroeste*** north-west
el ***norte*** north
nosotros/as we, us
la ***nota*** grade, mark
notar to notice
las ***noticias*** news
la ***novela*** novel
nuclear nuclear
nuestro/a our
Nueva York New York
nueve nine
nuevo/a new
el ***número*** number
numeroso/a numerous, large
nunca never
el ***objeto*** object
la ***obra*** work (of art, literature)
la ***obra de arte*** artwork
las ***obras*** roadworks, building works
observar to observe
ocho eight
ocupar to occupy
el ***oeste*** western (film)
la ***oferta*** offer
la ***oficina*** office
ofrecer to offer
oír to hear
el ***ojo*** eye
el ***olor*** smell
olvidar(se) to forget
once eleven
online online
la ***opción*** option
opinar to believe, think
la ***opinión*** opinion
la ***oportunidad*** opportunity
optimista optimistic
el ***ordenador*** computer, PC
la ***oreja*** ear
la ***organización*** organisation
organizar to organise
orgulloso/a proud
original original
el ***otoño*** autumn
otra vez again
otro/a other, another

paciente patient
el ***padrastro*** stepfather
el ***padre*** father
los ***padres (m. pl.)*** parents
la ***paella*** paella (rice and seafood dish)
pagar to pay
la ***página*** page
el ***país*** country
el ***paisaje*** landscape
el ***pájaro*** bird
la ***palabra*** word
el ***palacio*** palace
el ***pan*** bread
la ***pantalla*** screen
paparazzi photographer who follows famous people
el ***papel*** role, paper
para to, for, in order to
para siempre forever
el ***paracaidismo*** skydiving
parecer to seem
parecerse a to look like
la ***pared*** wall
la ***pareja*** couple, partner
el ***parkour*** parkour
el ***paro*** unemployment
el ***parque*** park
el ***parque temático/de atracciones*** theme park
la ***parte*** part
la ***participación*** participation
participar to participate, take part
el ***partido*** match, game
pasado/a (adj.) past, last
pasar to pass, spend
pasar de moda to be out of fashion
pasarlo bien to have a good time
la ***Pascua*** Easter
pasear to go for a walk
el ***paseo*** walk, stroll
el ***pasillo*** corridor
la ***pasión*** passion
el ***paso*** step
el ***pastel*** cake
las ***patatas fritas*** chips, fries
el ***patio*** yard, patio, playground

pedir to ask for, order
la ***pelea*** fight
pelear(se) to fight
la ***película*** film
el ***peligro*** danger
peligroso/a dangerous
el ***pelo*** hair
el/la ***peluquero/a*** hairdresser
pensar to think
peor worse, worst
pequeño/a small
perder to lose
perderse to get lost
perdonar to forgive
perezoso/a lazy
perfecto/a perfect
el ***perfil*** profile
el ***periódico*** newspaper
el/la ***periodista*** journalist
permitir to allow, permit
pero but
el/la ***perro/a*** dog
la ***persecución*** pursuit
la ***persona*** person
el ***personaje*** character (ie. in book, film)
personal personal
la ***personalidad*** personality
personalizado/a personalised
pesado/a heavy
pesar to weigh
el ***pescado*** fish
pesimista pessimistic
el ***peso*** weight
el ***pez*** fish
el ***pie*** foot
la ***piel*** skin
la ***pierna*** leg
pintar to paint
la ***pintura*** painting
la ***piscina*** swimming pool
el ***piso*** flat, apartment
la ***pizza*** pizza
el ***plan*** plan
planear to plan
el ***planeta*** planet
la ***planificación*** planning
el ***plano*** map, street plan
la ***planta*** plant
plantar to plant

el ***plástico*** plastic
la ***plataforma*** platform
el ***plato*** dish, plate
la ***playa*** beach
la ***plaza*** square
la ***plaza de toros*** bullring
la ***plaza mayor*** main square
poblado/a populated
pobre poor
poco/a little, bit
pocos/as a few, few, not many
poder to be able to
la ***policía*** police (force)
el ***pollo*** chicken
poner to put
poner fin a to bring an end to
ponerse to put on, to become
popular popular
por for
por ciento percent
por ejemplo for example
por eso so, therefore
por fin finally
¿por qué? why?
porque because
el ***portátil*** laptop
portugués/a (adj.) Portuguese
la ***posibilidad*** possibility
posible possible
positivo/a positive
practicar to practise
práctico/a practical
el ***precio*** price
precioso/a beautiful
la ***preferencia*** preference
preferir to prefer
la ***pregunta*** question
preguntar to ask a question
el ***premio*** award, prize
preocupar(se) to worry
preocuparse por to worry about
la ***preparación*** preparation
preparar to prepare
presentar to present, introduce

presentarse to introduce oneself
la ***presión*** pressure
la ***primavera*** spring
primero/a first
el/la ***primo/a*** cousin
principal main, principal
el ***principio*** beginning
la ***privacidad*** privacy
privado/a private
proactivo/a proactive
probablemente probably
probar to try, try out, test, sample
el ***problema*** problem
procesado/a processed
producir to produce
el ***producto*** product
la ***profesión*** profession
el/la ***profesor(a)*** teacher
profundamente deeply
profundo/a deep
el ***programa*** programme
prohibido/a forbidden, banned
prohibir to prohibit, ban
propio/a own
proteger to protect
la ***proteína*** protein
próximo/a next
el ***proyecto*** project
la ***prueba*** test, exam
publicar to publish
el ***público (n.)*** public
público/a (adj.) public
el ***pueblo*** village, town
el ***puente*** bridge, Bank holiday
el ***puerto*** port, harbour
puertorriqueño/a Puerto Rican
el ***puesto*** job, post
el ***punto*** point
puro/a pure
qué what
qué tal how is
¿Qué tal ...? How is/was ..., how are/were ...?
que yo sepa as far as I know
el ***quechua*** Quechua (indigenous language)
quedar to remain, to arrange to meet
quedarse to stay
quejarse to complain
quemar to burn
quemarse to get (sun) burnt
querer to want, love
el ***queso*** cheese
quién who
¿quién/quiénes? who?
químico/a (adj.) chemical
quince fifteen
la ***Quinceañera*** girl's 15th birthday (Lat Am.)
quitar to remove
rápidamente quickly
rápido fast, quick
raramente rarely
raro/a strange, odd, rare
el ***rato*** time, while
la ***razón*** reason
realista realistic
recargar to charge, recharge
la ***recepción*** reception
recibir to receive
reciclar to recycle
reciente recent
recoger to pick up, collect
recomendar to recommend
reconocer to recognize, acknowledge
recordar to remember
el ***recreo*** break, break time
el ***recuerdo*** souvenir
el ***recurso*** resource
la ***red social*** social network
reducir to reduce
regalar to gift
el ***regalo*** present, gift
regar to water, irrigate
el ***régimen*** diet
la ***región*** region
la ***regla*** rule, ruler
la ***relación*** relationship
relajado/a relaxed
relajante relaxing
la ***religión*** religion
religioso/a religious
el ***reloj*** watch, clock
repasar to revise
reportar to report
la ***reserva*** reservation
reservar to book
resolver to solve
respetar to respect
el ***respeto*** respect
respirar to breathe
responder to answer, reply
responsable responsible
el ***restaurante*** restaurant
el ***resto*** rest
el ***resultado*** result
la ***revista*** magazine
rico/a rich
el ***riesgo*** risk
el ***río*** river
el ***ritmo*** rhythm
robar to steal
la ***roca*** rock
romántico/a romantic
romper to break
la ***ropa*** clothes
roto/a broken
rubio/a fair, blond(e)
el ***ruido*** noise
la ***ruina*** ruin
el ***sábado*** Saturday
saber to know
sacar to take out, get
sacar fotos to take photos
la ***sal*** salt
la ***sala de juegos*** games room
el ***salario*** salary
salir to leave, go out
la ***salud*** health
el ***sándwich*** sandwich
sano/a healthy
el ***secreto*** secret
la ***sed*** thirst
el/la ***seguidor(a)*** follower
seguir to continue, follow
según according to
segundo/a (adj.) second
seguro/a safe, sure, secure
seis six
la ***semana*** week
la ***semana pasada*** last week
la ***Semana Santa*** Easter Week, Holy Week
sencillo/a simple
sentar to sit, seat
sentarse to sit (down)
el ***sentido del humor*** sense of humour
sentir(se) to feel
la ***separación*** separation
separado/a separated
separar to separate
ser to be
la ***serie*** series
serio/a serious
los ***servicios*** toilets
servir to serve
el ***sexo*** sex
siempre always
siempre que puedo whenever I can
la ***siesta*** siesta, afternoon nap
el ***siglo*** century
la ***silla*** chair
simpático/a nice, friendly
sin without
sin duda without doubt
sin embargo however
la ***sinagoga*** synagogue
sincero/a honest
sino but
el ***sistema*** system
el ***sitio*** place
el ***sitio web*** website
la ***situación*** situation
situarse to be located
sobre on, about
sobre todo above all
el ***sofá*** sofa, settee
el ***sol*** sun
soler to usually do something
solicitar to apply for
solo/a only, alone
soltero/a single
la ***sombra*** shadow, shade
soñar (con) to dream (about)
sonreír to smile
la ***sopa*** soup

sorprender to surprise
la ***sorpresa*** surprise
subir to ascend, go up, upload
subir a to get onto (transport)
el ***submarinismo*** scuba diving
sucio/a dirty
Sudamérica South America
el ***sueño*** dream
la ***suerte*** luck
sugerir to suggest
el ***supermercado*** supermarket
el ***sur*** south
suspender to fail (ie. exam)
táctil touch (ie. touch screen)
tal y como just as, exactly as
también also, as well
tampoco neither, either
tan so
tan ...como as … as
tanto/a so many, so much
tantos/as so many, as many
tardar to take (time)
tarde (adv.) late
la ***tarde (n.)*** afternoon, evening
el ***tatuaje*** tattoo
el ***teatro*** theatre, drama
la ***tecnología*** technology
la ***tela*** cloth, fabric
la ***tele*** TV, telly
el ***teléfono*** telephone
el ***teléfono móvil*** mobile phone
la ***telenovela*** soap opera
la ***telerrealidad*** reality TV
el ***telescopio*** telescope
la ***televisión*** TV, television
la ***temperatura*** temperature
el ***templo*** temple
temprano early
tener to have
tener calor to be hot
tener derecho a to have the right to
tener éxito to be successful
tener hambre to be hungry
tener lugar to take place
tener miedo to be afraid
tener que to have to
tener suerte to be lucky
el ***tenis*** tennis
terminar to finish
terrible terrible
el ***texto*** text
el ***tiempo*** time, weather, weather forecast
el ***tiempo libre*** free time
la ***tienda*** shop, tent
la ***Tierra*** Earth
el/la ***tío/a*** uncle/aunt
los ***tíos (m. pl.)*** uncle(s) and aunt(s)
típico/a typical
el ***tipo*** sort, type
tirar to throw, pull
tirarse to jump off
tocar to play (instrument, music)
todas partes everywhere
todavía still
todo all, the whole, everything
todos los días every day
tomar to take, have, drink, eat
tomar el sol to sunbathe
el ***tomate*** tomato
tonto/a silly, stupid
la ***torre*** tower
la ***tortilla*** Spanish omelette
tostado/a toasted
trabajador(a) hard-working
trabajar to work
el ***trabajo*** work, job
la ***tradición*** tradition
tradicional traditional
la ***traducción*** translation
traer to bring
el ***tráfico*** traffic
el ***traje*** suit, costume
tranquilo/a quiet, peaceful
la ***transmisión*** broadcast
el ***transporte*** transport
trasladarse to transport oneself
treinta thirty
el ***tren*** train
tres three
los ***Tres Reyes Magos*** the Three Wise Men
triste sad
tú mismo/a yourself
turbulento/a turbulent, stormy
el/la ***turista*** tourist
último/a last, latest
un montón de a lot (of)
único/a only, unique
el ***uniforme*** uniform
la ***universidad*** university
urbano/a urban
usar to use
el ***uso*** use
útil useful
utilizar to use
la ***uva*** grape
las ***vacaciones*** holidays
vale la pena it is worthwhile
valer la pena to be worth it
la ***variedad*** variety
varios/as several, various
el/la ***vecino/a*** neighbour
vegano/a vegan
vegetariano/a vegetarian
la ***velocidad*** speed
vender to sell
venir to come
la ***ventaja*** advantage
la ***ventana*** window
ver to see, watch
el ***verano*** summer
la ***verdad*** truth
verdadero/a true
verde green
la(s) ***verdura(s)*** vegetables
la ***vergüenza*** embarrassment
vestirse to get dressed
el/la ***veterinario/a*** vet
la ***vez*** time, occasion
viajar to travel
el ***viaje*** trip, journey
la ***vida*** life
la ***vida social*** social life
el ***vídeo*** video
la ***videoconsola*** video game console
el ***videojuego*** video game
viejo/a old
el ***viento*** wind
el ***viernes*** Friday
la ***visibilidad*** visibility, awareness
la ***visita*** visit
visitar to visit
la ***vista*** view
vivo/a vivid
volver to return, go back
votar to vote
la ***voz*** voice
el ***vuelo*** flight
ya now, already
ya no no longer, not … any more
ya que since, as
el ***zapato*** shoe
la ***zona*** area
el ***zumo*** juice